Demographic Responses to Economic Adjustment in Latin America

international union
for the scientific study
of population

The International Union for the Scientific Study of Population Problems was set up in 1928, with Dr Raymond Pearl as President. At that time the Union's main purpose was to promote international scientific co-operation to study the various aspects of population problems, through national committees and through its members themselves. In 1947 the International Union for the Scientific Study of Population (IUSSP) was reconstituted into its present form.

It expanded its activities to:
- stimulate research on population
- develop interest in demographic matters among governments, national and international organizations, scientific bodies, and the general public
- foster relations between people involved in population studies
- disseminate scientific knowledge on population.

The principal ways through which the IUSSP currently achieves its aims are:
- organization of worldwide or regional conferences
- operations of Scientific Committees under the auspices of the Council
- organization of training courses
- publication of conference proceedings and committee reports.

Demography can be defined by its field of study and its analytical methods. Accordingly, it can be regarded as the scientific study of human populations primarily with respect to their size, their structure, and their development. For reasons which are related to the history of the discipline, the demographic method is essentially inductive: progress in knowledge results from the improvement of observation, the sophistication of measurement methods, and the search for regularities and stable factors leading to the formulation of explanatory models. In conclusion, the three objectives of demographic analysis are to describe, measure, and analyse.

International Studies in Demography is the outcome of an agreement concluded by the IUSSP and the Oxford University Press. The joint series is expected to reflect the broad range of the Union's activities and, in the first instance, will be based on the seminars organized by the Union. The Editorial Board of the series is comprised of:

Demographic Responses to Economic Adjustment in Latin America

Edited by

G. Tapinos
A. Mason
J. Bravo

CLARENDON PRESS · OXFORD
1997

Oxford University Press, Great Clarendon Street, Oxford OX2 6DP

Oxford New York
Athens Auckland Bangkok Bogota Bombay
Buenos Aires Calcutta Cape Town Dar es Salaam
Delhi Florence Hong Kong Istanbul Karachi
Kuala Lumpur Madras Madrid Melbourne
Mexico City Nairobi Paris Singapore
Taipei Tokyo Toronto Warsaw

and associated companies in
Berlin Ibadan

Oxford is a trade mark of Oxford University Press

Published in the United States by
Oxford University Press Inc., New York

© IUSSP 1997

British Library Cataloguing in Publication Data
Data available

Library of Congress Cataloging in Publication Data

ISBN 0–19–829210–4

1 3 5 7 9 10 8 6 4 2

Typeset by Graphicraft Typesetters Ltd., Hong Kong
Printed in Great Britain by Biddles Ltd., Guildford & King's Lynn

Contents

Contributors

Reynaldo Bajraj	CELADE, Chile
Jere Behrman	Department of Economics, University of Pennsylvania, USA
Jorge Bravo	CELADE, Chile
Brígida García	El Colegio de Mexico, Mexico
Kenneth Hill	Department of Population Dynamics, John Hopkins University and the World Bank
David Lam	Department of Economics, University of Michigan, USA
Deborah Levison	Center for Population Analysis and Policy, Institute of Public Affairs, University of Minnesota, USA
José Alberto Magno de Carvalho	CEDEPLAR, Brazil
Andrew Mason	Program on Population, East–West Center and Department of Economics, University of Hawaii, USA
Philip Musgrove	The World Bank, USA
Orlandina de Oliveira	El Colegio de Mexico, Mexico
José Antonio Ortega-Osona	University of California at Berkeley, USA
Alberto Palloni	Center for Demography and Ecology, University of Wisconsin, USA
David Reher	Universidad Complutense de Madrid and Instituto de Demográfica, Spain
Eduardo Rios-Neto	CEDEPLAR, Brazil
Georges Tapinos	Institut d'Etudes Politiques de Paris and INED, France

Part I

The Framework

1 Economic Adjustment and Demographic Responses in Latin America: *An Overview*

REYNALDO BAJRAJ, JORGE BRAVO, AND GEORGES TAPINOS

Introduction

The purpose of this chapter is to provide an overview of economic adjustment in Latin America over the last decade and to review the still sparse but growing evidence relating to the demographic responses associated with such changes. First, we present the economic background to the analyses of the demographic fluctuations, which are examined in the second part of the chapter.

We use the general term 'adjustment' despite the fact that economic crises and adjustment policies are closely interrelated and that it is very difficult or even impossible to disentangle one from the other. Besides, although macroeconomic stabilization efforts can be distinguished conceptually from the more structural changes and reforms[1], in practice both types of intervention have been undertaken simultaneously during the last decade in the Latin American region. In the 1960s and 1970s, many stabilization programmes were implemented in Latin America and the Caribbean, usually connected with loans provided by the International Monetary Fund (IMF). Many of these met with only partial success, and then only for short periods of time. Complaints began to be voiced that *structural* conditions impeded the success of conventional stabilization policies. The most common argument was that it was difficult or impossible to change the behaviour of the public sector regarding its current deficit, unless its relative size in the economy was changed and its functions were redefined. In the 1980s this vision broadened, generalized, and emerged in the operations. The IMF began to require the approval of structural adjustment programmes, usually financed by the World Bank, in order to carry out the short-term stabilization operations.

The ease and extent with which this initiative spread in the 1980s was due in part to the prolongation and severity of the crisis in that decade. We will take a brief look at this crisis by drawing a very broad outline of it, and by describing the adjustment of the external and internal gaps that preceded and followed it. Then, we shall consider their apparent effects on demographic variables, based on the evidence available.

---

[1] Short-term stabilization policies aim at the restoration of some financial equilibrium, while structural reforms are oriented towards the transformation of certain basic relations in the economy on a medium- to long-term basis.

Crisis and Adjustment in Latin America

Economic crisis in the 1980s

The expression 'the lost decade' is now widely applied to the 1980s, denoting the adverse economic evolution of the Latin American region during this period. In the 1960s and 1970s, the Gross Domestic Product (GDP) had grown by 5.7 per cent annually, while in the 1980s it grew at the rate of only 1.1 per cent. *Per capita* GDP decreased by about 10 per cent during the decade, at an average annual rate of nearly –1 per cent (see Table 1.1). The decade began with severe internal and external imbalances. The deficit in current accounts reached 5 per cent of the GDP in 1980–1, which was obviously unsustainable in the long term[2]. Its counterpart, indebtedness, had become three and a half times the value of annual exports.

The internal imbalances were no less substantial: the public sector deficit was equivalent to six or seven points of GDP in Brazil and Bolivia, and was greater than 11 per cent in Mexico and Argentina, although there were exceptions such as Venezuela and Chile. Urban unemployment, which was moderately high in many countries in 1980, grew during the first half of the 1980s to over 13 per cent in Colombia, Chile, Panama, Uruguay, and Venezuela, and has stayed on average somewhat above pre-crisis levels (see Table 1.1). Finally, the inflation rate was as high as 100 per cent annually in Argentina and Brazil, whereas countries such as Mexico and Colombia, with traditionally low inflation, had an inflation rate of approximately 30 per cent—a rate which in the 1960s and 1970s had led Argentina and Brazil to be suffering from chronically high inflation.

It was in the context of these imbalances that the crisis erupted. The detonator was on the external front: in August 1982—in connection with the Mexican moratorium—the commercial banks, which were the principal owners of the US$ 90 billion debt increase in 1980–1, abruptly ceased their new loans to the region. In the following two years the region was forced to bring to zero its annual current account deficit of 40 billion dollars. Which of these gaps closed, and which did not? How were the closures achieved? In general, the fast bridging of the external gap was brought about by force. The internal imbalances, on the other hand, experienced wide oscillations. There were some improvements, as in the case of the public sector deficit; but generally, the disequilibrium remained the same or worsened, as was the case with unemployment and inflation.

Two circumstances made the external adjustment particularly hard. One was the situation in the international markets and the commercial policies of the OECD countries, which translated into reduced demand for Latin American exports and a decline in the terms of trade. The other was the evolution of interest rates: the LIBOR rate, that had hitherto fluctuated around 2 per cent in real terms, reached

---

[2] These averages hide great differences between countries: the decrease in per capita GDP (10 per cent on average) was more than 20 per cent in countries such as Argentina, Venezuela, and Peru; the current account deficit, which was 5 per cent of GDP in 1980–1 for the region as a whole, was over 12 per cent in Chile, and so on.

	GDP (US$m)	Growth rate of GDP per capita (% per year)		Percentage Urban	Urban unemployment rate (%)			Growth rate of per capita public expenditures (% per year)	
	1990	1960–80	1980–90	1990	1980	1985	1990	Health 1980–85	Education 1980–85
Argentina	2,324	2.0	-2.3	83	2.6	6.1	7.4	-3.6	-6.8
Bolivia	591	2.8	-2.5	45	7.1	5.8	9.5	-4.0	-11.4
Brazil	1,898	6.9	-0.5	67	6.2	5.3	4.3		
Colombia	1,418	3.5	1.7	64	9.7	14.1	10.3	1.3	2.0
Costa Rica	1,469	3.2	-0.5	43	6.0	6.7	5.4	-10.5	-7.8
Chile	2,599	1.5	1.2	81	11.7	17.0	6.5	3.9	-5.8
Dominican Republic	1,092	3.9	-0.3	50				-10.7	-6.4
Ecuador	1,355	6.1	-0.4	47	5.7	10.4	8.0	-7.9	-6.2
El Salvador	658	1.6	-1.5	43					
Guatemala	802	3.1	-1.8	37	2.2	12.0	6.4	-15.1	-10.5
Haiti	206	0.7	-2.0	24				-0.1	-2.6
Honduras	609	2.4	-1.1	35	8.8	11.7	7.1	-3.9	9.2
Mexico	2,326	4.8	-0.7	66	4.5	4.4	2.9	-5.5	-3.7
Nicaragua	446	0.3	-4.0	51	18.3	3.2	12.0	0.2	15.2
Panama	1,512	5.3	-1.4	50	10.4	15.7	16.8	2.9	2.6
Paraguay	1,299	5.1	0.1	42	3.9	5.1	6.6	14.2	-2.4
Peru	854	1.7	-2.8	64	7.1	10.1	8.3	2.6	1.6
Uruguay	2,166	1.7	-0.5	85	7.4	13.1	9.3	-3.5	-6.7
Venezuela	3,221	-0.3	-2.1	79	6.6	14.3	10.5	3.4	-1.4
Average	1,413	3.0	-1.1	71	7.4	9.7	8.2	-2.1	-2.4

Note: All averages are unweighted, except for the case of the urbanization rate, which is weighted by the country population.

Sources: GDP: CEPAL estimates, on the basis of official statistics; percentage urban: CELADE (1991), *Latin America: Percentage Urban 1990*, Demographic Bulletin, 24/47; unemployment rates and public expenditures: *Statistical Yearbook for Latin America and the Caribbean* (1991 edition), CEPAL, Santiago, Chile.

a historical maximum of 6 per cent in 1981 and stayed above 4.5 per cent until 1986, attaining a new peak of 6.1 per cent in 1984. Added to this was the procyclical withdrawal of new loans. The net capital inflow was reduced abruptly to insignificant levels, and profit and interest payments rose, so that the transfer of resources to the region was radically transformed. Net capital inflows in 1980 and 1981 of 11 billions annually gave way to large net capital *outflows* in 1982, a situation which continued until 1991, the first year in which there was again a positive transfer.

One cannot help making a historical comparison to assess the dimension of this transfer effort. Fully aware of the dangers and limits of exercices of this kind, we shall compare the transfer of resources from Latin America to the rest of the world with the famous war reparations paid by Germany after the First World War. Between 1925 and 1932 the latter were equivalent to 2.5 per cent of Germany's gross domestic product, and to 13.4 per cent of its exports. Between 1982 and 1985 in Latin America the net remittances were equivalent to 4.2 per cent of GDP and represented 25.7 per cent of the sub-continent's exports. Incidentally, similar results are obtained if one uses the French reparations after the war of 1870 as a comparison. The conceptual difficulties relating to such comparisons are obvious; the point is raised simply to give a rough impression of magnitude of the effort involved.

What happened on the domestic front? According to neo-classical theory both the internal and external imbalances are very simply explained: excess of internal expenditure over and above the product produces a deficit in the current account. The policy recommendation for this is a restriction on expenditure, and a change in relative prices—for example, through devaluation—to stimulate the production of tradable goods and divert consumer demand from these towards those that are non-tradable. If, in general, the principal cause of overspending is the public deficit, then devaluation should be accompanied by a restrictive fiscal policy. Furthermore, these types of measures are complementary in as much as what is desired is to avoid the public deficit producing inflationary effects that in turn erode the real value of the devaluation and its consequent impact.

Recent experience shows that this approach is effective insofar as the external sector is concerned, although at an enormous recessive cost. It also shows that the recipe is less effective for the internal imbalances due to three types of problems (Meller 1992). Firstly, the overspending may be caused primarily by the private sector. An example is Chile, which had its great external imbalance with a surplus public budget in 1978–81. Secondly, when there is a large public deficit (the most frequent case) and at the same time the payments on interest rise, the necessary contraction in operational cost in order to reach a budget balance is not determined independently of the said interest payments. Mexico is a case in point, albeit somewhat extreme: in 1985–6 interest payments by the government rose to 14.6 per cent of GDP, from 4.4 per cent in 1981. The operational deficit in Mexico during those years decreased from 7 of to 0 per cent of GDP, but the real deficit, after interest payments, rose to 14.5 per cent. Finally, precisely because the interest payments were so large, whenever there was a strong devaluation aimed at closing the external gap, a contradictory effect appeared in the public deficit, since the amount of national currency that the state had to spend to pay the interest on all the debt nominated in hard currencies, whether internal or external debt, increased in the same proportion as the devaluation. A good part of the frustrations already mentioned on the internal front, namely persistent public deficits and even more persistent inflation, can be explained through such a contradictory (rather than complementary, as is often maintained) relationship between the different measures adopted to close the two types of gaps.

To sum up: the region began the 1980s with severe internal and external imbalances; an external shock made the current account deficit unsustainable; interest rate and terms-of-trade conditions developed unfavourably, and all this led to a huge recessive adjustment. This adjustment closed the external gap and allowed a large transfer of resources to the exterior, but a good number of the internal imbalances remained.

Macroeconomic policies

Let us briefly review the policy measures undertaken. Three courses of action regarding structural reforms are currently favoured by the multilateral agencies: (1) state reform, which requires fiscal discipline on the expenditure side and on the taxation side, and privatization; (2) liberalization and deregulation, which includes liberalization of external trade (e.g. no quotas, no prior permits), low customs duties, liberalization of the financial markets, no discriminatory treatment against foreign investment, and, as far as possible, freedom of movement for all capital; and (3) increased openness, in a context of growing freedom of international trade.[3]

How were these reforms applied? As far as fiscal reforms are concerned, operational expenditures were greatly reduced: during 1985–9, surpluses of 1 or 2 per cent of the GDP appeared in Brazil, Mexico, and Colombia, while Argentina and Bolivia achieved small deficits. This occurred despite the reduction of fiscal revenues by between two and four points of the GDP due to the recession and, in some cases, to ineffective tax reforms. The final result of these changes was that deficits of mainly operational origins of 6–10 per cent turned into deficits typically between 3 and 7 per cent, composed principally of interest on the public debt.

Privatization was a policy instrument that gained momentum through the decade. Examples go from forerunners such as Chile, which began with a great impetus as far back as the 1970s, through cases of a certain gradualism, such as Mexico, to cases of great speed, though relatively late, such as Argentina in 1991–2. These policies sought to increase efficiency and competition in the long term, and to

---

[3] A less publicized element is the liberalization of the labour market, with the sole exception of the transitory freezing of salaries during shock programmes, oddly promoted in some cases in conjunction with liberalization measures.

decrease the size and the deficit of the public sector in the short term. No less important, however, was the idea that privatization gives a strong sign of a 'change of régime', which it is hoped will inspire trust in the economic policies as a whole, reducing inflationary expectations.

The external deregulation was substantial. Tariffs fell by half in the majority of countries, their structure was simplified and most of their quantitative restrictions abolished. The devaluation in real terms was also very strong. Typically, the value of the dollar in 1990 is significantly higher than in 1980; it was about 80 per cent higher in Argentina, Chile, Colombia, and Venezuela. Peru and Brazil are exceptions, but both had begun the decade with very undervalued currencies in comparison with the average for Latin America.

Taken as a whole, the group of measures produced two great 'losers' in most cases, both of which are relevant for demographic behaviour: investment and equity. Investment was reduced by half during the first two years of the decade, as it was the variable most frequently used to adjust the operational public deficit. Private investment demand fell as a result of the recession, at a time when the internal and external supply of savings was also declining. The investment ratio (in relation to GDP) fell from about 22 to 16 per cent in Brazil, from 25 to 19 per cent in Mexico and Venezuela, from 23 to 17 per cent in Peru, and from 22 to 8 per cent in Argentina. This large drop in investment places great strain on the economy and is no less serious an impediment to future growth than the burden of external debt.

The decade's other great loser was equity. The real purchasing power of wages fell much more than the per capita GDP in several countries between 1980 and 1990. In Mexico it fell by about 22 per cent while the GDP per capita fell by 7 per cent. In Peru and Venezuela, real salaries fell by no less than half, while the GDP per capita fell by between 20 and 30 per cent. Unemployment increased significantly by the mid-1980s, and it was still high in many countries in 1990. The primary distribution of income became more regressive. Data for the metropolitan areas of Argentina, Brazil, Colombia, Costa Rica, Uruguay, and Venezuela show that, in all cases, the top quartile of income earners (i.e. that 25 per cent of the population with the highest incomes), came out better off than the average: in Argentina and Brazil, the top quartile increased its real income while everybody else's decreased. The proportion of the population living below the poverty line increased to about 40 per cent for the region as a whole.

In most cases, this deterioration was not compensated for by social spending. On the contrary, as a result of fiscal adjustments and the reduction of public expenditures, outlays on health and education per capita almost everywhere registered smaller values in 1990 than in 1980: in Colombia and Venezuela they were 5 per cent less; in Chile, 10 per cent less; in Argentina, 15 per cent less. Public expenditures decreased, on average, by rather more than 2 per cent per year during 1980–5 (see Table 1.1). These figures, although not strictly comparable across countries or over time, clearly reveal a deterioration in social spending. It is mainly through its social costs that adjustment impinges on the demographic variables.

Demographic Responses

Demographic variables and economic adjustment

The evidence regarding the demographic consequences of economic adjustment in the region is still rather sparse. Mason (Chapter 2 below) recalls the analytical channels and reviews the major findings, taking a worldwide approach. Let us briefly mention the main demographic conjectures that have been expressed and then put into perspective the contributions in this volume, along three main lines of research: policy and institutional factors, short-term fluctuations in vital rates, and family labour force responses.

Mortality and, more probably, morbidity, might increase as a consequence of the worsening of living conditions. The decrease in income for the lower strata of the population might imply less, or less rich, food intake, though this type of expenditure should show little downward elasticity. The drop in public investment might affect sanitation infrastructure, but this might not have immediately visible effects. More important, hygienic habits and preventive attitudes towards diseases need not change abruptly. But public expenditure, as well as private expenditure, on health care might decrease, and this could have a noticeable effect on morbidity and, ultimately, on mortality.

Fertility could be affected, in principle, in either of two differing ways. If the traditional relationship between poverty and high fertility holds, then an increase in fertility could be expected. On the other hand, it is most probable that cultural changes which, together with economic growth in the 1970s, led to decreases in fertility will not be easily or rapidly reversible. Rather, if people plan their families so as to offer their children higher standards of care, nutrition, education, etc., then it is possible that in the face of economic adversity, decisions to have children may be postponed (or, more plausibly, decisions to marry may be postponed, with the attendant postponement of planned pregnancies). Which of those possibilities prevail is therefore an open empirical question.

Migration could also be affected, in cases where the preferred locations for economic activities geared to the export market differ from those oriented to the domestic market: one should expect migrants to be attracted to the former, because their relative weight increases with structural adjustment. If the exports which are increased are mainly of agricultural origin, as is the case in many Latin American countries, then urbanization might be slowed down, which in turn may affect the average evolution of fertility and mortality–morbidity. This hypothetical effect is in contrast to those resulting from agricultural crises originating in climatic changes that lead to bad harvests.

Generally speaking, two main difficulties arise when an attempt to identify and measure the demographic consequences of adjustment is made. The first is that the latest available data refer to the early 1990s; that is to say, only the most immediate consequences of the economic changes of the 1980s are captured. The second difficulty, not peculiar to the exercise of examining the consequences of structural adjustment, is nonetheless a significant one. To assign demographic changes to a particular set of socio-economic policy measures is to differentiate actual demographic behaviour and dynamics from what might have been in the absence of such policy. If mortality kept decreasing, for example, this does not necessarily mean that it is invariable with respect to economic policy. We might need to compare rates of decrease or, more generally, analyse deviations from otherwise expected values. Moreover, these expected values cannot be simple extrapolations from the past. It may well be that the economic situation, if dealt with by means of a given (different) set of policies, would have deteriorated even further, with consequently more acute effects on mortality. A third set of policies could have allowed for mortality to take an in-between path. In other words, there is no such thing as *the* impact of structural adjustment on mortality but, rather, there are as many impacts as possible comparisons with the presumed effects of alternative (plausible) policy packages.

Some studies have made use of survey data at two points in time to make 'before and after' analyses, while others have used yearly data series, in order to assess the short-term deviation from the trend and relative impact of institutional and behavioural factors, and to measure the lags involved. 'Before and after' exercises are useful in some respects (e.g. they allow the direct comparison of adjustment and non-adjustment periods), but even those based on more than just a few observations in time do not show the pattern of lag effects, except in a very limited way. Moreover, what happens 'after' cannot be exclusively attributed to the crisis or to adjustment, but to all events that follow the period 'before'. This latter difficulty is overcome, to a large event, by the short-term analyses.

Policy and institutional factors

Policy and institutional factors have been an issue of major interest. By use of yearly data series, Bravo (1992) examined trends in mortality due to certain causes in Costa Rica, Chile, and Guatemala. He found that, during the 1980s, mortality was affected more in Costa Rica than in Chile, despite the fact that Costa Rica had achieved slightly better health and mortality indices than the latter, and that it had a less severe crisis from which it recovered more quickly. Part of the explanation is that per capita expenditures in health and other social services were relatively more protected in Chile (see Table 1.1), and that some policies effectively concentrated resources on high-risk groups. Guatemala's fluctuations, on the other hand, were usually greater than those occurring in the other two countries, but were highly unsystematic in their response to economic changes. Its more sizeable rural population and low coverage in terms of public health facilities make it less vulnerable to macroeconomic shocks (economic fluctuations were measured by changes in the GDP) or fiscal retrenchment, and at the same time, more vulnerable to events such as epidemics or bad harvests.

A first set of studies in this volume (Musgrove, Behrman, Chapters 3 and 4) considers the impact of policy and institutional factors—at the family and state level—on demographic variables. The way in which public budgets were allocated, in particular the relative adjustments in investment and operational expenditures (Musgrove, Chapter 3 below), constitute important filters of the health and mortality consequences of economic changes that should be considered when the experience in particular settings is interpreted. Indeed, concern has been expressed about the effect that the crisis and adjustment could have on nutrition. Changes in food policies can have an impact on nutrition and on the health of the population, in as much as they affect the price of food products, when either direct subsidies to consumption or production or indirect subsidies are withdrawn, or when quantitative restrictions are set up. Behrman (Chapter 4 below) uses an economic household model of the determinants of nutritional health status, to assess the channels through which individuals and households respond to changes in these determinants, and discusses the policy implications of the impact of structural adjustment on food policy and nutrition.

Short-term fluctuations in vital rates

Some work has concentrated on the study of *short-term* fluctuations in marriages, births, and deaths on the basis of methodology developed by Lee (1990, and references therein) and Galloway (1988) that has been widely applied to historical settings. These studies examine the lag patterns of demographic responses in greater detail. Reher (1990) carried out what is probably the first modern statistical study of short-term demographic–economic fluctuations in the region. Using Mexican data series from the eighteenth century, he found significant and rather immediate responses of nuptiality, fertility, and mortality to economic changes, which were indexed by food prices. Already in 1927, Prebisch had carried out a pioneering analysis of short-term demographic changes in Argentina during the late nineteenth and early twentieth century (see Prebisch 1991). This study did not make use of the (now standard) modern statistical methods, but the findings are strikingly similar to those of Reher (1990), and even to some twentieth-century analyses to be discussed next, except for the case of mortality, for which Prebisch does not find a meaningful response.

As far as the twentieth century is concerned, and more specifically the post-Second World War period, a different conclusion is reached by Reher and Ortega (Chapter 6 below). They consider three Latin American countries—Argentina, Chile, and Uruguay—and make use of a set of sophisticated statistical methods to examine short-term changes over time. The links between fluctuations in living standards and demographic behaviour appear to be weaker than those in pre-transitional populations, with high demographic rates and a standard of living close to the subsistence level.

The study by Hill and Palloni (1992) on short-term responses to crises in Latin America is one of the most comprehensive to date on the subject. Using data for

seven Latin American and Caribbean countries, they find that marriages are positively related to economic conditions in the same year, that the response of births
is generally one year lagged, and that infant mortality and the mortality of women
aged 20 to 59 years are negatively related to economic changes at lag 0. Although
they report few statistically significant coefficients, they find systematic patterns
across countries that are consistent with expectations and the hypothesized mechanisms. Their findings illustrate some of the general patterns found and also some of
the country specificities. When marriages respond significantly (as is the most
common case), they do so contemporaneously, with little or no evidence of rebounds.
In countries where births react significantly (which occurs in a slightly lower proportion of cases) the largest response takes place after a lag of one year, as expected.
Infant mortality either does not respond at all, or does so contemporaneously, but
the responses are rarely statistically significant. Rebound effects are typically present.
Non-infant deaths almost never respond in any significant way to economic fluctuations (one notable exception being in the case of Guatemala), but when they do,
it is more frequently a phenomenon concentrated in adult women.

The demographic significance of the short-term mortality responses may be better
appreciated when the total effect it produces on a summary measure such as life
expectancy at birth is considered. Following Palloni and Hill (Chapter 5 below) an
estimate for a 'median' Latin American country implies that a reduction in GDP of
10 to 15 per cent—not an uncommon occurrance in the region during the 1980s—
results in a loss of nearly one year in life expectancy in the medium term. The
effect is mainly attributable to the response of infant deaths.

Regarding the national contexts in which these relations are observed, let us
mention that Chile has somewhat better average economic indicators than Costa
Rica, though the latter has a less concentrated income distribution and slightly more
favourable mortality indices. Both have generally better socio-economic indicators
than Guatemala, which has a much more important rural and indigenous population, and higher demographic rates as well. Despite the large differences in infant
mortality between Costa Rica and Guatemala, the responses of both countries to
economic fluctuations are very similar, at least in the very short term (0 and 1 years
lagged). Economic fluctuations affect births with a lag of 0 or 1 year depending,
in part, on the degree of association between formal unions and births, which is
relatively tight in Guatemala, less so in Chile, and very loose in Costa Rica.

Family labour force responses

A third set of issues concerns the labour market. How and to what extent did
households adjust to the economic crises? Evaluation of the effects is all the more
difficult since interactions between labour demand and labour supply factors are
present in the observed time series and make it difficult to assess causality links.
The adjustment mechanisms of the labour supply are examined by distinguishing
between the impact of the withdrawal from the labour market caused by decreased

earnings (that is, the discouraged worker effect) and the effect of the increase in labour supply to offset the reduced standard of living resulting from the decrease in wages of the already active family members (that is, the added worker effect).

The evolution of gross activity rates, without distinction between levels of education, is difficult to interpret, due to the general upward trend of female activity rates. An indirect way to assess the relative impact of these effects is to classify households according to socio-economic groups. The test of the additional worker hypothesis implies that the poorest women increase their labour supply during the crisis, and will be the first to withdraw from the labour market at the time of the recovery. Indeed, if female labour supply is positively related to level of education, and negatively related to the number of young children in the household, the additional worker hypothesis would involve a higher increase in activity rates for the poorest, least educated women, and an increase in labour supply regardless of the number of children. Moreover, the participation in the labour market of women heads of households, usually among the poorest in the population, would increase too.

Contributions in this volume, concerning either a particular country (Mexico, Argentina, Chile, Brazil) or a comparison between a set of different Latin American countries, reach mixed conclusions regarding the additional worker hypothesis, which vary according to the type of secondary household member considered. The work of García and Oliveira (Chapter 10 below), and that of Lam and Levinson (Chapter 9 below) on Brazil clarify the nature of the mechanisms concerned. García and Oliveira show that the observed increase in female labour force participation between 1981 and 1987 has a complex pattern. The crisis induces a decrease in the withdrawal from the labour market of young women, as increase in the activity rates of older women, more important participation by less educated women, and increased activity by women in legal or consensual unions.

The contribution of Lam and Levinson aims particularly to identify long-term trends and the changes caused by the crisis and by recovery. They show that in the 'long' run (1977–90), the higher the level of education, the greater the increase in married women's activity rates. Considering more specifically the 1983 crisis and the 1986 recovery, it appears that the increase in female activity during the recession, and the decrease during the recovery, are greater for women of a low educational level. This confirms the counter-cyclical effect of activity rates of married women. In other words, the effect of the additional worker that appears with the crisis enhances the long-term trend of the rise of female activity rates, although this short-term effect cannot be considered as the main explanation of the longer-term tendency.

An increase in children's labour might be expected to be another consequence of the crisis and of adjustment. Such an outcome does not seem to be verified by the cases examined. A decrease in child activity is sometimes observed, and might correspond to the increase in mothers' activity, as a result of a substitution of children for mothers in the area of domestic work. Much more has yet to be learned about how the labour force behaviour of family members affects basic demographic variables such as marriage patterns, fertility decisions, or mortality.

Case studies

Most of the available studies offer little direct evidence of the particular effect of adjustment policies, apart from the distinction that some of them make between responses during adjusting and non-adjusting time periods (for example, Palloni and Hill, Bravo, Chapters 5 and 7 below). The problem is more complex, less well defined, and therefore less tractable. Nevertheless, more can be learned from the experience of particular countries by combining statistical analyses with the consideration of institutional factors that are known to have been important in specific adjustment contexts. Two monographs on Chile and Brazil are discussed along these lines in the contributions by Bravo, and by Rios-Neto and Magno de Carvalho (Chapters 7 and 8 below).

In the case of Brazil, in the analysis of short-term variations in economic variables and vital rates in the city of São Paulo, Rios-Neto and Magno de Carvalho show for the 1916–88 period a positive impact of GDP on marriages and births, a negative elasticity between GDP and the infant mortality rate, and a pro-cyclical relation between GDP and activity rates. Considering more specifically the post-Second World War period the results are similar, as far as marriages and births are concerned. However, the relationship between GDP and infant mortality rate turns pro-cyclical, an unexpected result attributed by the authors to stronger health policies and nutritional programmes during the last few decades that might have wiped out the underlying negative relationships.

The latter result is consistent with the findings reported in the chapter on Chile by Bravo. He finds that infant mortality responds in the expected negative fashion to economic fluctuations and that it displays the usual 'rebounds' found in other studies; the size of the responses, however, is quite moderate and the statistical significance is low. On the other hand, the responses of marriages and births are substantial, highly significant, and display the expected rebound lag pattern. In some cases, there appear to be extra-economic events, sometimes indirectly related to the economic changes and reforms, that seem to have great importance in shaping demographic responses. For example, the abrupt changes in nuptiality and births in Chile (and in Uruguay as well) at the beginning of the 1970s may have been affected by the climate of political instability that had been building up since the middle 1960s, and by the events that followed the military coup in 1973. The reaction of marriages right after the worst of the economic recessions is over and as soon as the first signs of recovery appear may be indicative of the sensitivity of these variables in some Latin American countries to *expectations* regarding the near future, which are formed in part on the basis of policy announcements.

Discussion

The evidence contained in the present volume speaks mainly to the short-term effects of economic change. In some cases, it allows for a comparison of the demographic responses during the 1980s, the most recent region-wide adjustment period, with those of previous decades. On the whole, the evidence shows demographically significant short-term effects of economic changes on marriages and births and, for the most part, relatively muted mortality effects. Mortality responses, although rarely statistically significant, show systematic patterns: infant and child mortality are the most affected by short-term economic changes and display expected lag patterns. The overall size of the demographic responses shows a broad downward trend over the present century, although in some cases, responses seem to have become slightly more significant during the recent adjustment period. In the countries examined, the labour force responses are found to be more significant for less educated, young and older adult women in consensual unions and weakest for children. The volume does not include specific studies on migration responses, although these could be very important in many countries that have undergone significant structural economic change during the last two decades.

Taking a panoramic view of the volume's findings, one might be intrigued as to why the demographic responses are not more substantial than reported, given the profound economic changes experienced by the Latin American countries during the last few decades. Part of the answer has already been alluded to in the previous sections, which point to methodological difficulties in identifying and measuring effects that are composed of a series of causal connections that the available data do not allow to be fully explored. Considering the careful selection of relevant information and the use of appropriate analytical methods, problems in the data used do not seem to be determinant on this point. Moreover, as discussed in the following chapters, even clear-cut empirical links do not have a unique or direct causal interpretation, as the relationships are in practice conditioned to a varying degree by the social policy filters and behavioural responses at the level of individuals or families, that can moderate or largely compensate for the direct effects of economic changes. In this regard, the present publication, as a first attempt systematically to assess the main demographic responses to economic crises and adjustment in the Latin American region, should contribute towards identifying the relevant hypotheses and the appropriate data that may be productively explored in future research.

REFERENCES

Behrman, J., 'The Effect of Structural Adjustment on Food Policy and Nutrition', Chapter 4 below.

Bravo, J. (1992), 'Economic Crises and Mortality: Short and Medium Term Changes in Latin America', Proceedings of the Conference on the Peopling of the Americas, 3, Veracruz: International Union for the Scientific Study of Population, 439–56.

—— , 'Demographic Consequences of Structural Adjustment in Chile', Chapter 7 below.

Galloway, P. (1988), 'Basic Patterns in Annual Variations in Fertility, Nuptiality, Mortality and Prices in pre-industrial Europe', *Population Studies*, 24/2, 275–303.

García, B. and Oliveira, O. de, 'Economic Recession and Changing Determinants of Women's Work', Chapter 10 below.

Hill, K. and Palloni, A. (1992), 'Demographic Responses to Economic Shocks: The Case of Latin America', Proceedings of the Conference on the Peopling of the Americas, 3, Veracruz: International Union for the Scientific Study of Population, 411–38.

Lam, D. and Levison, D., 'Structural Adjustment and Family Labour Supply in Latin America', Chapter 9 below.

Lee, R. D. (1990), 'The Demographic Response to Economic Crisis in Historical and Contemporary Populations', *Population Bulletin of the United Nations*, 29, ST/ESA/SER. N/29, New York: United Nations, 1–15.

Mason, A., 'The Response of Fertility and Mortality to Economic Crisis and Structural Adjustment Policy during the 1980s', Chapter 2 below.

Meller, P. (1991), 'Adjustment and Social Costs in Chile during the 1980s', *World Development*, 19/11 (special issue, November 1991), 1545–1661.

Musgrove, P., 'Economic Crisis and Health Policy Response', Chapter 3 below.

Ortega-Orsona, J. A. and Reher, D., 'Short-term Economic Fluctuations and Demographic Behaviour: Some Examples from Twentieth-Century South America', Chapter 6 below.

Palloni, A. and Hill, K., 'The Effect of Economic Changes on Mortality by Age and Cause: Latin America, 1950–90', Chapter 5 below.

Pascale, R. (1988), *Sobre Ajuste y Crecimiento*, Banco Central del Uruguay, Departamento de Investigaciones Económicas, Serie Estudios 18.

Prebisch, R. (1991), 'Anotaciónes Demográficas', in Notas de Población, Special issue in honour of Dr Raúl Prebisch, 19/54, Santiago: CELADE.

Ramos, J. (1985), 'Stabilization and adjustment policies in the Southern Cone, 1974–1983', *CEPAL Review* 25, April 1985.

Reher, D. (1990), 'Coyunturas económicas y fluctuaciones demográficas en México durante el siglo XVIII', *História e Populacao: Estudos sobre América Latina*, São Paulo.

Rios-Neto, E. and Magno de Carvalho, J. A., 'Demographic Consequences of Structural Adjustment: The Case of Brazil', Chapter 8 below.

Villalobos, F. (1986), 'Las políticas de ajuste y el proceso de industrialización: Uruguay 1980–85', *Revista Uruguaya de Ciencias Sociales*, 11/2 Montevideo.

2 The Response of Fertility and Mortality to Economic Crisis and Structural Adjustment Policy during the 1980s: *A Review*

ANDREW MASON

Introduction

The purpose of this chapter is to review the demographic experience of the 1980s and to assess the impact of economic crisis and structural adjustment on fertility and mortality. There are two principal concerns. The first is that structural adjustment policies have had adverse and unanticipated effects on mortality or fertility, undermining important social objectives of development. A second possibility is that mortality has increased or fertility decline has slowed because of economic problems which are unrelated to structural adjustment policies. If this is so, certain policies might be justified—for example, increasing expenditures on health care—that conflict with prescriptions espoused for adjustment purposes. Despite the importance of this topic, it is not possible to distinguish the impact of deteriorating economic conditions in many developing countries from the impact of structural adjustment policies *per se*.

Although economic development leads to lower fertility in the long run, the few studies that have been carried out concur that, in the short run, fertility is pro-cyclical. Thus, it is doubtful that slower or negative economic growth has led to higher fertility, or to more rapid population growth, for that matter. Of course, as continued economic problems impede development efforts, fertility reduction objectives could be undermined. But to the extent that structural adjustment policies re-establish the conditions necessary for economic development, policies to reduce fertility would be complemented. The primary way in which adjustment policies could have an adverse impact is that fiscal austerity may undermine family planning programmes. Information about the extent of budget cuts is limited and experience with privatization programmes insufficient to reach any firm conclusions.

With few exceptions—for example, the famine-induced mortality increase in Ethiopia—mortality has continued its downward trend in developing countries despite the economic problems of the 1980s. In some countries, it has probably declined more slowly than it would have done under better circumstances, and in some localities it has risen in recent years. But it is difficult to establish the extent to which this has happened, and to identify the underlying causes.

Assistance by Dolly Testa in preparing this manuscript is greatly appreciated.

Mortality gains in developing countries can be attributed, in large part, to long-term processes such as increased literacy, improved urban infrastructure, and better health care systems. The extent to which these and other fundamental factors have suffered during the 1980s may not be apparent for years, if ever. There are quantifiable short-term responses of mortality, especially infant mortality, to economic fluctuations. The evidence from Latin America seems clear on this point, although the responses are relatively modest. Undoubtedly, the vulnerability is much greater in Africa where incomes are lower and the health care system less developed, but there is no evidence on this issue.

Fertility

We would like to address two questions in this section. First, have rates of child-bearing among women living in developing countries been influenced by recent economic problems and structural adjustment policies? Second, are the fertility responses temporary and of little demographic significance or have there been more fundamental, long-lasting changes?

Previous research on the determinants of fertility sheds quite a bit of light on these issues, but much of it is indirect. First, we know that fertility responds to economic change. Historical studies show that even in pre-industrial societies, child-bearing responded to economic fluctuations. And in developing countries which have not yet adopted modern family planning practices, the use of traditional contraceptive methods, changing age at marriage, and physiological mechanisms provide the means by which childbearing varies.

Second, we know that fertility declines with development. Policies and programmes that speed the development process will, in general, speed the fertility transition. Of course, this says nothing about particular aspects of development, and some policies may have little impact on fertility and other policies may lead to increased fertility.

Third, we know that the short-term response of fertility to economic factors may be quite different from the long-term response. Low-income countries may have high rates of fertility, but couples do not usually respond to unemployment by bearing more children. Most studies have found that fertility is pro-cyclical, temporarily rising in good times and declining in bad.

Fourth, we know that the public sector and international donors have played an instrumental role in promoting family planning and lowering rates of childbearing. A reduced commitment to these programmes in countries with high fertility rates can be expected to lead to slow fertility decline.

Unfortunately, we have no conclusive evidence about the impact on fertility of recent economic events in developing countries. Part of the problem can be traced to inadequate data. For many developing countries, current and reliable data on fertility and family planning programmes are not available. A second and major problem is that our models are not sufficiently developed to analyse aggregate trends in fertility and disentangle the impacts of short-term economic phenomena from long-term social and economic change, changing culture, and changing government policy.

This section organizes the discussion of fertility using a well-known framework. (Bulatao and Lee 1983). Childbearing in any country is a product of factors that affect the supply of children, the demand for children, and the costs of regulation. At early stages of the demographic transition, variation in fertility is dominated by supply side factors: for example, age at marriage, and fecundability. At late stages, fertility is dominated by the demand for children or factors that influence a couple's desired completed family size and the timing of their childbearing. And at inter-mediate stages, contraceptive costs, including availability, play an important role. Thus, the impact of economic fluctuations may vary widely depending on a country's position within the demographic transition.

Supply-side factors

In a pre-contracepting society, or non-contracepting segments of any society, variation in fertility is determined by supply-side factors which affect the age at which women begin their childbearing, the mean birth interval, and the age at which childbearing ceases. Of the five proximate determinants identified by Bongaarts and Menken (1983), age at first exposure to intercourse and variation in post-partum infecundability are by far the most important determinants of variation in natural fertility rate.

The age at which women are first exposed to intercourse is determined partly by biology (the age at onset of menarche) and partly by social convention (the age at first marriage). Bongaarts and Menken (1983) examine sources of variation in a natural fertility regime and find that the differences observed among early and later marrying populations are sufficient to account for five additional births, holding other proximate determinants fixed.

Most assuredly, changing economic conditions within developing countries do not produce ten-year changes in the average age at marriage. But studies that are reviewed in more detail below conclude that changes in the unemployment rate and the level of per capita income do generate noticeable changes in marriage age and, in turn, rates of childbearing. Variation in the age at onset of menarche can also affect age at first exposure to intercourse and the supply of children, but only in the few countries where early marriage is prevalent and influenced by age at menarche[1] or in countries where early premarital sexual activity is common, as in the Caribbean. The most convincing direct evidence for a link is reported by Udry and Cliquet (1982). Among two early marrying populations, Pakistanis and ethnic Malays

---

[1] It is very rare for women to marry before reaching menarche. In Yemen, about 11 per cent of ever-married women aged 15–19 have not yet reached menarche, but in thirteen other developing countries for which data are available, 96 per cent of ever-married 15–19 year olds in Mauritania, 98 per cent of those in Sudan, and 99 per cent of those in the other countries had reached menarche (Singh and Ferry 1984).

in Malaysia, differences in age at menarche resulted in a substantial difference in age at first marriage and age at birth of first child.

Can economic conditions affect age at onset of menarche? In a number of related studies, Frisch (1975, 1978) shows that malnutrition can delay menarche by two to three years. Thus, severe economic problems or the elimination of food subsidies could depress childbearing to the extent that nutritional levels are adversely affected.[2] As addressed in more detail below, it is unclear that nutritional levels have suffered greatly. Moreover, even if chronic malnutrition has increased, the impact on current childbearing is probably modest. Bongaarts (1980) employed computer simulation techniques to assess the impact of a two-year delay in age of menarche in a population with a young age at marriage and found that current fertility would decline by less than 5 per cent.

Variation in postpartum infecundability is identified by Bongaarts and Menken (1983) as the second important proximate determinant of natural fertility. Postpartum infecundability is determined primarily by the duration and, probably, the intensity of breastfeeding and, in some societies, by social taboos against intercourse following birth.[3] The duration of postpartum infecundability can vary from three months in contemporary developed countries to up to two years in developing countries where extended breastfeeding is practised.

There are several obvious mechanisms by which economic change could influence breastfeeding practices. Formal sector employment which leads to separation of mother and child undermines breastfeeding. More educated and higher-income mothers are generally less likely to breastfeed in developing countries. Moreover, currency devaluation will increase the price of imported formula, leading mothers to substitute breast for bottle feeding. One would expect, then, that economic downturn and adjustment policies would encourage breastfeeding, leading to longer postpartum amenorrhea and somewhat lower rates of childbearing. The effect of severe malnutrition on the quantity of breast milk reinforces the pro-cyclical response of childbearing by encouraging more intensive breastfeeding and extending the period of postpartum amenorrhea (Gray 1983). The effects, however, are relatively small except in cases of severe malnutrition.

To sum up, then, a variety of mechanisms exist by which the supply of children can respond pro-cyclically to economic fluctuations. The most important is probably variation in the age at marriage. Physiological factors are complementary but probably play a minor role except in cases of widespread famine or severe economic dislocation. But even where the use of modern contraceptives is limited, traditional methods may allow couples to postpone or reduce their childbearing. The influence of economic conditions on the demand for children is the issue to which we now turn.

---

[2] There is also substantial variation in the age of menopause which may be linked to nutrition, but the impact on completed family size or current fertility will be small given the low rates of childbearing among women in their forties (Gray 1983).

[3] Postpartum taboos against sexual intercourse are particularly widespread in Sub-Saharan Africa, but it seems implausible that they are influenced, in the short term, by changing economic conditions.

Demand-side factors

Most research on the demand for children has relied on the new household economics approach that emphasizes the impact of long-term or permanent changes in income or productivity on completed family size. To the extent that economic fluctuations lead households to revise their expectations about lifetime earnings, the new household economic model and supporting empirical research provides a useful guide to the likely response of childbearing couples. But current fertility is influenced by timing decisions, as well, that may respond in unique fashion to temporary economic fluctuations. Although there are few studies of cyclical fertility, we will also discuss what is known on the topic below.

The standard new home economics model of fertility treats children as consumer goods. Were it not for a number of important complications, children would be like any other normal good—increased income would lead to increased demand for children (Becker 1960). Three aspects of childbearing have an important bearing, however, on the relationship between the economic circumstances of the family and completed family size. First, children are produced. Because they require an intensive use of mothers' time, an increase in wages of women entails both a substitution and an income effect. Couples can afford more children but the opportunity cost of children increases, as well. If the substitution effect dominates, couples will choose to bear fewer children. The opportunity cost of children may be negligible in many developing countries, however. In rural societies, the conflict between work and childrearing is considerably less than in industrialized economies where work and home are physically separated.

Second, the satisfaction that couples derive from children depends on both the number and the 'quality' of their children. As income rises, couples may choose to substitute quality for quantity so that total expenditure on children increases but not necessarily the number of children (Becker and Lewis 1973 and Willis 1973).

The third qualification is particularly germane to the context of less developed countries (LDCs). The underlying premise of the new home economics model of childbearing is that children are net users of household time. But where children require relatively little exclusive attention and engage in productive activities themselves, they can be net suppliers of household time. Under these conditions, a general increase in wages will reduce rather than increase the net price of children and encourage higher rates of childbearing (Lindert 1983).

Many studies of childbearing in more developed countries (MDCs) have confirmed Becker's original hypothesis that children are a normal good and, if properly measured—that is, controlling for the value of time—an increase in income should lead couples to bear more children. But a much cloudier picture emerges from studies of LDC childbearing. Mueller and Short (1983) reviewed twenty-two macro-level studies of the income fertility relationship based mostly on international cross-sections. Only a single study consistently found a positive relationship between fertility and income and the great majority found no significant relationship at all.

On the other hand, micro-level studies are more supportive of a positive income relationship. Even here, though, results have been far from uniform.

The impact of short- rather than long-term changes in income have attracted little attention, but Ben-Porath (1973) distinguishes 'permanent' responses to economic change from 'transitory' responses. Current economic downturns in today's developing countries presumably have both transitory and permanent effects on fertility. As households revise their expectations about lifetime economic circumstances, we might expect revision in desired completed fertility. But current childbearing will be influenced, as well, to the extent that households revise the timing of their childbearing in response to transitory economic circumstances.[4] Ben-Porath offers two arguments for a pro-cyclical fertility response. First, a downturn creates uncertainty about permanent income, encouraging couples to postpone *irreversible* fertility decisions. Second, in the face of liquidity problems, couples may choose to time their childbearing so as to match variation in family size (and consumption 'needs') to variation in income. However, a third factor may elicit a counter-cyclical response. Because childrearing is a time-intensive activity, the opportunity cost of rearing children declines during periods of rising unemployment. Just as young adults choose to remain in school during periods of high unemployment, young women may choose to bear more children.

Costs of regulation

Structural adjustment policies affect the costs of contraception in two different ways. First, deficit reduction efforts may affect funding for government-sponsored family planning programmes, limiting either the availability of contraceptives or inducing increased charges for contraceptives. Second, exchange rate adjustments or other policies designed to reduce current account deficits will increase the costs of imported contraceptives. This would increase costs in both the public and the private sector.

Recent data on family planning expenditures in Asia, where the public sector is dominant, present a mixed picture for the 1980s. In the Philippines, the budget allocation for family planning dropped in 1983 to one-third of the 1981 level. In Indonesia, family planning expenditure increased at a remarkable pace until 1983, but actually declined in 1984 and grew much more slowly thereafter. On the other hand, Bangladesh has maintained expenditures on family planning at a high level despite its economic problems (Ross *et al.* 1988).

A decline in expenditures need not result in a decline in services (or an increased price to consumers). Wages constitute a large portion of costs in many family planning programmes so that real costs may have declined with real wages in countries experiencing negative growth. Moreover, family planning efforts often rely heavily on community groups whose members may work on a volunteer basis.

---

[4] Of course, decisions to delay childbearing will also affect completed family size as it will increase the likelihood of this falling short of a couple's desired completed family size.

The recent decline in expenditure in the Philippines, for example, was accomplished by a more effective utilization of volunteer labour that may have actually improved family planning service delivery.

A potentially important source of increased costs in some countries is the direct price of contraceptives. The importance of contraceptive supplies varies considerably from country to country, but anywhere from 10 per cent up to 40 per cent of family planning budgets can be devoted to purchasing contraceptives. More importantly, many countries rely on foreign sources so that prices are sensitive to exchange rate fluctuations. Four major Asian developing countries—China, India, Indonesia, and Korea—are self-sufficient or nearly self-sufficient when it comes to contraceptives. A number of Latin American countries manufacture oral contraceptives, but all import more contraceptives than they produce. Egypt aside, African countries are entirely dependent on imports to supply their family planning programmes (Ross *et al.* 1988).

To summarize, research on fertility determinants generally supports the thesis that economic events during the 1980s should have depressed fertility. Most supply-side and demand-side mechanisms support a pro-cyclical response in fertility. Moreover, two counter-cyclical mechanisms could dominate in some circumstances: (1) reduced wages and employment among women would lower the opportunity costs of childbearing; and (2) deteriorating family planning programmes could result in higher costs of regulation. Many of the mechanisms described are temporary in nature so that as economic conditions improve, fertility could be expected to rebound.

Evidence on the secular response of fertility

There is clear evidence that severe economic crisis can have a pronounced impact on fertility in the short run. One well-documented case is the Dutch famine of 1944–5, induced by a Nazi embargo on the movement of all goods within occupied Holland in retaliation for a strike by Dutch rail workers. Stein *et al.* (1975) demonstrate the close association between food availability in urban areas and births nine months later. As the food ration declined from 1,700 to around 700 or 800 calories per day, monthly births dropped from around 4,000 to as few as 1,700.

Three additional cases have been well documented for contemporary developing countries. Extensive flooding in Bangladesh in 1974 and 1975 destroyed a substantial portion of the rice crop, driving up rice prices by more than 100 per cent. The crude birth rate dropped to only 27.6 births per thousand population between April 1975 and March 1976 as compared with birth rates ranging from 40 to 48 prior to the famine. The 1984–5 drought in Dafur, Sudan, led to a 25 per cent decline in the crude birth rate in the south and close to a 50 per cent decline in the north (de Waal 1989). Ashton *et al.* (1984) and Coale (1984) document the demographic impact of the economic crisis in China associated with 'the great leap forward'. Average daily food energy declined from over 2,100 calories in 1958 to just over 1,500 calories in 1960, and the total fertility rate dropped from 6.1 births per woman in the 1957–8 fiscal year to 3.4 births per woman in the 1960–1 fiscal year (Ashton *et al.* 1984).

Studies of these severe crises have emphasized the physiological link between famine and fecundity and sexual activity, and ascribe a secondary role to volitional efforts to reduce childbearing in the face of economic adversity. The evidence on this issue is understandably skimpy, but in the Dutch case, for example, fertility rates declined by less for first-parity births than for higher-parity births. This finding suggests that delayed marriage was not a major proximate determinant of declining fertility.

These examples establish outer bounds for the potential impact of economic crisis, and demonstrate that, if economic conditions deteriorate sufficiently to induce famine, the impact on fertility can be quite substantial. Examination of data on births after normal conditions are restored indicates that famine has no lasting impact on fertility and that fertility typically exceeds normal levels immediately following a fertility crisis. In all three cases cited above, birth rates rebounded to levels equal to or exceeding those persisting prior to the crisis.[5] Obviously, the reduced fertility (and higher mortality) associated with famine has permanently affected the population size. Simulation studies by Watkins and Menken (1985) show that a severe two-year famine which resulted in a 110 per cent increase in the death rate and a drop in the birth rate of one-third would result in a population that is 7 per cent smaller after 90 years (see, also, Komlos 1988; Palloni 1988; and Watkins and Menken 1988). There is no evidence, however, that crises of the sorts described above have a lasting impact on the rate of population growth or the timing of the fertility transition.

A number of studies of the impact of moderate economic fluctuations on fertility have been undertaken in the MDCs. Early studies demonstrated that high unemployment delayed marriage and reduced marital fertility in the US (Kirk 1960; Silver 1965). The Ben-Porath (1973) study of fertility fluctuations in Israel may be more instructive because of the analysis of different socio-economic groups. As has been found by early US studies, both marriage and fertility in Israel were procyclical in the 1950s and 1960s. Moreover, changes in the unemployment rate had a statistically significant effect for both Jewish and non-Jewish populations and— among the Jewish population—for those originating in Africa, Asia, Europe, or America. The elasticity of fertility with respect to the employment rate was estimated to vary from 0.6 to 1.3. More or less, then, a one percentage point increase in the unemployment rate induced a one per cent reduction in the birth rate.

A number of studies that have examined the response of marriage and marital fertility to economic fluctuations in pre-industrial Europe may also be relevant to today's LDCs (see Palloni 1989 for a recent review). For example, Lee (1981) in his analysis of England from 1541 to 1871, found that marital fertility and nuptiality

---

[5] The presence of fertility exceeding normal levels after a crisis is mostly a physiological phenomenon. More women will be 'at risk' because fewer will have given birth recently and higher infant mortality rates will decrease the average duration of postpartum amenorrhea for women who have given birth.

were both pro-cyclical. Price changes generated a strong negative response in marital fertility, peaking at a lag of 9 or 10 months, and a negative response in marriage during the same year. Although fertility rebounded at a lag of 24 months, the cumulative effect of price increases over five years was strongly negative.

Marriage and fertility in seven Latin American countries dropped below their long-term trends during the Great Depression. Given contraceptive practices of the time, most variation in fertility could probably be traced to changes in age at marriage. Crude birth rate data for ten Latin American countries shows that the number of births declined more rapidly or dropped from steady levels between 1930 and 1935 (Palloni 1989).

Most available contemporary evidence for developing countries is confined to the Latin American context. Much is in this volume. The Hill and Palloni analysis (Chapter 5) of economic crisis and demographic change examines the short-term impact of per-capita private consumption on births and marriages in seven Latin American countries and births by order for a subset of four countries for which the required data are available. In Chile, economic fluctuations had a substantial contemporaneous impact on marriages and first births and a lagged impact on first births and higher-order births. In the other countries studied, however, the estimated coefficients were generally not statistically significant. The signs of the coefficients were often consistent with the maintained hypotheses that marriage is pro-cyclical, but there was little evidence that births were affected by economic fluctuations. Bravo (Chapter 7) analyses the impact of per-capita GDP and the unemployment rate on demographic trends in Chile and reaches conclusions that are generally consistent with the Hill and Palloni findings. Ortega-Osona and Reher (Chapter 6) reach similar conclusions in their analyses of Argentina and Chile.

Goldani *et al.* (1989) examines the impact of the debt crisis on marriage and fertility in Brazil. They point out that the rate of first marriage dropped by 27.4 per cent between 1980 and 1984 and that the total fertility rate declined by 20 per cent between 1980 and the first half of 1984 as compared with a 6 per cent decline between 1977 and 1980. Marriage and fertility are also found to respond pro-cyclically to wages (Rios-Neto and de Carvalho, Chapter 8).

The research on the response of fertility to economic crisis provides an incomplete picture. In some Latin American countries, economic decline apparently led to delayed marriage and lower rates of childbearing. In many Latin American countries, however, there is little evidence of a substantial effect. Little is known about the impact in Africa.

Mortality

Identifying the channels by which mortality improvements in developing countries have been achieved provides some guidance with respect to the potential effects of economic crisis and structural adjustment policies. First, much of the evidence points to the central role played by the public sector as an agent of reduced mortality.

Of the countries which have achieved very rapid improvements in mortality, many (Sri Lanka, Cuba, Costa Rica, and China) are notable for the pervasiveness of their public sectors. Moreover, many of the channels by which mortality is reduced are areas with significant public sector activity. The most immediate and direct role of the public sector is in the provision of individual and public health services, including health education, immunization, malaria eradication, and primary health services. Musgrove (Chapter 3) provides a very informed discussion of economic crisis and health policy.

There are three other areas in which the public sector may have played a major role in reducing mortality. Public works programmes have improved the quality of the water supply and sanitation systems, leading to a reduction in environmental contamination. Increased commitment to education and, especially, a commitment to primary school education for all in many developing countries has had a beneficial impact on each of the proximate determinants of mortality, from improving personal illness control and nutrition to improving maternal factors—that is, reduced childbearing, longer birth intervals, and later age at first birth. A final public sector activity with a clear potential for influencing mortality is government food policy, including agricultural subsidies, price supports, and supplemental feeding programmes. In a recent survey of food policies, Pinstrup-Anderson (1985) concludes that the living standards and nutritional status of the poor have been adversely affected by the elimination of cheap food policies because the poor spend such a high proportion of their income on food and because supplies have not increased as rapidly as had been hoped. Furthermore, many of the poor have not enjoyed the benefit of a higher income because they are not involved in agricultural production. In sum, a significant deterioration in the provision of public services potentially could have an important adverse impact on health and mortality. Behrman (Chapter 4) points out the variety of mechanisms that can ameliorate the impact of changing food policies.

Health and mortality conditions are not determined solely by public sector activity. Preston's influential studies (1975, 1980, 1985) of international variation in life expectancy have demonstrated a close cross-sectional relationship, at the national level, between mortality and relevant dimensions of economic development such as literacy, the level and distribution of per capita income, and food consumption. A steady improvement in the material standard of living, and all that goes with it, makes a major contribution to steady, long-term improvements in mortality conditions.

Thus, there can be little doubt that slower economic growth or negative economic growth, where it has occurred, has deleterious long-term consequences for reducing mortality, just as it has adversely affected other important dimensions of social and economic progress. Some of the consequences of slower growth might be immediately apparent—for example, reduced expenditure on health care or food. Others, such as slower improvements in educational attainment, will emerge with considerable delay. It is equally true that structural adjustment policies, to the extent that they succeed in re-establishing sustainable, long-term economic growth, will have beneficial long-term effects on mortality conditions. Several questions remain, however. First, do structural adjustment policies entail short-term effects on mortality that can and should be avoided? Second, are the short-term mortality consequences of economic crisis sufficiently severe that extraordinary measures are required, even if they are contrary to structural adjustment objectives?

Government programmes

A reasonable empirical starting point for answering the first question is to examine whether the level of public services has deteriorated as a result of reductions in government expenditures undertaken to reduce substantial government deficits. Available evidence indicates that public sector efforts have suffered in recent years. Pinstrup-Anderson (1987) examines government spending on health, education, and food programs during the 1970s and 1980s. Expenditures on food subsidies in countries with major food programmes have increased less rapidly than general prices but the real benefits to consumers may have increased in some countries because world agricultural prices have declined. Colombia and Sri Lanka have undertaken explicit policies to reduce the scope of food subsidy programmes, but none of the ten countries surveyed has more effectively targeted programmes at the poor.

Changes in expenditure in the social sectors have varied considerably from country to country and from region to region, but per capita expenditures on health have declined in seven countries in Africa, fourteen countries in Latin America, three countries in the Middle East, and four countries in Asia. Per capita expenditures on education have declined in five African countries, ten Latin American countries, and in two countries in both the Middle East and Asia. In general, capital expenditures have been more vulnerable than recurrent expenditures. Thus, the impact on health care and, hence, mortality may be spread over a number of years and not concentrated solely in the years in which expenditures have declined.

For a number of other reasons, it is unlikely that the level and quality of government social services have declined as substantially as per capita public expenditures. First, many social sectors tend to be relatively labour-intensive and reductions in public expenditures often have been realized through a decline in real salaries rather than staff cuts. (See Macedo 1984 on Brazil, for example).[6]

Second, to the extent that government services are cut, selective reductions may mitigate the adverse impact on mortality. In Chile, for example, a substantial cut in health expenditures resulting from the 1975–6 recession was accompanied by a shift in health policy towards a concentration on primary care for mothers and newborn infants that may have minimized the impact on infant and child mortality (Foxley and Raczynski 1984). Behrman and Deolalikar (1989) describes a number of cases in which fiscal savings have been achieved through the targeting of food

[6] This is not to suggest that the high wage content of recurrent expenditure is necessarily a good thing. To the extent that fiscal austerity prevents increasing expenditures on non-salary items, e.g. books and drugs, the success of public programs will be limited.

subsidies that have reduced the cost of cheap food policies without substantial adverse impact on the poor, although they seem more optimistic about the success of such efforts than Pinstrup-Anderson. In five Latin American countries studied by Musgrove (Chapter 3 below) investment was reduced very sharply, protecting recurrent expenditure.

Finally, those receiving public sector services undertake action that mitigates the adverse impact of public policy. As public health services decline in quality or availability, individuals may turn to the private sector or engage in self-treatment. Some recent evidence shows that significant reductions in food expenditure are achieved with little nutritional sacrifice (see Behrman and Deolalikar 1989 and the references cited therein).

Unfortunately, it is difficult to assess the importance of these qualifications and the extent to which the decline in public expenditures may have affected the quality of social services. Even on a country-by-country basis, it is difficult to determine the extent of deterioration in public services and the impact on health and morbidity in either the short or long run.

Evidence on mortality trends

Studies of recent trends in mortality agree in one important regard—economic crisis and structural adjustment typically have not led to an increase in mortality. Hill and Pebley (1988), for example, examine quinquennial data on the proportion of children dying before age five and find only one country, Ghana, in which mortality increased during the 1980s. Palloni (1989) and Bravo (Chapter 7) examine mortality trends in Latin America and find no cases in which mortality has increased. This does not preclude the possibility that mortality decline has slowed in recent years. Thus, the central question remains: is mortality today higher than it would otherwise have been because of the economic crises developing countries have faced and the adjustment policies they have pursued?

Several nagging problems preclude a definitive answer to this question. First, only limited data on mortality conditions are available in many developing countries. Although a number of studies based on annual statistics 'compiled' by the World Bank have been published (Zuckerman 1987 and Kakwani 1988 are examples) a great majority of the data points are linearly interpolated, or extrapolated using estimates for five-year intervals prepared by the UN Population Division. Such data may be useful for comparing the mortality levels from one country to the next or for gauging the broad trends in mortality decline, but are clearly inadequate for analysis of annual variation in mortality and its relationship to structural adjustment.

The quinquennial estimates of mortality provided by the UN Population Division are more reliable in the sense that a larger proportion of the data points are based on actual data rather than extrapolation or interpolation. Even so, a large portion of the figures, especially values reported for sub-Saharan Africa, are not based on real data (Hill and Pebley 1988).

The second difficulty is identifying the expected trend in mortality in the absence of economic crisis or structural adjustment. This is a counterfactual exercise that requires a complete and precisely estimated model of mortality. In the absence of such a model, available studies have taken relatively simple approaches to this issue. Preston (1985) considers whether absolute declines in life expectancy have been more modest in recent years. Hill (1985 and 1988) examines percentage declines and declines along a logistic. Behrman and Deolalikar (1988) employ a quadratic to estimate the long-term trend and assess whether data deviate from the estimated trend. Palloni (1989) uses a cubic to fit very long time series and pre-economic crisis mortality trends in Costa Rica as a model for shorter-term analysis.[7] Bravo uses a cubic fitted to annual data for 1950–90 for four Latin American countries. Hill and Palloni (Chapter 5) use a centred moving average to represent the long-term trend in mortality. Essentially, researchers have taken one or two approaches to identifying a counterfactual trend by which to judge the mortality experience of the 1980s. The a priori approach assumes that mortality decline has slowed if the percentage decline, absolute decline, or similar simple measure is smaller than in previous years. The difficulty is the lack of theoretical foundation for long-term trends in mortality. Most obviously, mortality rates have a fixed lower limit of zero which precludes a constant absolute decline in mortality rates. The second approach to characterizing the long-term trend is data-based. The potential pitfalls of this approach are rather obvious. Using a sufficiently flexible functional form would allow many different patterns to be characterized as consistent with the long-term trend. These patterns may not always coincide closely and thus may, in some cases, lead to ambiguous results.

Despite the inherent difficulties of research in this area, several recent studies provide support for the view that mortality decline has slowed during the 1980s. Palloni (1989) examines trends in infant mortality in Latin America. Extensive analysis shows that in seven out of ten countries, the rate of mortality decline during the 1980s slowed relative to the decline experienced during the 1970s and those countries with the greatest decline in real wages suffered the greatest slowdown in mortality. Cornia (1987) reviews results from case studies of ten countries. In two cases—São Paulo in Brazil, and Ghana—infant mortality is reported to have increased at some point during the 1980s, whereas in Chile, the Philippines, and South Korea the rate of decline is reported to be less than the trend. Several recent studies (Bravo 1992 and Chapter 8 below; Hill and Palloni 1992; and Palloni and Hill, Chapter 6 below) have examined short-term fluctuations in mortality and have consistently found an inverse relationship between infant mortality and per capita income or similar economic measures. How significant is the impact of economic fluctuations? Palloni and Hill (Chapter 6 below) estimate that a 10 per cent drop in GDP would generate a decline in life expectancy of 0.7 years, mostly attributable to changes in infant mortality.

---

[7] The use of a polynomial to represent a trend requires particular caution on the part of the researcher because the function need not be monotonic over the time period analysed. In principle, one could conclude that an increase in infant mortality was on trend.

Not all recent research supports the thesis that mortality has been adversely affected by economic crisis. Behrman and Deolalikar (1989) review results of their study of Jamaica in which they analyse 1984–5 health inputs and outcomes coincident with the implementation of a structural adjustment programme. Using a quadratic equation to represent secular trends, they find little evidence to support the view that health characteristics have departed from their long-term path, despite conclusions to the contrary by Boyd (1988). Hill and Pebley (1988) examine quinquennial data on the proportion of children dying before age five and, Ghana aside, find no evidence of a slowdown and for the countries for which data are available, evidence of an accelerated decline. Only in the case of Asia is there evidence of a slowdown in the rate of mortality decline on a regional basis.

Where does this leave us? First, research on the determinants of mortality suggests that many of the economic problems that developing countries have encountered during the 1980s should adversely affect mortality. However, this research does not adequately address timing issues and the extent to which mortality change might lag changes in income, nutrition, or education. The available evidence does suggest that long-term social and economic development is more important than short-term fluctuations. Second, the link between the economic situation and mortality conditions is not set in concrete. At the household level, a variety of actions can be taken to ameliorate the adverse impact of economic contraction on mortality. At the macro level, governments, assisted by international donors, have achieved impressive gains in mortality even at fairly low material standards of living. However, reductions in government expenditures in many countries has reduced the public health care resources and impaired the ability of the system to deal with any emerging health problems. Third, the likely impact of adjustment policies, *per se*, depends on the success of those policies. If short-term increases in unemployment and reductions in income growth yield more rapid and broadly based economic development, mortality conditions may be improved by adjustment policies. Fourth, data are inadequate to judge whether the economic crisis or adjustment policies have adversely affected mortality, in general. Many countries have continued to achieve substantial improvement in mortality; a few have experienced slowdowns or even mortality reversals; for many countries, we do not know.

Concluding Remarks

Reviewing recent research on fertility and mortality and the impact of structural adjustment and economic crisis leads to two important conclusions. The first is that the information available to track mortality and fertility has many limitations. The problem is particularly troubling because the data inadequacy is greatest in the poorest countries—the very countries where economic crisis surely had its greatest impact.

The second important conclusion is that people in many developing countries have a remarkable ability to minimize the impact of severe economic crisis. Many countries experienced major and prolonged declines in real income, high rates of unemployment, rapid inflation, and significant cuts in government programmes. Under the circumstances, one would expect demographic impacts literally to leap off the page. In a few countries they do, but in most they do not.

The existing studies are mixed in their assessment about the demographic impacts, but there is no evidence of a widespread decline in childbearing or increase in mortality. In some Latin American countries, fertility and mortality do not seem to have been affected at all.

Our view of the 1980s may be considerably different ten years on from what it is today. Recent studies may have seriously underestimated the impact on fertility and mortality. The response of fertility and mortality to economic recovery, if it continues, should provide important clues to the social costs of economic crisis during the last decade.

REFERENCES

Ashton, B. *et al.* (1984), 'Famine in China, 1958–61', *Population and Development Review*, 10/4 (December), 613–46.

Becker, G. S. (1960), 'An Economic Analysis of Fertility', in *Demographic and Economic Change in Developed Countries*, Universities–National Bureau Conference Series, 11, Princeton, NJ: Princeton University Press, for the National Bureau of Economic Research.

—— and Lewis, H. G. (1973), 'On the Interaction between the Quantity and Quality of Children', *Journal of Political Economy*, 81 (March–April), S279–88.

Behrman, J. R. (1988), 'The Impact of Economic Adjustment Problems on Health and Nutrition in Developing Countries', in Bell, David E. and Riech, Michael R. (eds.), *Health, Nutrition and Economic Crises: Approaches to Policy in the Third World*, Dover, MA: Auburn House, 103–46.

—— and Deolalikar, A. B. (1989), 'Health, Nutrition and Macroeconomic Adjustment with a Human Face: The Analytical Basis for the UNICEF Advocacy and a Case Comparison', Conference on Social, Cultural and Behavioural Factors Affecting Health: What is the Evidence?, Australia National University, Canberra, 15–19 May 1989.

Ben-Porath, Y. (1973), 'Short-term fluctuations in Fertility and Economic Activity in Israel', *Demography*, 10 (May), 1985–204.

Bongaarts, J. (1980), 'Does Malnutrition Affect Fecundity? A Summary of the Evidence', *Science*, 208, 564–69.

—— and Menken, J. (1983), 'The Supply of Children: A Critical Essay', in Bulatao, R. A. and Lee, R. D. (eds.), *Determinants of Fertility in Developing Countries*, New York: Academic Press.

Boyd, D. (1988), 'The Impact of Adjustment Policies on Vulnerable Groups: The Case of Jamaica, 1973–1985', in Cornia, G. A., Jolly, R., and Stewart, F. (eds.), *Adjustment with a Human Face*, Oxford: Clarendon Press, 125–55.

Bravo, J. (1992), 'Economic Crises and Mortality: Short and Medium-term Changes in Latin America', Proceedings of the Conference on the Peopling of the Americas, Veracruz: International Union for the Scientific Study of Population.

—— 'Demographic Consequences of Structural Adjustment in Chile', Chapter 7 below.

Bulatao, R. A. and Lee, R. D. (1983), (eds.), *Determinants of Fertility in Developing Countries*, New York: Academic Press.

Coale, A. J. (1984), *Rapid Population Change in China, 1952–1982*, Committee on Population and Demography, 27, Washington, DC: National Academy Press.

Foxley, A. and Raczyunski, D. (1984), 'Vulnerable Groups in Recessionary Situations: The Case of Children and the Young in Chile', in Jolly, R. and Cornia, G. A. (eds.), *The Impact of World Recession on Children*, Oxford: Pergamon Press, 53–76.

Frisch, R. E. (1975), 'Demographic Implications of the Biological Determinants of Female Fecundity', *Social Biology*, 22, 17–22.

—— (1978), 'Population, Food Intake, and Fertility', *Science*, 199, 22–30.

—— (1979), 'Nutrition, Fatness and Fertility: The Effect of Food Intake on Reproductive Ability', in Moseley, W. H. (ed.), *Nutrition and Human Reproduction*, New York: Plenum Press, 91–121.

Goldani, A. M., McCracken, S. D., and Pullum, S. W. (1989), 'Demographic Change and Stability in Brazil during a Period of Economic Crisis', paper prepared for the Annual Meetings of the Population Association of America, Baltimore, MD, 30 March–1 April 1989.

Gray, R. (1983), 'The Impact of Health and Nutrition on Natural Fertility', in Bulatao, R. A. and Lee, R. D. (eds.), *Determinants of Fertility in Developing Countries*, New York: Academic Press.

Hill, K. (1985), 'The Pace of Mortality Decline Since 1950', *Quantitative Studies of Mortality Decline in the Developing World*, World Bank Staff Working Paper 63, 55–96.

—— and Palloni, A. (1992), 'Demographic Response to Economic Shocks: The Case of Latin America', Proceedings of the Conference on the Peopling of the Americas, Veracruz: International Union for the Scientific Study of Population.

—— and Pebley, A. R. (1988), 'Levels, Trends and Patterns of Child Mortality', Workshop on Child Survival Programs: Issues for the 1990s, Johns Hopkins University, 20–21 November 1988.

Kakwani, N. (1988), 'The Economic Crisis of the 1980s and Living Standards in Eighty Developing Countries', CAER Paper 25 (February), University of New South Wales, Center for Applied Economic Research.

Kirk, D. (1960), 'The Influence of Business Cycles on Marriage and Birth Rates', *Demographic and Economic Change in Developed Countries*, National Bureau of Economic Research, Princeton University Press, 241–57.

Komlos, J. (1988), 'On the Role of Crises in Historical Perspective: Comment', *Population and Development Review*, 14 (March), 159–64.

Lee, R. D. (1981), 'Short-term variation: vital rates, prices and weather', in Wrigley, E. A. and Schofield, R. S., *The Population History of England 1541–1871*, Cambridge, MA: Harvard University Press, 356–401.

Lindert, P. (1983), 'The Changing Economic Costs and Benefits of Having Children', in Bulatao, R. A. and Lee, R. D. (eds.), *Determinants of Fertility in Developing Countries*, New York: Academic Press.

Macedo, R. (1984), 'Brazilian Children and the Economic Crisis: Evidence from the State of São Paulo', in Jolly, R. and Cornia, G. A. (eds.), *The Impact of World Recession on Children*, Oxford: Pergamon Press, 33–51.

Martorell, R. and Ho, T. J. (1984), 'Malnutrition, Morbidity and Mortality', in Mosley, W. H. and Chen, L. C. (eds.), *Child Survival: Strategies for Research, Population and Development Review*, Supplement to Vol. 10, 25–48.

Mueller, E. and Short, K. (1983), 'Effects of Income and Wealth on the Demand for Children', in Bulatao, R. A. and Lee, R. D. (eds.), *Determinants of Fertility in Developing Countries*, New York: Academic Press.

Musgrove, P., 'Economic Crisis and Health Policy Response', Chapter 3 below.

Palloni, A. (1988), 'On the Role of Crises in Historical Perspective: Comment', *Population and Development Review*, 14 (March), 145–58.

—— (1989), 'Population Trends and Economic Crises in Latin America: Is there any evidence of a relation?', Annual Meeting of the Population Association of America, Baltimore, MD, March 1989.

—— and Hill, K. 'The Effects of Economic Changes on Mortality by Age and Cause: Latin America, 1950–90', Chapter 6 below.

Pinstrup-Anderson, P. (1985), 'Food Prices and the Poor in Developing Countries', *European Review of Agricultural Economics*, 12, 1/2.

Preston, S. H. (1975), 'The Changing Relation Between Mortality and the Level of Economic Development', *Population Studies*, 29 (July), 231–48.

—— (1980), 'Causes and Consequences of Mortality Declines in Less Developed Countries During the Twentieth Century', in Easterlin, R. A. (ed.), *Population and Economic Change in Developing Countries*, Chicago: University of Chicago Press, 289–341.

—— (1985), 'Mortality and Development Revisited', *Quantitative Studies of Mortality Decline in the Developing World*, World Bank Staff Working Paper 63, 97–122.

Ross, J. A., Rich, M., Molzan, J. P., and Pensak, M. (1988), *Family Planning and Child Survival: 100 Developing Countries*, New York: Columbia University Press.

Silver, M. (1965), 'Births, Marriages, and Business Cycles in the United States', *Journal of Political Economy*, 73, 237–55.

Singh, S. and Ferry, B. (1984), *Biological and Traditional Factors that Influence Fertility: Results from WFS Surveys*, Comparative Studies 40, London: World Fertility Survey.

Stein, Z., Susser, M., Saenger, G., and Marolla, F. (1975), *Famine and Human Development: The Dutch Hunger Winter of 1944–45*, New York: Oxford University Press.

Udry, J. R. and Cliquet, R. L. (1982), 'A Cross-Cultural, Examination of the Relationships between Ages at Menarche, Marriage, and First Birth', *Demography*, 19 (February), 53–64.

de Waal, A. (1989), 'Famine Mortality: A Case Study of Dafur, Sudan, 1984–85', *Population Studies*, 43 (March), 5–24.

Watkins, S. C. and Menken, J. (1985), 'Famines in Historical Perspective: Reply', *Population and Development Review*, 11 (December), 645–75.

—— —— (1988), 'On the Role of Crises in Historical Perspective: Reply', *Population Review*, 14 (March), 165–70.

Willis, R. J. (1973), 'A New Approach to the Economic Theory of Fertility', *Journal of Political Economy*, 81 (March–April), S14–69.

Part II

Policy and Institutional Factors

3 Economic Crisis and Health Policy Responses

PHILIP MUSGROVE

Introduction: The Nature of the Question

'Health Policy' is something less well defined and much less quantitative than the phenomena demography normally deals with, so it seems appropriate to begin by explaining just what questions will be treated in what follows. This will also serve to make it clear that the approach of this paper is rather skeptical and conceptual, and has little new empirical information to offer.

Economic crisis versus structural adjustment

It is difficult to distinguish the demographic consequences of structural adjustment from the reactions to the economic crisis which provokes the need for adjustment— whether or not that adjustment is part of a formal programme involving short-term foreign assistance and policy advice from institutions such as the World Bank. Thus it is not clear that whatever bad consequences for health occur should be attributed to the adjustment programme (Cornia 1989) rather than to the economic mismanagement, sheer bad luck, or other factors causing the crisis. Focusing on the adjustment process may mean supposing that the alternative was not to adjust, rather than supposing that the only choice a country faced was *how* to get its macro-economy back into balance, and *how soon* to start doing so. Whether adjustment looks like needlessly throwing the car into a skid and a possible collision, depends on whether the alternative looks like going over a cliff. The general question is whether the economic crisis, including such responses to it as a formal adjustment programme, has had any systematic effect on health policy. Specific policy changes may be part of, or linked to, specific decisions on adjustment, but they need not be: they may be contemporaneous reactions to aspects of the crisis itself.

Connections to demographic phenomena

Ultimately, one wants to know what happened to births, deaths, age distributions, and other quantifiable demographic variables. This chapter does not carry the story that far, except for a brief discussion of previous empirical research on the health consequences of the crisis of the (early) 1980s. One of these sources (Grosh 1990) concentrated on expenditure on health care; the other (Musgrove 1988) also considered the output of services and the outcomes for health in the population. But since next to nothing was known about morbidity, the scant evidence available on health outcomes concerns mortality.

Here the emphasis is on what, if anything, happened to health policy. It is possible *a priori* that crisis or adjustment made for substantial changes in health policy, but without having much effect on anyone's health status. It is just as possible that there were large effects on morbidity and mortality, but that these had little to do with any official policy. To consider the likelihood of these and other possible outcomes, it will help first to think of the channels by which an economic downturn can affect health, and then to consider whether and how policy—particularly health policy—may be important in each of those channels.

Channels for health effects of economic crisis

Almost anything can affect one's health, and almost nothing in a modern economy is immune from the effects of economic contraction: so there is hardly any limit to the ways that economic crisis might affect the health of the population. Many of the possible channels are, however, likely to be quantitatively unimportant, affecting very few people or changing the incidence or prevalence of disease or other variables by insignificant amounts. Figure 3.1 (modified from Musgrove 1988) shows the principal ways by which an economic crisis could be expected to have significant effects on health. The diagram is incomplete in two demographically important respects: it does not show any of the mechanisms likely to affect birth rates, and because it has no spatial dimension it does not suggest impacts on migration.

Some of the channels portrayed are direct—that is, they modify the likelihood of getting sick or hurt, or dying—while others are indirect, in that they pass through the health care system and would show no effect if the crisis did not affect that system. To the extent that publicly provided (or publicly subsidized) health care is free to users, it is particularly important what happens to the publicly-funded health sector. Health outcomes suffer most when the public health system shrinks in size or becomes less effective just when, because of lost employment, income, or insurance coverage, people's need for it increases. Whether the relation between need and demand for health care changes during an economic downturn is one of the major questions to which policy might be addressed.

In principle, one or more kinds of public policy are relevant to every channel of mediation between economic events and demographic outcomes, including health. Some of these, such as policies affecting prices, wages, and employment, are crucial to adjustment programmes. Health policy can affect only some of the channels although, on a broad definition, these effects can reach far beyond the narrower decisions concerning the public provision of medical care. The diagram distinguishes those paths for which health policy is most relevant, in both the broad sense, including regulation and incentives, and in the narrow sense of spending public resources to buy or produce health care.

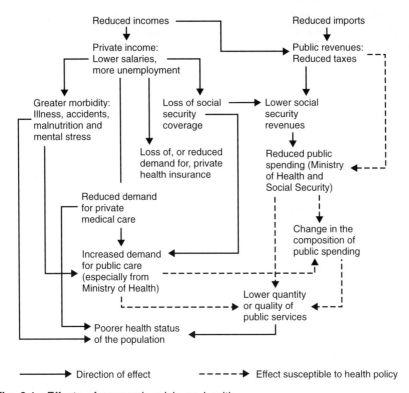

Reduced incomes ——————
Private income:
Lower salaries,
more unemployment

Reduced imports
Public revenues:
Reduced taxes

Greater morbidity:
Illness, accidents,
malnutrition and
mental stress

Loss of social → Lower social
security
coverage

Lower social
security
revenues

Loss of, or reduced
demand for, private
health insurance

Reduced public
spending (Ministry
of Health and
Social Security)

Reduced demand
for private
medical care

Change in the
composition of
public spending

Increased demand
for public care
(especially from
Ministry of Health)

Lower quantity
or quality of
public services

Poorer health status
of the population

————▶ Direction of effect   – – – – ▶ Effect susceptible to health policy

Fig. 3.1 Effects of economic crisis on health
Source: Adapted from Musgrove (1988, Cuadro [Table] 3–1).

The reach and importance of health policy

Health policy is essentially unable to affect people's employment and income at the moment of a crisis, however much the provision of health care may overcome disabilities and raise people's productivities in the long run. The direct *economic* effects of economic downturn on health are therefore beyond the reach of health policy. Other direct effects, however, may be more amenable to control: health policy affecting the environment, and public health measures generally, are examples. Among the indirect effects, it is not only the public provision of care that responds to health policy; it may be just as important to determine who has access to social security medical care, or to regulate the private insurance market. In general, it can be expected that these indirect consequences of policy become more important as the economy, and the health sector, become more differentiated and complex. In a poor country where few people can afford private doctors and all hospital care is publicly provided, public policy affects health through fewer channels than in a richer country with a large private medical sector and substantial private insurance. Thus, apart from differences in the specific health policies of one and another country, there are differences in the *reach* of policy; this is reason enough to suspect that simple relations between policy and outcomes will be hard to find or nonexistent, that what is true of Nicaragua or Bolivia will not characterize Argentina or Brazil.

Health Policy: Definition, Ambiguity, and Attribution

Up to this point, the phrase 'health policy' has been used as though it needed no definition and presented no ambiguity: it should be possible to tell what a policy is, whether and how it has changed, what caused any such change, and what effect that might be expected to have on health and demographic variables. On closer examination, all these assumptions appear questionable.

What do we mean by health policy?

Consider two extreme possible meanings for these words. One is that health policy is defined by the declarations of governments, in the broadest terms and at the highest political level. In that sense, every government that participated in the Alma Ata Conference in 1978 has a policy of giving priority to primary health care (World Health Organization 1978). Everything else—the definition of strategies for implementation, the decisions about investment, budget allocation, and regulation—would then be just the expression or working out of the policy. The limitations of this view are well known: what governments (and others) do, does not necessarily follow from what they say. In any case, what was said is often left so vague that it is hard even to tell whether a given action or decision is consistent with the supposed 'policy'.

At the other extreme, everything that a government does can be regarded as revealing or conforming to an implicit policy: 'real' policy is the sum of actions. But this is no easier to interpret, because actions are so numerous, and so often apparently inconsistent, that policy may be too complex to mean anything more general. Policy itself may also be contradictory, which is hard to tell from the absence of policy. We are left with the puzzlement of Alice, listening to the White Knight explain the difference between the Thing, and the Name of the Thing, and What the Thing is Called, and What the Name of the Thing is Called (Carroll 1865, chapter 8). At the very least, it must be recognized that policy may be defined at different levels of generality, and bear different relations to what actually goes on in a health sector. Change in policy is therefore at least equally complicated, and different policies could change in inconsistent directions under the same, or simultaneous but unrelated, impulses.

How can we tell if policy has changed?

Clearly a change in rhetoric is a different thing from a change in activity, so whether a change in policy has occurred depends on whether one is concerned with words or deeds. But there is another dimension to policy change which is more subtle and probably more important than the distinction between saying and doing. That is the *conditional* reach of a policy, the period over which and the circumstances under which it is supposed to apply.

Consider a Ministry of Health whose budget has for several years been growing at 5 per cent per annum, and which has routinely devoted 10 per cent of the budget to capital investment. In the first year of an economic crisis—of unpredictable depth and duration—the budget is cut by 10 per cent (the same as for the government budget generally), and all investment is stopped, leaving the recurrent budget the same as the year before. Was there a change of policy? If 'policy' meant a constant share for investment, then clearly policy changed. But if it meant never reducing recurrent expenditure, then there was no change in policy, and the stoppage of investment was necessary to uphold the policy.

This simple example illustrates two important issues. First, it is neither easy nor fair to infer policies solely from certain actions. Criticizing the outcome is a different matter, and does not depend on what happened to policy along the way. Second, governments have competing objectives—to keep investing to expand services, but also to try never to cut existing services—and in general, *they do not really have policies for reconciling those conflicts* when suddenly choices have to be made. Policies are seldom or never spelled out with all the 'ifs' and 'buts' that circumstances may impose, particularly if that would require a long planning horizon. As another example, there are good reasons why public expenditure on health care should be counter-cyclical, to cope with the fluctuation of needs mentioned earlier (Musgrove 1984), but no government in Latin America has such a policy. It would imply a privileged position for health in recessions (which every Minister of Health would endorse), but require reduced spending or at least reduced growth in boom times (which no Minister seems prepared to accept). It seems more nearly the case that there is one policy in good times and another in bad times, with no policy for getting from one situation to the other.

Attributing causes and effects

Much of the focus on the possible damage from recession and adjustment is on the issue of public spending, but the more interesting questions about health policy are not so narrow. Is there a shift among different kinds of interventions? Between one institution and another for delivery of care? Between hospital and ambulatory care? Does the government change its mind about user fees or internal prices and tariffs? Does it change the way staff are hired, assigned, or promoted? Does it change the way inputs other than staff are ordered and allocated, or the way they are paid for and the way they are combined with human inputs? Change in any of these dimensions may carry implications for the budget, but the impact may be very different from what the money amounts would suggest, and even run in the opposite direction.

An economic crisis is likely to have two kinds of adverse effects on health. It reduces people's incomes and therefore both exposes them to increased risk of getting sick and makes it harder for them to buy medical care if they need it; and it reduces government revenues and therefore makes it harder to provide or subsidize health services. Health policy cannot do anything about the loss of income, whether individual or public, but it can affect all three of the possible consequences just described.

A good health policy, or a good change in existing policy, would maintain the output of those services most essential to health, or even extend them, for the counter-cyclical reason mentioned earlier. It would reduce waste in the system both in the sense of technical inefficiency or lower than possible output for given inputs, and in the allocative sense of giving priority to those interventions which buy the greatest increase in health status per dollar spent (Jamison, Mosley, Measham, and Bobadilla 1993). Moreover, to the extent that economic hardship was regressive, policy would become offsettingly progressive, taking particular care to protect the poor. The latter aspect is usually described as 'equity', although it is only one of the possible meanings of equity in a health care system (Musgrove 1986). Thus the opportunity for good change in policy is greater, the worse policy was before the crisis. It is easier to fast, if one is too fat to start with, and it is easier to become more efficient or progressive if the system was initially wasteful or regressive. *Ceteris paribus*, we should expect improvements in health policy to be correlated negatively with the quality of prior policy.

Policy or policy change is bad if it reduces service coverage more than necessary, reduces it more than proportionally for the most valuable services, cuts back more on services to the neediest, or makes provision less efficient by (further) unbalancing the combination of inputs. The better a system was functioning before an economic shock, the greater the risk that it will become less effective or more regressive or inequitable. Because policy can be judged by four distinct criteria— total coverage, allocative efficiency, technical efficiency, and progressivity—it is obvious that many possible policy changes look good on one criterion and bad on another, with their total effect uncertain. Such ambiguous policies are particularly likely to have redistributional effects, benefiting or protecting some groups and worsening the situation of others. A priori, policies such as introducing or raising user fees fall into this category, with their outcome depending on what happens to demand, to net revenues, and to purchases of inputs.

What Happened in Latin America in the 1980s?

There were substantial changes in declared policy or actual public practice in many countries all over the world during the 1980s. In some cases these changes resulted from political upheaval rather than simply economic pressure; the formerly communist countries of eastern Europe, such as Romania (Fox 1992) or Poland (World Bank 1992), provide the most striking examples. In other cases, changes in the health sector have followed economic shock, as in Indonesia after the collapse of oil prices (World Bank 1991) or in Ghana, following an adjustment programme that began in 1983 and led to substantial change in budgets and (temporarily) in real user fees (Berk 1992). These cases illustrate the diversity of causes leading to changes in health policy and the variety of possible responses and outcomes. The range of events in Latin America has been somewhat narrower, but it still shows the importance of political and ideological as well as economic factors in affecting health policy.

Declared policy change: words as policy

One approach to the question of how health policy responded to economic stress would be to review all the constitutional and legal changes affecting health over the decade in as many countries as possible. A study by Fuenzalida-Puelma and Scholle Connor (1989) limited the analysis of health policy to what is specified in national constitutions and certain major laws. Not surprisingly, these documents refer primarily to the *right* to health or health care, and sometimes to the duty of the state or government to guarantee or provide it. (The constitution of Guyana goes so far as to declare a right to a happy life, free of disease.) The degree to which rights and duties are spelled out depends very much on the age of the constitution, and on whether the country has a common law (formerly English) or civil law (formerly Spanish, Portuguese, or French) tradition. Nineteenth-century documents such as the constitutions of 1853 in Argentina or 1886 in Colombia (or 1787 in the United States), do not even mention health explicitly. Newer charters, particularly those adopted during the 1970s or 1980s in such countries as Brazil, Cuba, Ecuador, El Salvador, Guatemala, Guyana, Honduras, Nicaragua, Panama, and Peru are much more explicit, sometimes declaring it the duty of the state to provide care (Panama) or to provide it free to the indigent (El Salvador) or to everyone (Cuba).

Over the long run, the analysis of constitutional provisions shows a clear increase in the social importance of health and health care, and a steady expansion of 'rights', generally in the direction of universal access. When budgets fall and services are curtailed or allowed to deteriorate in quality or equity, however, the disjunction between actual practice and the goals espoused in the law becomes temporarily wider. Certainly the law, at this level of generality, offers no guide to what will actually happen under economic pressure.

Evidence on spending: budgets as policy

What a government actually spends on health is commonly taken as a test of whether it has 'put its money where its mouth is'. If public expenditure on health care were to change substantially when nothing in the economic environment or in the burden of disease faced by society had changed, that would indeed be an indication that policy had changed, that health had acquired greater or lesser priority among claims on public resources. An economic crisis is obviously a poor time for that kind of test, since the economic environment changes abruptly, and that in turn may directly increase the burden of ill-health. It is still possible to ask the simpler question whether health expenditure was relatively protected or not, but even then there are at least three reasonable denominators to compare it to: population, total public spending, and gross domestic product. These three ratios do not necessarily move together, and even if they do, it is not clear what that indicates about policy.

Estimates of these ratios for thirteen countries, for 1980–5 or 1980–6, are shown in Table 3.1. The data refer to consolidated public sector spending, including subnational governments, in four cases and to the central government only in the other nine. All data are shown as real, country-specific indexes, using 1982 as the base year. This was the year the debt crisis began, and for many countries was therefore the last relatively normal budgetary year, with sharp retrenchment occurring in 1983 or 1984. (Costa Rica and El Salvador are notable exceptions, where spending declined substantially between 1980 and 1982.)

In every country except Honduras and Venezuela, public spending per person on health was lower, sometimes much lower, in the mid-1980s than it had been at the start of the decade. Whether expenditure could have been maintained more generally, despite falling incomes, is an open question; it would certainly have required a strong counter-cyclical commitment. The absence of any policy to give health more priority in times of hardship is also shown by the decline in the share of GDP which governments devoted to the sector: again, Honduras and Venezuela are exceptions.

It may be more reasonable to judge policy by comparing health spending with total public spending. This indicator also fell in most countries, often quite sharply, indicating that health lost in relative budgetary priority. The results are more varied both within and among countries, however. The share rose, at least temporarily, in Brazil, Ecuador, Mexico, and Uruguay—suggesting that there was no continuous policy but rather a year-to-year improvisation. Certainly these were not, in most countries, years in which conditions were favourable to defining and implementing stable, future-oriented policies.

Inputs and outputs: allocation and provision as policy

The expenditure estimates just presented have been purged, so far as possible, of general price inflation. It is, however, virtually impossible to standardize them for price changes specific to the health sector, or for changes in the mixture of inputs used or outputs produced: no one has made up the indices necessary for such deflation. Particularly during economic turmoil, it cannot be assumed that there is a stable relation between dollars spent and health gains produced. It is therefore natural to look specifically at some crude measures of sectoral output and at the absolute or relative amounts of different inputs used.

Given the magnitude of the decline in expenditure, it is surprising to find that public sector health output, in the form of ambulatory consultations and hospitalization, generally did not fall proportionately in the five countries where these measures were studied (Musgrove 1988: 40–53). There is a great deal of variation among countries and from year to year, but no evidence that output depended linearly on budgets. Four possible reasons may be suggested:

1. Investment was reduced very sharply, at least at the start of the crisis, so that recurrent expenditure was partly protected. This clearly happened in all countries.

2. Real salaries fell, so that although there was no reduction in public sector health staff, the cost of employing them declined. The tendency of employment to grow even during the crisis suggests that one of the few constant policies of most governments was to provide jobs for as many medical graduates as possible. The evidence on salaries is more mixed; these fell more often than not, however, indicating that medical personnel paid part of the cost of budget reductions. This is a reminder that 'health policy' is not only policy about patients and their needs, but also about staff and their demands, and that a major policy problem is to reconcile these two groups' claims.

3. Existing inefficiencies in the use of resources were reduced, by providing more ambulatory and less hospital care, or more preventive and less curative care, or by making better use of low-level staff relative to doctors, or by improving the balance among staff, drugs, and other inputs. Here the evidence is extremely mixed. Musgrove (1988) found almost no data by which to judge either allocative or technical efficiency. Hospital use increased in Honduras, largely because several new hospitals had been completed just before the recession began. It would have been a change of policy *not* to put them into operation, and consistent policy meant shortchanging ambulatory care. In Brazil, there was a clear policy to hold down hospitalization and direct more resources to non-hospital care (Piola and Vianna 1991). Grosh (1990) found evidence of reductions in the already low ratios of nurses to doctors, suggesting that inefficiency actually increased in several countries during the 1980s. And in the case of social security medical care in Peru, Petrera (1989) found that expenditure on drugs was cut drastically while staff increased, clearly indicating a worsening of inefficiency.

4. Quality declined, so that consultations and hospitalizations made poorer contributions to health improvements than before. This idea is hard to distinguish from that of reduced efficiency, and there is almost no direct evidence bearing on it—no evidence, in particular, of lower gains in healthy life years or other outcome measures.

These four possible explanations refer to total output in the form of consultations and hospitalizations. It is a different question whether health outcomes varied in relation to sectoral output. Almost nothing systematic could be found out about allocation among different programmes or health problems. However, immunization programmes were generally protected and this probably helps account for the continued decline in infant mortality in several countries during the 1980s.

What do these fragments of evidence say about how health policy reacted to the budget reductions? The short answer has to be, not much: what evidence there is, is too incomplete and inconsistent, and often is based on very crude indicators. Nonetheless, two conclusions suggest themselves. One is that there is a cost to changing policy, even when changed circumstances require it. The choice may be between leaving new investments idle, and using them even though cheaper or

Table 3.1 Indices of public expenditures on health (central government or total public sector) in thirteen Latin American and Caribbean countries, 1980–86 (1982 = 100)

Country, concept and coverage	1980	1981	1982	1983	1984	1985	1986
Argentina (consolidated public sector)							
Per capita	149	127	100	148	47	53	64
As share of total public spending	121	111	100	125	42	47	55
As share of GDP	127	118	100	145	45	55	64
Bolivia (central government only)							
Per capita	219	134	100	91	88	85	60
As share of total public spending	124	103	100	103	94	73	70
As share of GDP[a]	200	125	100	100	100	100	75
Brazil (central government only)							
Per capita	108	99	100	81	82	91	96
As share of total public spending	104	104	100	91	104	113	78
As share of GDP	94	96	100	85	87	89	89
Chile (consolidated public sector)							
Per capita	96	94	100	82	75	76	67
As share of total public spending	98	93	100	84	72	70	63
As share of GDP	94	79	100	84	74	74	63
Costa Rica (consolidated public sector)							
Per capita	205	136	100	109	108	106	110
As share of total public spending	142	114	100	94	89	91	91
As share of GDP	178	124	100	109	102	102	103
Dominican Republic (central government only)							
Per capita	99	110	100	102	89	77	85
As share of total public spending	83	93	100	93	99	84	82
As share of GDP	100	109	100	100	91	82	91
El Salvador (central government only)							
Per capita	132	114	100	94	95	76	69
As share of total public spending	131	105	100	107	83	89	72
As share of GDP	112	106	100	94	94	75	69

Ecuador (central government only)							
Per capita	84	108	100	89	87	88	
As share of total public spending	94	108	100	106	106	95	
As share of GDP	84	107	100	95	92	92	
Honduras (central government only)							
Per capita	103	98	100	100	95	93	105
As share of total public spending	105	114	100	94	78	76	95
As share of GDP	94	92	100	102	96	95	108
Jamaica (central government only)							
Per capita	91	95	100	90	71	64	57
As share of total public spending	88	93	100	92	90	91	86
As share of GDP	92	94	100	89	72	69	61
Mexico (central government only)							
Per capita	90[a]		100	93	94	95	83
As share of total public spending	100[b]		100	94	97	114	
As share of GDP			100	100	99	100	93
Uruguay (central government only)							
Per capita	91	104	100	91	91	93	
As share of total public spending	120	119	100	111	113	131	
As share of GDP	83	93	100	97	100	102	
Venezuela (consolidated public sector)							
Per capita	92	100	100	131	108	115	
As share of total public spending	94	92	100	157	147	155	
As share of GDP	85	95	100	140	120	130	

[a] Calculated from estimates to one digit only, in original source.
[b] Figures for 1979.

Sources: Argentina, Bolivia, Chile, Costa Rica, Dominican Republic, El Salvador, Jamaica and Venezuela: Grosh (1990), Tables A.II.R, A.II.9, A.II.19, A.II.24, A.II.29, A.II.34, A.II.39, A.II.44, A.III.5, and A.II.6; Brazil, Ecuador, Honduras, Mexico and Uruguay: Musgrove (1988), Cuadro [Table] 3-1. Gaps in table indicate data missing in original sources.

more effective programmes had to be cut back, as seems to have occurred in Honduras. Because investment in buildings and people takes a long time to mature, quick and substantial changes in input use are difficult and costly. Second, while it might be possible to define coherent policy change with respect to one objective, there is no easy way to take account of competing objectives. This is true not only when allocating resources to different treatments, which means making choices among patients, but also when sharing the burden of recession between patients and health sector workers. The burden seems to have been shared quite differently in different countries.

Improvisation, coping, and interest group struggles

The foregoing discussion suggests that not only has there been no uniform response to economic crisis and adjustment across countries in Latin America but that even within any one country, 'policy change' has usually not been well defined or internally consistent. Implicit policy, indicated by how much is spent and on what, has of course changed, but in an often erratic fashion. Moreover, the explicit enunciation of policy, particularly when embodied in constitutions, laws, and statements for political public consumption, may have little to do with reality.

Significant, coherent shifts of policy can be debated and implemented. But that process is not automatic, takes more time than an abrupt economic crisis allows (at least in the first year or two), and is likely to respond to other, long-term factors independent of the crisis. Particularly in the short run, what happens is much more a matter of *coping* with the immediate financial pressures, *improvising* adjustments within the public health sector, and *struggles* between interest groups over who and what is to be protected, or sacrificed. These are messy processes, which helps explain both the year-to-year variation in expenditure and service production and the frequent inconsistency between what is said and what is done.

Coping is what administrators of clinics and programs have to do, when their budgets are cut or they face some other restrictions such as failure to deliver drugs and supplies. Traditionally, Latin American public health systems have been grossly overcentralized, so that administrators cannot reallocate budgets significantly, make their own personnel decisions, or otherwise respond effectively to resource shortage. This problem long antedates the economic crisis, and would need fixing even if no recession had occurred; the crisis has merely made more painfully evident the inefficiency such centralization imposes.

Improvising means trying to adjust policy in the short run, usually without an adequate conceptual basis. Particularly in the first years of a crisis, improvising is nearly all that can be done: there is too little experience from which to predict the consequences of policy changes, and the system usually starts so far from equilibrium that many different possible changes appear to make sense or at least to offer some good effects. Many improvisations are implicitly revealed in the budget, but as was argued above, it is hard to read any clear policy shift out of them. What is needed is detailed research on what actually happened at the level of programmes and facilities, who took the relevant decisions, and what if any difference they made. Some research exists, particularly in the case of Brazil (Piola and Vianna 1991; Couttolenc 1991), but in most countries rather little is known about the details of policy improvisation.

Struggling for resources and control goes on all the time within governments and among the interest groups affected by the crisis in health care finance, but it can be expected to intensify when funds are reduced. Ideally, policy means a decision about who is to bear the burden, who is to win and who is to lose. These decisions are seldom made clearly or enforced consistently, and the results often escape the control of those trying to make health policy. For example, doctors in Honduras secured most of the budget increases in the form of higher salaries for themselves, blocking any expansion of services (Musgrove 1988, Chapter 6). In Brazil, the largest struggle has been over the sharing of funds and responsibilities among the federal, state and municipal governments, with revenue-sharing determined outside the health sector and central health policy having to adjust to the new financing pattern (Piola and Vianna 1991).

Exogenous trends in policy

In the absence of economic crisis and adjustment the need to cope and the pressure to improvise would have been much less, and it would have been easier to accommodate the normal struggles between interest groups. But there would still have been some strong scientific and intellectual or ideological currents running in the Latin American health sector, and it is reasonable to suppose they would still have had some influence on health policy. Three such tendencies are those towards specific, cost-effective interventions, particularly those applied in 'child survival' programmes (Task Force for Child Survival 1990); towards privatization in the provision of services (Roth 1987; World Bank 1987); and towards 'cost recovery' or user fees at public facilities (Jimenez 1987; Griffin 1988).

Each of these ideas has been sold on the grounds that governments' economic difficulties require them to concentrate on what works best and costs least—that faced with a crisis, they cannot afford the 'luxury' of high-cost, ineffective care (usually identified with hospital care), or of inefficient public provision, or of free care for everyone in the population. But these ideas would surely have been pressed on governments even if no crisis had occurred; what the crisis did was to make it harder for governments to resist them on purely ideological grounds. At least, this is the case for privatization and for user fees, ideas which most Latin American governments generally rejected before the 1980s, but which have subsequently been embraced with varying degrees of enthusiasm and desperation.

The peculiar case of Brazil

In some of the smaller countries, particularly those in Central America which are relatively dependent on foreign assistance and especially on help from USAID, policy change can be strongly pushed by a combination of financial need and external conceptual or ideological pressure. These pressures are less effective in larger and more self-sufficient countries, and what happens to policy can be correspondingly more complex. Brazil is probably the most studied example. As in other countries, there was a sharp reduction in central government health care spending at the beginning of the crisis (1983–84), and this provoked a search for 'fat to burn' or opportunities to reduce waste and inefficiency (Piola and Vianna 1991). Partly for this reason, and partly for perceived equity reasons, there was also a push to curtail hospital services and expand ambulatory care. At the same time, Brazil shows some tendencies that were generated domestically and with little or no reference to the economic situation. These include the near-universalization of social security coverage, even to people not contributing to the system; the express inclusion of an unlimited 'right to health' in the new Constitution of 1988; an *increase* in the public provision of care, at the expense of public finance for privately provided care through contracts with the social security system; and a devolution of both money and responsibilities, including the transfer of control over health facilities and the transfer of personnel, to states and municipalities. All these changes have much more to do with the democratization of the country in the 1980s than with anything else.

Brazil also illustrates the improvised, turbulent nature of health policy reform to an extreme degree, because of the struggles among levels of government, agencies of the federal government, and interest groups. The country has had three substantial efforts at reform in the last decade, and while they are consistent in some respects, there are also instances of reversal (Couttolenc 1991; Piola and Vianna 1991). Thus the decentralization of services under the 1988 SUDS (Unified and Decentralized Health Systems) operated through the states, which determined how much of their newly acquired federal money and facilities to turn over to municipalities, whereas the subsequent 1990 SUS (Single Health System) reform reasserted federal control and provided for the social security system to deal directly with municipalities.

Concluding Reflections

It is difficult to reach any substantial and defensible conclusions about the relation between economic crisis and health policy, so these final reflections are not so much a summing up as suggestions of other questions to contemplate.

How much does health policy matter?

Health policy responds to many factors, some of them political and some quite ideological, in addition to the economic circumstances that constitute a crisis or the adjustment to one. That alone makes it difficult for health policy to change quickly and sensibly if a crisis arises. Most 'policy change', leaving aside the most general pronouncements of goals or wishes, involves a great deal of coping with adversity, improvisation, and struggle among competing interests. That means that what actually happens is unlikely to correspond exactly to declared policy, and generally has to sacrifice some objectives to satisfy others. Together these two arguments suggest that the importance of policy, and of changes in policy, is overrated. Perhaps the rhetorical component should be ignored altogether, and the real component judged simply by how much health improvement is obtained, relative to money spent. Good results mean, implicitly, good policy; bad results mean something needs to be changed.

The limitation of this view, of course, is that bad results by themselves do not tell one *what* needs to be changed. And if policy is (part of) what mediates between inputs and outputs, then one has to look at policy to see what is, or has gone, wrong. So the argument that 'policy matters', and that good policy is preferable to bad policy, survives this skeptical view. What may not survive is any simple notion of a one-to-one correspondence from economic phenomena to health policy, and from there to health outcomes. There is similarly not much reason to believe in a relatively uniform, systematic response to economic crisis across countries or even across a few years in one country. From the scant empirical evidence, it is hard to say how much health policy has mattered recently in Latin America; and while much past and present policy can be roundly criticized on theoretical grounds, it is hard to tell how much better outcomes might have been with better policies.

Dealing with crisis and adjustment: are there any lessons?

There is no shortage of attempts to answer this question, in both theoretical and empirical terms (Bell and Reich 1988). Even if the economic crisis of the 1980s turns out to have had little impact on life and death in Latin America, it largely halted the expansion of public health coverage, probably reduced the quality and accessibility of care, and severely shook the public institutions which had to cope with it or adjust to it; so it is natural to try to derive lessons from the experience. Most of the lessons really amount to suggestions for *better* policy, which would be just as relevant if there had never been a crisis. To concentrate on cost-effective interventions, to favour the poor and those most at risk, to finance the system on a sound basis, to avoid duplication of effort, to use prices and fees both for internal efficiency and to steer demand in appropriate directions, to buy and use inputs in the right proportions—all this excellent advice may carry more weight when governments are broke and desperate, but it will make just as much sense if economic growth resumes and health budgets expand. There is even a potentially perverse effect, in that any public health sector which becomes lean and efficient will have no 'fat to burn' if confronted with a future retrenchment. A little bit of waste in good times is a protection in bad times; how much waste ought to be tolerated depends, unfortunately, on the likely duration and severity of bad times, which are hard to predict.

This suggests that governments need policies not only for a point in time, but for a course over time. To have to change policy when budgets are cut—or to need to do so, but fail to come up with anything but panicky improvisation—indicates that the pre-crisis policy did not adequately contemplate the possibility of a crisis or spell out what to do about it. A medium-term policy should have built into it the 'expansion path' of the sector, both when budgets are rising and when they are falling; it should already say what to cut and what to save, if resources drop by X per cent. Like all plans, such a policy would need to be revised every year, because what to do depends on what one is already doing or has the capacity to do. But it should avoid the need to introduce entirely new policies purely under financial pressure, and it should forbid the kind of retrenchment which guarantees reduced efficiency because some inputs are protected while others are abandoned. It might even build in a counter-cyclical protection for health care. This kind of policy— actually a portfolio of contingent plans, of 'what to do if' policies—seems to have been conspicuously lacking in Latin America at the beginning of the 1980s, and that, as much as the pressures of adjustment, may account for the reduction in effective health protection in the early years of the crisis.

REFERENCES

Bell, D. E. and Reich, M. R. (eds.) (1988), *Health, Nutrition and Economic Crises: Approaches to Policy in the Third World*, Dover, MA: Auburn House.

Berk, D. A. (1992), personal communication, 19 May.

Carroll, L. (1865), *Through the Looking Glass*, Macmillan.

Cornia, B. A. (1989), 'Investing in human resources: health, nutrition and development for the 1990s', *Journal of Development Planning*, 19/159.

Couttolenc, B. (1991), 'Change in the Brazilian health system: key issues for SUS', Latin American Country Department I, Human Resources Division, World Bank, Washington, DC.

Fox, L. (1992), *Romania: Human Resources and the Transition to a Market Economy*, World Bank Country Report, Washington, DC.

Fuenzalida-Puelma, H. and Scholle Connor, S. (1989), *The Right to Health in the Americas: a Comparative Constitutional Study*, Washington, DC: Pan American Health Organization.

Griffin, C. C. (1988), 'User charges for health care in principle and practice', Seminar Paper 37, Economic Development Institute, World Bank, Washington, DC.

Grosh, M. E. (1990), *Social Spending in Latin America: The Story of the 1980s*, World Bank Discussion Papers 106, Washington, DC.

Jamison, D. T., Mosley, W. H., Measham, A. R., and Bobadilla J. L. (eds.) (1993), *Disease Control Priorities in Developing Countries*, New York: Oxford University Press for the World Bank.

Jimenez, E. (1987), *Pricing Policy in the Social Sectors: Cost-Recovery for Education and Health in Developing Countries*, Baltimore: Johns Hopkins University Press.

Musgrove, P. (1984), 'Health care and economic hardship', *World Health*, October.

—— (1986), 'Measurement of equity in health', *World Health Statistics Quarterly*, 39.

—— (1988), 'Crisis Económica y Salud: la experiencia de cinco paises latinoamericanos en los años ochenta', unpublished study, Pan American Health Organization, Washington, DC.

Petrera, M. (1989), 'Effectiveness and efficiency of Social Security in the economic cycle: the Peruvian case', in Musgrove, P. (ed.), *Health Economics: Latin American Perspectives*. Pan American Health Organization, Washington, DC.

Piola, S. F. and Vianna, S. M. (1991), 'Políticas e prioridades do sistema único de saúde–SUS', Latin American Country Department I, Human Resources Division, World Bank, Washington, DC.

Roth, G. (1987), *The Private Provision of Public Services in Developing Countries*, New York: Oxford University Press.

Task Force for Child Survival (1990), *Protecting the World's Children: A Call for Action*, Fourth International Child Survival Conference, Bangkok, 1–3 March.

World Bank (1987), *Financing Health Services in Developing Countries: An Agenda for Reform*, Washington, DC.

—— (1992), 'Poland, health system reform: meeting the challenge', Report 9182-POL, Washington, DC (restricted circulation).

—— (1991), *Indonesia: Issues in Health Planning and Budgeting*, World Bank Country Report 7291, Washington, DC.

World Health Organization (1978), *Alma-Ata 1978: Primary Health Care*, Geneva.

4 The Effect of Stuctural Adjustment on Food Policy and Nutrition

JERE BEHRMAN

I. Introduction

Most Latin American economies have been dominated by structural adjustment efforts in the past decade. Such efforts in a sense have a short-term character in that they are attempting to remedy aggregate economic imbalances so that medium and long-term growth can be sustained. But often the efforts themselves have fairly long durations, albeit in some cases with substantial fits and starts. Moreover, successful structural adjustment programmes are likely to change critical relative prices and policies from what they were before structural adjustment. Therefore such structural adjustment efforts may have had important demographic consequences through impacts on income, prices, the social sectors, and human resource investments.

One channel through which structural adjustment efforts may have important demographic impact is through food policy and nutrition. In most structural adjustment programmes there are considerable changes in policies that affect food prices and quantities, though only a subset of these may be designated explicitly as 'food policy' changes. The changes in food prices and quantities, in turn, may have substantial effects on the quantity, quality, and the composition of foods consumed, and thus on nutrient intakes. Changes in nutrient intakes, together with other changes such as those in time use and in the disease environment, may alter anthropometric and clinical indicators of nutritional and health status.

In this chapter, I address the question: what do we know about the impact of structural adjustment in Latin America on food policy and nutrition? I organize my comments by first presenting a simple economic household model of the determinants of nutritional and health status, since the proximate determinants of nutritional and health status are at the micro individual and household level. Then I use this framework to discuss: (1) the channels through which the food policy component of structural adjustment programmes may affect the reduced-form determinants of individual nutritional and health status; (2) how individuals and households respond to the changes in the reduced-form determinants of individual nutrition and

This chapter is closely related to the other chapters in this volume that were originally presented as papers at the conference on 'Mortality and Health' because of the interactions between health, morbidity, mortality, and nutrition. It also is related to recent papers by Aguirre (1991), Altimir (1991), Castaneda (1991), de Janvry (1991), Hoffman (1991), Morales (1991), Ruel and Garrett (1991), Stewart (1991), Thompson (1991), and Trejos (1991).

health status induced by structural adjustment programmes; and (3) policy implications regarding the impact of structural adjustment on food policy and on nutrition.

II. Simple Economic Modelling of Proximate Determinants of Nutritional and Health Status

Within a simple economic model of household behaviour, there is a production function for nutritional and health status for the ith individual in the kth household in the tth period (H_{ikt}) that depends on proximate factors such as nutrient intakes (N_{ikt}), other health-related goods and services (C_{ikt}), time use (T_{ikt}) for which the time use of other household members than the individual (e.g. that of mothers for child nutritional and health status) may be important so i may take on values for such other individuals, disease (D_{ikt}), genetic endowments (G_{ik}), the environment (E_{ikt}), and stochastic factors (u_{ikt}), all given the nutritional and health status of the previous period ($H_{ik,t-1}$):

$$H_{ikt} = H(N_{ikt}, C_{ikt}, T_{ikt}, D_{ikt}, G_{ik}, E_{ikt}, H_{ik,t-1}, \ldots, u_{ikt}), \tag{1}$$

where all of the variables may be vectors with multiple entries.

This is purely a technical/biological relation. Food policy changes as part of structural adjustment programmes may affect nutritional and health status if they affect any of the right-side variables in this relation, including—but not limited to—nutrient intakes. But many of the right-side variables, including nutrient intakes, reflect constrained choices of the household. Therefore to explore the impact of food policy changes on nutritional and health status, it is necessary to consider what determines household behaviour.

Within a simple household model, behaviour is determined by maximizing an intertemporal objective function (which may reflect some intrahousehold bargaining process) subject to a set of production functions such as in relation (1), past realizations of assets of individual household members (A_{ik}) including those for nutritional and health stocks (H_{ik}), full prices (including nominal and time costs for all goods and services bought and sold including those for products, labour and credit) for current and future time periods (P), reaction functions for private and public transfers for current and future time periods (TR), quantitative policies such as food and credit rationing for current and future time periods (Q), exogenous income components for current and future time periods for each individual (Y_{ik}), an intertemporal budget constraint, and stochastic disturbances (v_{kt}). For many of these variables at any point of time the future values are not known, so future expectations must be used (and perhaps other moments of the distributions of future values of the relevant variables if individuals are not risk-neutral). This constrained maximization leads to reduced-form conditional demand relations for all outcomes determined by the household in the tth period (Z_{kt}), including the nutritional and health status of each individual in the household in the tth period:

$$Z_{kt} = Z(A_{ik}, H_{ik}, G_{ik}, P, TR, Q, Y_{ik}, v_{kt}),\tag{2}$$

where i is over all individuals in the kth household.

Relations such as (1) and (2) exist for all individuals in all households in the economy.[1] These household behavioural relations, embodied in a large set of relations for supplies and demands in all markets and for policies in the overall economy, provide the basis for making a number of points about what we do and do not know about the impact of structural adjustment in Latin America on food policy and, through food policy changes, on nutritional and health status. I group my observations on this topic with respect to three broad issues in the following three sections of this paper.

III. Channels through which the Food Policy Component of Structural Adjustment Programmes may Affect the Reduced-Form Determinants of Individual Nutritional and Health Status

The direct channels through which changes in food policy as part of structural adjustment programmes have impact on individual nutritional and health status is through changes in food prices (in P) and in quantitative policies such as food rationing (in Q). While in some developing country contexts (e.g. South Asia, North Africa) food policy has operated considerably through food rationing, in Latin America the primary direct channel for food policy has been through food pricing. Structural adjustment programmes have affected food price in part through direct price changes—for instance, due to elimination of food subsidies—that normally are categorized as food policy changes. Prior to structural adjustment efforts, many Latin American governments attempted to keep real prices of food low through a combination of direct price ceilings, explicit consumer and/or producer subsidies, food export prohibitions or limitations, and overvalued exchange rates.[2] In some developing countries efforts to encourage production with producer subsidies partially to offset overvaluation and at the same time to delink urban food prices from producer food prices resulted in large total subsidies as part of the food policy that contributed to large governmental deficits. But food prices were affected as much or more in many cases through indirect policies—for instance, overvaluation —that normally may not be thought of as food policy, but may be very important in determining relative food prices, than by direct food price policies such as taxes, subsidies, and price ceilings. Krueger, Schiff, and Valdes (1988), for example, suggest that for sixteen developing countries that they have investigated (including Argentina, Brazil, Chile, Colombia, and the Dominican Republic in Latin America), the (negative) indirect effects on the incentives for production of agricultural exportables (including foods) were about two and a half times as large as the direct effects in the late 1970s. These negative incentive effects, by keeping agricultural

---

[1] Some households, of course, may be single-individual households.

[2] Pinstrup-Andersen, Jaramillo, and Stewart (1987) review this experience and the impact of structural adjustment on food prices.

relative prices low, of course tended to keep the relative prices of food and other agricultural commodities low for consumers and other users. If structural adjustment programmes were to eliminate all of the previous direct and indirect effects on food and other agricultural prices, they would thus operate much more through the indirect effects than through the direct effects that are usually the focus of so-called 'food policy.'

In the process of structural adjustments price ceilings have been removed, food subsidies lessened or eliminated[3], taxes and quantitative limitations on food exports lessened or eliminated, and domestic currencies devalued. The net impact of these changes has tended to be lessening of the distortions in the domestic price structures as compared with international price structures, reductions in food subsidies, and immediate increases in relative food prices—particularly for foods that are internationally tradable or which are close substitutes in production or consumption for goods that are internationally tradable.

The poor seem particularly vulnerable to food price increases since they spend relatively large shares of their incomes on food[4]. Have such real food price increases reduced the inducements for the poor in Latin America to consume foods? The answer to this question is not as straightforward as it might seem for at least four reasons.

First, food price subsidies in most countries prior to structural adjustment were *not* effectively targeted on the poor. Generally, most such subsidies went to middle and upper income classes in urban areas, while most of the poor have been in rural areas (Pinstrup-Andersen 1993). Moreover, even for the urban poor who have received such subsidies, often they have been for limited quantities of foods so that substantial quantities were also purchased at unsubsidized prices.

Second, since staple foods are important wage goods, lower food prices due to subsidies may have permitted lower nominal wages, and therefore lower real incomes, of the poor[5]. That is, employers in both the public and private sectors may have been more able to pay lower nominal wages and still hire the labour that they desired than they would have been without the food subsidies. This may have been possible because the food subsidies meant that the real wages in terms of purchasing power were higher than they would have been without them. If so, the removal of the food subsidies may have been accompanied by nominal wage increases by employers to obtain the labour that they desired, which mitigated declines in real wages due to elimination of the subsidies[6].

---

[3] A number of countries, including Brazil and Mexico, cut explicit food subsidies substantially in the 1980s. Mexico, for example, cut such subsidies sharply between 1983 and 1984 as part of a shift from a general to a targeted programme, which Lustig (1992) claims caused a serious deterioration in the real purchasing power of the urban poor. Subsequently, however, general subsidies were increased and in the late 1980s operated alongside targeted programmes.

[4] Abugattas and Lee (1991), for example, report that the poorest income quintile in Lima, Peru, spent 64 per cent of their income on food in 1985–6 and 67 per cent in 1990.

[5] Crucial to this point is the distinction between nominal wages (e.g. wages in pesos) and real wages (i.e. the purchasing power of wages in terms of what food and other goods and services they can buy).

[6] To the extent that this is true for the public sector, reductions in governmental deficits due to the removal or reduction in food subsidies are offset partially by increased wage payments.

Third, food price subsidies may contribute to governmental deficits and thereby inflation, which tends to erode the purchasing power of the poor relatively greatly because the poor have less access to mechanisms to shelter themselves from inflation (such as indexed domestic income sources and foreign assets)[7]. The reduction in food price subsidies as part of food policy changes in structural adjustment programmes, therefore, may indirectly help protect the purchasing power of the poor from the extent of inflation that otherwise would have occurred.

Fourth, the poor are heterogenous with regard to the relation of their income sources to food prices. Therefore policies that change food prices may have widely different effects on the real incomes of the poor. Moreover, these effects may vary substantially with the time horizon.

For example, Pinstrup-Andersen (1993) suggests that it is useful to consider six types of poor households:

1. semi-subsistence farmers;
2. low-income market-oriented farmers;
3. landless agricultural workers;
4. low-income rural landless non-agricultural workers and self-employed;
5. low-income urban workers in the internationally tradable sector; and
6. low-income urban workers and self-employed in the non-tradable sector.

Let us consider first the rural households in the first four groups. Semi-subsistence farmers and low-income market-oriented farmers who produce their own food are protected from negative effects of food price increases on their incomes and, if anything, have greater incentives to increase their real income through selling food (or more food) at the higher prices. Landless agricultural workers and low-income market-oriented farmers who are net purchasers of food, in contrast, are likely to experience a reduction in their real incomes due to higher food prices. These real income reductions due to higher food prices may or may not be offset by increases in income due to higher prices for the goods which they are engaged in producing (food and/or other commodities). The overall impact on their incomes depends on which of these effects predominates. In the short run, low-income market-oriented farmers are more likely to benefit than landless agricultural workers because the former are likely directly to reap some of the product price gains from structural adjustment, while the latter depend on increased agricultural labour demands or reduced agricultural labour supplies. Studies such as that by Krueger, Schiff and Valdes (1988) mentioned above suggest that these gains may be considerable, particularly through indirect effects such as exchange rate devaluations. The available evidence also suggests that, while the composition of agricultural production may change, aggregate agricultural supplies (and therefore aggregate agricultural labour demands) and not very responsive to the relative price changes engendered in the initial stages of structural adjustment programmes (see, for example, Binswanger 1990). For there to be larger effects in the medium and longer run, it

---

[7] See, however, the footnote 6.

is probably important that the structural adjustment programme encompasses improvements in agricultural and related market infrastructure (such as adaptive research, better communications, and transportation) for which governments are likely to have comparative advantages in direct production or in providing subsidies because of increasing returns to scale and public goods characteristics (see Section V). With such complementary developments, agricultural supplies and agricultural labour demands are more likely to increase over time. Finally, it should also be noted that in the rural sectors there are considerable numbers of low-income rural landless *non*-agricultural workers and self-employed. These individuals and households are likely to benefit from the any improved terms of trade for agricultural goods, which is a likely outcome of structural adjustment programmes, because they are engaged substantially in the provision of goods and services for the agricultural producers, who are likely to gain income from increased prices even in the short run, and perhaps increased supplies in the longer run. Of course in response some households may switch into this category from other categories (such as landless agricultural workers and low-income market-oriented farmers who are net food purchasers) who may on balance be disadvantaged by food price and other changes induced by the structural adjustment programmes. Pinstrup-Andersen (1993) claims that, as a result of such changes, in rural areas in Latin America during the turbulent economic crises and adjustment efforts of the 1980s poverty remained about the same (after declining in the 1970s), though he does not indicate what happened due to adjustment efforts *per se*. It is interesting to note, however, that structural adjustment may occur concurrently with considerable increases in rural incomes and reductions in rural poverty. The Indonesian experience in the mid-1980s is striking in this regard. Huppi and Ravallion (1990) report that during this adjustment period the head count measure of rural poverty fell from 53 to 38 per cent for farm labour and from 44 to 31 per cent for self-employed farmers, and that national poverty fell from 33 to 22 per cent. They claim that these gains occurred in substantial part because of expansion in agricultural exports and government protection of rural consumption at the expense of investment.

Now let us consider the effects on the urban poor. The impact of food price increases on this group is almost certainly negative since the increased prices reduce the purchasing power of a given level of nominal income and are not likely to increase urban nominal income. The broader aspects of structural adjustment programmes may have substantial effects that favour the urban poor who are engaged in tradable activities over those engaged in nontradable activities (that is, the fifth category above over the sixth category above). But, as Pinstrup-Andersen (1993: 8–9) notes, the big losers from food price changes associated with structural adjustment programmes among the poor in Latin America were undoubtedly in urban areas, in many of which poverty rates increased in the 1980s. But he also emphasizes: 'Without counterfactual information it is, of course, not possible to assess the magnitude of these deteriorations relative to a situation without adjustment or the more likely scenario of an alternative adjustment package. What is apparent is that changes in food price policies during adjustment generally result in higher consumer prices for food relative to changes in nominal wage rates for the poor including, but not limited to, official minimum wage rates. The change in real food prices, i.e. changes in nominal food prices relative to other prices, varies among countries and over time and no generalizable pattern is apparent.' That is, in addition to the effects on prices and quantities, food policies, or wider policies associated with structural adjustment, may cause others of the right-side determinants in relation (2) to change. Therefore, confident identification of the impact of food policy changes alone is not easy.

IV. How Individuals and Households Respond to the Changes in the Reduced-Form Determinants of Individual Nutritional and Health Status Induced by Food Policy Changes as Part of Structural Adjustment Programmes

If food policy changes undertaken as part of structural adjustment programmes change the right-side variables in the reduced-form demand relations for nutritional and health status in relation (2), how do households respond? This is an important question since, just because variables such as food prices may change a great deal in structural adjustment programmes, it does *not* necessarily follow that nutritional and health status will change substantially. The reason for this is that there are many substitution or coping mechanisms that are possible. Whether or not they are important in the real world is an empirical question about which there is some limited, but suggestive evidence. However, for at least two reasons one cannot just look at the 'facts' to see what the impact of food policy changes has been on nutritional and health status in Latin America: First, it is not only food policy that has changed: substantial changes have been occurring throughout the economy. Since many of these other changes are correlated with the food policy, to explore the impact of food policy changes it is necessary to control for these other changes in the analysis. Second, to evaluate the impact of food policy changes associated with structural adjustment, one must have some notion of what the situation would have been without structural adjustment. The appropriate counterfactual presumably is *not* a continuation of the situation immediately before structural adjustment since it is precisely because that situation appeared unsustainable, due to various imbalances, that the structural adjustment programmes were initiated.[8]

Good estimates of the relations introduced in Section II, particularly of relation (2), may help us to gain an insight into the impact of the variables affected by food policy on nutritional and health status. Such estimates can control for other changes that have been occurring at the same time, and permit the evaluation of counter-

---

[8] Efforts to evaluate the impact of structural adjustment programmes with aggregate data are plagued by these problems. Yet recent aggregate studies that attempt to deal with the counterfactual problems, such as Behrman and Deolalikar (1991) and Maasland and van der Gaag (1991) find much less evidence of negative effects than claimed in earlier studies such as Cornia, Jolly, and Stewart (1987, 1988).

factual situations. However, is it difficult to obtain good estimates of such relations, for a number of reasons that cannot be ignored. Estimation of the parameters of relations such as (1) and (2) from the sort of information that is usually available poses various problems. One problem in estimating relation (1) is that many of the right-side variables in this relation reflect choices made by the household. If, for example, more nutrient intakes are allocated to household members who are inherently weaker (for example, lower values of G_{ik}) or to those who use more nutrients in their activities (associated with T_{ikt}) and if these simultaneous relations are not controlled in the estimation, the impact of nutrient intakes on nutritional and health status is likely to be underestimated. Likewise, if unobserved endowments (G_{ik}) affect past as well as current health status, as seems plausible, only if those endowments are controlled in the estimation procedure can consistent estimates be obtained of the impact of past nutritional and health status on current status, and thus, for example, the extent of catch-up growth possible. Another example is the fact that in many data sets there is no information on individual nutrient intakes (N_{ikt}), but only on nutrients available to the household. That the nutrients available to the household may be distributed unevenly relative to needs, and may be allocated to other uses than intakes for household members (food may be given to employees or guests, or may be wasted) means that misleading inferences may be drawn unless such possibilities are controlled for in the empirical analysis. Yet other problems may arise because of functional forms of estimated relations—for instance, there may be sharp nonlinearities so that the very poor behave differently from those who are better off, which may be missed with linear relations—and because quality considerations such as those related to micronutrients may be missed due to the nature of the data. In general terms, the basic point is that data and estimation problems may cause the stochastic terms (i.e. u_{ikt}, v_{kt}) *not* to be independent of the right-side variables in the estimated relation, so that inconsistent estimates of the parameters of interest are obtained. In a number of cases, whether or not these problems are controlled for seems to make a considerable difference in the parameter estimates.

   With these caveats, I now turn to several dimensions of available empirical estimates, referring to other developing regions as well to Latin America because of the paucity of studies that address these problems satisfactorily. The most direct impact of food policy changes on nutritional and health status in the Latin American context would seem to be through food prices, which—as noted above—tend to increase under structural adjustment programmes through a combination of direct and indirect policy changes (such as, respectively, reduction in food subsidies and devaluation). Since most of the evidence about nutrient demands is from cross-sectional data, the available evidence is based on limited food price variation. Estimated own-price elasticities for basic staples tend to be negative, and often larger for poorer households than for better-off households (see, for example, surveys in Alderman 1986, Behrman and Deolalikar 1988, and Deaton 1988). Williamson-Gray (1982) estimates a compensated own-price elasticity of Brazilian cereals demand of −0.74 for the poor, −0.16 for middle-income households, and close to zero for upper-income households.[9] Such results suggest that the poor shift their food composition considerably when relative food prices change. Such compositional shifts obviously have implications for nutrient intakes, but they do not necessarily mean reductions in basic nutrient intakes. The consumption of basic nutrients such as calories might even increase if consumers turn from more expensive to cheaper sources of nutrients (for example, from meats to cereals, from processed rice to coarse cereals, and from more to less processed food for calories). Several studies indicate considerable price responses in demands for calories and other basic nutrients by estimating directly a variant of relation (2) with nutrients as the dependent variables (see, for example, Strauss 1984; Pitt and Rosenzweig 1985; Behrman and Deolalikar 1987, 1990). However, a number of these responses are positive, suggesting that such compositional shifts may be important because people turn to cheaper sources of basic nutrients. This reasoning would suggest that at least the response in basic nutrients such as calories to price increases in the basic staple is likely to be inverse. This result is found by some of these studies, but not by all them. Thus, to the extent that food policy changes undertaken as part of structural adjustment programmes work through increasing food prices, the evidence suggests that such effects do not have as clear-cut an impact on nutrient intakes as seems to be assumed by many. Furthermore, the limited available estimates of relation (1) suggest that nutrient intakes have less precise and less substantial effects on nutritional and health status as measured by anthropometric, morbidity and clinical measures than seems to be assumed by many—although perhaps partly due to the kind of problems in estimating this relation satisfactorily, that have been noted above.[10]

Another mechanism through which food price policy changes may alter nutritional and health status is through changing real income, as discussed in Section III. A decade ago there seemed to be a broad consensus that changing real income was a powerful way to alter nutrient intakes, and presumably thereby nutritional and health status. The World Bank (1981: 59), for example, stated this position forcefully: 'There is now a wide measure of agreement on several broad propositions . . . Malnutrition is largely a reflection of poverty: people do not have income for food . . . The most efficient long-term policies are those that raise the income of the poor.' This position appeared to be buttressed by estimates that the elasticity of basic nutrient consumption (usually calories) with respect to income for the poor in developing countries was of the order of magnitude of 0.7 or more, so that a 10 per cent decline in income would result in a decline of 7 per cent or more in calories consumed. Such elasticities would seem to suggest that if food policy

[9] The elasticity of food demand with respect to a price indicates the percentage change in the quantity demanded relative to the percentage change in the price. A compensated price elasticity is one that is calculated holding real income (or, more precisely, satisfaction) constant in order to isolate the response to prices from the response to income. A compensated own-price elasticity of –0.74 for cereals for Brazilian poor means that in response to a 10 per cent increase in cereal prices these households reduce consumption of cereals by 7.4 per cent due to the price effect alone.

[10] Behrman and Deolalikar (1988) survey the available results and discuss some of the estimation problems.

changes in structural adjustment cause reductions in real income for some of the poor, such as those living in urban areas and landless agricultural labourers, there may be a substantial cost in terms of reduced nutrient intakes.

Since the early 1980s, however, there have been two strains of literature that bring into question the magnitude of such effects.

The first strain questions whether the nutrient elasticities with respect to income are anything like as high as previously thought. Some recent studies argue that the previous estimates overstate substantially the true responses of nutrient intakes to income because they ignore intra food group substitution, nutrients that are available to the household that—as income rises—increasingly go to other purposes than for nutrient intakes of household members (for example, to guests, employees, waste), and other measurement problems (see, for example, Behrman and Deolalikar 1987; Bouis and Haddad 1992). Estimates that control for such possibilities imply elasticities of nutrient intakes with respect to income that are from a tenth to a fourth the magnitudes suggested in the previous paragraph, in the 0.05–0.25 range. Even the estimates that allow for strong nonlinearities for the very poor (such as Strauss and Thomas 1992 for Brazil), while controlling for other measurement and estimation problems, are at the upper end of this range rather than at levels three to four times higher as was suggested by earlier conventional wisdom. Thus the impact of changes of real income on nutrient intakes appears to be much less than was thought by many a decade ago. This means that the negative effects of income on nutrient intakes for any poor groups who suffer at least initial income losses are likely to be much smaller than often claimed—and the increases in nutrient intakes for those who have income gains are also likely to be much smaller than often claimed. A 10 per cent change in income is likely to lead to a 1 or 2 per cent change in basic nutrient intakes, not an 8–13 per cent change. Of course changes in income may also have an impact on nutritional and health status through changing other right-side variables in relation (1), for example through changing health-related consumption, a topic covered in other chapters.

The second strain of recent literature that brings into question the great importance of income effects on nutrition and health status relates to the role of private interhousehold transfers in developing countries (see, for example, Cox and Jimenez 1991, 1992; Kaufmann and Lindauer 1986; Lucas and Stark 1985; Ravallion and Dearden 1988; Rosenzweig 1988; Rosenzweig and Stark 1989; and Townsend 1994). These studies suggest that in a number of contexts private transfers are substantial —particularly where there is little of governmental assistance—and provide a safety net for those whose real incomes fall for any of a number of reasons including, in the case of the urban poor and agricultural net food purchasers, food price increases as part of a structural adjustment programme. Although the available data make it hard to be sure to what extent the motive for such transfers is altruism rather than insurance, at least for the poorer recipients altruism appears to be part of the motive. Whatever the motives, the supply of private transfers would seem to depend not only on current relative incomes, but also on expected future incomes. The greater the expectations that future incomes will increase, the greater is likely to be the current supply of such private transfers for altruistic reasons and possibly for insurance reasons. The greater the transfers to poorer households, whatever the motives behind these, the less will reductions in the real labour earnings of net food purchasers adversely affect nutrient intakes and other components of nutritional and health status.

Of course the extent of the impact of food policy changes on nutritional and health status depends in part on the mechanisms for smoothing consumption over time, the determinants of transfers, and expectations for future developments. The more efficacious the mechanisms, for example, the less is likely to be the response of nutritional and health status to food price increases and related real income declines. In the absence of such mechanisms, there is a question about the extent to which resources can effectively be transferred over time by adjustments in nutritional and health status. That is, in terms of anthropometric indicators, to what extent is catch-up growth possible? Although catch-up growth is not likely to be a substitute for good markets, the more it takes place, the less permanent and thus less severe will be the impact of any current short falls in nutritional and health status due to food policies or to any other cause. While there has long been speculation about such possibilities, until recently there have been no efforts to estimate whether or not there is catch-up growth in the framework presented in Section II in which growth may depend on unobserved endowments. Recent preliminary estimates that control for such a possibility (Behrman, Deolalikar and Lavy 1994) indicate that there is significant catch-up growth, but that it is less than completely compensatory.

V. Policy Implications Regarding Problems in Interpreting from Available Information. What is the Impact of Structural Adjustment on Food Policy and on Nutrition?

From an economic perspective, there are two major reasons for undertaking policies—efficiency and distribution. The efficiency motive for policies relates to the possibility, at one point in time or over a period of time, of obtaining more production or consumption with the same resource use by rearranging the way in which society uses its productive inputs, the composition of output that it produces, or the composition of goods and services that it consumes. For example, if minimum wages for the formal manufacturing sector are too high too few workers may be employed in that sector and too many employed in agriculture, or if prices of petrochemical products do not reflect the pollution and congestion costs of using these products society may use too many of them, or if the private gains from providing so-called 'public goods' such as information (for which more for one member does not come at the expense of less for another) are less than the social gains inadequate quantities of such goods are likely to be provide. In all of these cases, with the same resources, consumption and growth would probably be increased by greater efficiency if distortions were removed so that the prices on which entities made their consumption and production decisions were purged of distortions so that they were reflective of true marginal social benefits.[11]

The distribution motive for policies reflects the fact that, without policy interventions, the distribution of outcomes may be different from that desired. For example, the poorer members of society may have more limited access to resources, consumption, and human resources than socially desired. There is a difficult question of how to determine what is 'socially desired'—that is, how to aggregate individual preferences to obtain social preferences—but there seems to be a widespread perception that the poor in many societies, including those in most Latin American countries, have inadequate consumption and human resources.

How might food policy, and food policy changes under structural adjustment in Latin America, be considered in the light of efficiency and distributional concerns?

The changes generally introduced as part of structural adjustment programmes to move domestic relative food prices towards international relative food prices are likely to be a move towards greater efficiency. The lessening or removal of price distortions is likely to result in greater incentives for the production of agricultural exportables, including in most cases domestic production of many foods. The extent of expansion of agricultural production, as noted above, is likely to depend in part on the adequacy of public sector roles in various areas in which market failures are likely because of strong scale economies and public goods characteristics: basic and applied agricultural research, information about nutrition, and market, transportation, and communication infrastructure. Many of these factors relate more to the supply of than to the demand for food, so an active food policy based on efficiency considerations may shift towards more of a supply-side orientation. However, there may also be some important areas regarding information where there are efficiency arguments for an active governmental policy on the demand side related to food policy. For instance, information about nutrient qualities of food is not likely to be disseminated sufficiently rapidly by private entities because its primary purpose is to serve the public good. Such information may become much more important in periods of structural adjustment due to the relative price and income changes induced by the structural adjustment programme that are likely to result in changes in quantities, qualities, and composition of food consumed. Thus policies that support the dissemination of information about nutrition may be an important part of food policy changes in structural adjustment programmes for efficiency reasons.

With regard to distributional concerns, as noted above, the impact of food price increases well may tend to increase the command over resources of some important

[11] There is a qualification due to the so-called 'second best' argument. According to this, removal of any one distortion (such as that due to the difference between the private and social costs of petrochemical production) does not necessarily improve efficiency if there are other distortions, as there almost always are. The point is illustrated by considering a situation in which there are two distortions that more or less offset each other, but if one is removed the other dominates with a more negative impact than previously. In the complexities of the real world with great knowledge imperfections, however, the most sensible prior assumption would seem to be that removing any particular distortion is likely to result in more efficiency unless there is explicit evidence to the contrary. See Behrman (1990) for further discussion of efficiency concerns and human resource investments in the development process.

groups of rural poor, especially if there are accompanying policy changes to alleviate the restraints on agricultural growth as well as an increased demand for rural labour due to market failures such as those mentioned in the previous paragraph. Thus for many of the poor there may well be a convergence of interests for both efficiency and distributional reasons. For the urban poor, however, such a convergence seems much less likely: in their case, real food price increases that may well be more efficient are likely to result in less, rather than more, real income. In the longer run the structural adjustment of the economy will, all being well, increase the demand for labour, and thus increase the real income of the urban poor through a number of means, including by reducing or eliminating various distortions that discriminate against the use of unskilled and semiskilled labour. At the start of the adjustment programme, however, unless there are policies that help to mitigate the immediate negative impact that food policy changes associated with the structural adjustment programme are likely to have on the urban poor, these individuals are likely to suffer a reduction in their real income that may lead to deterioration in nutritional and health status. Devising policies that are effective in avoiding this outcome without seriously undermining the structural adjustment programme, however, may not be easy. Well-targeted food subsidies for basic staples, for example, may mitigate such effects on the urban poor without putting enormous pressure on governmental budgets; however, they create disincentives for agricultural expansion. Moreover, they are not likely to have the support of the middle and upper classes if indeed they are well-targeted on the poor, and may help to undermine the credibility of the adjustment effort by encouraging other interest groups to claim the right to special policy treatment.

VI. The Mexican Shift from Generalized Food Subsidies to Targeted Food Subsidies under the Structural Adjustment Programme[12]

Prior to 1990 food subsidies in Mexico were given through generalized price discounts. But, as is well known, such subsidies may not be sufficiently well targeted to yield substantial benefits to the poor. The basic staple that received the generalized price subsidy, although not the only one, was tortillas. Data from the 1984 National Income–Expenditure Survey shows that per capita tortilla consumption is pretty much the same, regardless of income level. The implication of these findings is straightforward; if, as some estimates suggest, around 20 per cent of the population constitutes the truly poor, then only 20 cents out of every peso of subsidies to tortilla consumption reached the very poor—and an equal amount reached the richest fifth of households.

Since 1990 a new strategy of targeted subsidies has been implemented in Mexico that tries to reach the very poor at lower overall fiscal cost through increasingly targeted interventions. The new strategy eliminates the use of generalized price

---

[12] This discussion builds upon material prepared by Santiago Levy for a Box on 'Targeted Food Subsidies in Mexico' in Behrman, 1993. Other papers by Friedmann, Lustig, and Legovini, 1992, and Lustig, 1992, also discuss the background to these Mexican programmes and related matters.

subsidies and replaces them by directly targeted subsidies. The main programme for this is the Tortilla–Solidaridad Programme.

In urban areas, targeted families for the Tortilla–Solidaridad programme are selected by social workers. Means-testing for the beneficiaries occurs through an income criterion, and not through anthropometric indicators that could serve as direct measurements of malnutrition. Any family earning less than two monthly minimum wages qualifies for the programme to receive one kilogram of tortillas free per day. Data from the National Income–Expenditure Survey show that even the poorest urban families consume an average of two kilograms of tortillas daily. Thus, the amount of the tortillas delivered clearly does not meet these families' needs. This implies that the consumption decisions of the poor are not distorted by the programme: at the margin, the price of tortillas which the urban poor have to pay is the market price. The subsidy is therefore identical to a direct income transfer, equal to the amount of tortillas delivered times the market price. Although superficially the Tortilla–Solidaridad Programme is seen as providing food for the poor, it is *de facto* an income transfer programme, and contains no provisions that directly focus on the existence of malnutrition or on causes of malnutrition unrelated to income. The transfer given through this programme to an urban family in the second decile of the income distribution is equal to approximately 5 per cent of its monthly income; for families in the first decile the transfer is somewhat higher.

The Tortilla-Solidaridad Programme covers 2.3 million families, 684,000 of them located in Mexico City. In 1992, the estimated annual fiscal cost was US$ 170 million. Interestingly, between 1990 and 1992, the fiscal cost increased by less than 30 per cent, while the number of families in the programme increased by more than 150 per cent. This has been possible because the strategy of targeted subsidies lessens wastage of public funds through transfers to those above the poverty line and makes the administration process more efficient. The delivery mechanisms have by now become somewhat sophisticated: families are given a magnetic card where their daily purchases are recorded; a card-reading machine, also records the number of tortillas delivered by any 'tortilleria' or food store. This in turn allows the owner of the food store to charge the government for the cost of the programme. The delivery mechanism thus works through private operation of the distribution system, minimizing incentives to cheat and to divert resources to other groups; no special stores or distribution networks are required. The key points of intervention by the government are distributing the cards, and covering store owners' costs.

The transition towards directly targeted subsidies has not been complete, how-ever. Most of the changes have been concentrated in urban areas, where the imple-mentation of the programme is easier. In the rural areas food support is still being offered through generalized price discounts, though these discounts are only offered in selected stores operated through CONASUPO, the government agency in charge of food distribution. The CONASUPO stores are supposedly located in remote and poor rural communities, where the spillover of the benefits associated with generalized price discounts to the non-targeted population is minimized. Further, to the extent that these communities are in remote areas, transport costs serve as a natural barrier limiting the opportunities for arbitrage and containing fiscal costs. Thus, the generalized price subsidies offered in the rural areas are semi-targeted subsidies, where the element of targeting derives from locational considerations. This programme does, however, affect the consumption decisions of villagers by changing the prices that they face in addition to changing their incomes.

If the Tortilla-Solidaridad programme is evaluated in terms of the transfer of income to the urban poor and the saving of fiscal resources, the results are clearly positive. On the other hand, this kind of means-tested programme has problems from an incentive-structure viewpoint since it implies a marginal income tax for the urban poor. Families whose income increases from below two minimum wages to over that amount are disqualified from the programme. This effect may or may not be strong enough to discourage families from increasing their income by their own means. Moreover, although termed a 'food and nutrition programme' Tortilla-Solidaridad is in fact basically an income transfer program, as noted above, and empirical estimate discussed above suggest that the impact of income on nutrient intakes is quite small, though there may be larger effects on other determinants of nutrients. A fuller evaluation would require further research to investigate the income disincentives of the programme, the extent of its effects on nutrition, and its effects through the fiscal budget. However, on the basis of currently available information and considerations such as those summarized in earlier sections as well as in this discussion, it is not clear that either the apparently fairly successfully targeted Tortilla-Solidaridad Programme or the generalized food subsidies that preceded it in urban areas and still exist in remote rural areas has much effect on nutrition, even though the programme may have desirable effects on urban poverty alleviation.

Musgrove (1991) has reviewed 104 food distribution programmes operating in nineteen countries of the region in 1990 at a cost of US$ 1.6 billion per year. His findings show that the conclusion above—that the impact on nutrition of the Mexican food and nutrition programme is probably very small—holds true for the region generally. He suggests that this is due to a number of factors (such as too little expenditure in some countries, ineffective spending in many programmes, and an attempt to attain too many goals in others), but he places considerable emphasis on the failure to monitor most programmes with regard to their stated nutritional improvement aims (and not just expenditure of resources or provision of food). In view of the considerable uncertainty about how policies work and how individuals and households behave in response to them, it would be of considerable use to undertake more careful information gathering, monitoring, and analysis of food policy and nutrition programmes in Latin America.

REFERENCES

Abugattas, J. and Lee, D. R. (1991), 'The Economic Crisis, Policy Reforms and the Poor in Peru during the 1970s and the 1980s', paper presented at the Workshop on Macroeconomic Crises, Policy Reform and the Poor in Latin America, October 1991, Cali, Colombia.

Aguirre, P. (1991), 'The Impact of Crises on Low Income Urban Households in Argentina. How the Very Poor Survive', paper presented at the Workshop on Macroeconomic Crises, Policy Reform and the Poor in Latin America, October 1991, Cali, Colombia.

Alderman, H. (1986), *The Effects of Income and Food Price Changes on the Acquisition of Food by Low-Income Households*, Washington, DC: International Food Policy Research Institute.

Altimir, O. (1991), 'Magnitud de la Pobreza en America Latina en los Anos Ochenta', paper presented at the Workshop on Macroeconomic Crises, Policy Reform and the Poor in Latin America, October 1991, Cali, Colombia.

Behrman, J. R. (1990), *Human Resource Led Development?* New Delhi: ARTEP/ILO.

—— (1993), 'Investing in Human Resources', *Economic and Social Progress in Latin America: 1993 Report*, Baltimore, MD: Johns Hopkins University Press for the Inter-American Development Bank, 187–255.

—— and Deolalikar, A. B. (1987) 'Will developing country nutrition improve with income? A case study for rural south India', *Journal of Political Economy*, 95, 108–38.

—— —— (1988), 'Health and nutrition', in Chenery, Hollis B. and Srinivasan, T. N. (eds.), *Handbook on Economic Development*, 1, North Holland Publishing Company, Amsterdam, 631–711.

—— —— (1990), 'The intrahousehold demand for nutrients in rural south India: Individual estimates, fixed effects and permanent income', *Journal of Human Resources*, 25, 665–96.

—— —— (1991), 'The poor and the social sectors during a period of macroeconomic adjustment: empirical evidence for Jamaica', *World Bank Economic Review*, 3, 291–313.

—— —— and Lavy, V. (1994), 'Dynamic Decision Rules for Child Growth in Rural India and the Philippines: Catching Up or Staying Behind?', Philadelphia, PA: University of Pennsylvania, mimeo.

Binswanger, H. (1990), 'The policy response of agriculture', *Proceedings of the World Bank Annual Conference on Development Economics 1989* (Supplement to *World Bank Economic Review* and *World Bank Research Observer*), 231–58.

Bouis, H. E. and Haddad, L. J. (1992), 'Are estimates of calorie-income elasticities too high? A recalibration of the plausible range', *Journal of Development Economics*, 39, 333–64.

Castaneda, T. (1991), 'The Impact of Macroeconomic and Sectorial Policy Reforms on Poverty, Household Food Security and Nutrition in Chile during the 1970s and 1980s', paper presented at the Workshop on Macroeconomic Crises, Policy Reform and the Poor in Latin America, October 1991, Cali, Colombia.

Cornia, A. P., Jolly, R. and Stewart, F. (eds.) (1987), *Adjustment with a Human Face: Volume 1*, Oxford: Clarendon Press for UNICEF.

—— —— —— (1988), *Adjustment with a Human Face: Volume 2*, Oxford: Clarendon Press for UNICEF.

Cox, D. and Jimenez, E. (1991), 'Private Transfers and the Effectiveness of Public Income Redistribution in the Philippines', Washington, DC: World Bank.

—— —— (1992), 'Social Security and Private Transfers in Developing Countries: The Case of Peru', *World Bank Economic Review 6*, 155–69.

Deaton, A. (1988), 'Quality, quantity, and spatial variation of price', *American Economics Review*, 78, 418–30.

de Janvry, A. (1991), 'Politically Feasible and Equitable Adjustment: Some alternatives for Ecuador in the 1980s', paper presented at the Workshop on Macroeconomic Crises, Policy Reform and the Poor in Latin America, October 1991, Cali, Colombia.

Friedmann, S., Lustig, N., and Legovini, A. (1992), 'Social Spending and Food Subsidies during Adjustment in Mexico', paper presented at IUSSP and CEDEPLAR Seminar on the Demographic Consequences of Structural Adjustment in Latin America, 29 September–2 October 1992, Belo Horizonte, Brazil.

Hoffman, R. (1991), 'Economic Crisis and Poverty in Brazil during the 1980s', paper presented at the Workshop on Macroeconomic Crises, Policy Reform and the Poor in Latin America, October 1991, Cali, Colombia.

Huppi, M. and Ravallion, M. (1990), 'The Sectoral Structure of Poverty during an Adjustment Period: Evidence for Indonesia in the mid-1980s', Washington, DC: World Bank.

Kaufmann, D. and Lindauer, D. L. (1986), 'A model of income transfers for the urban poor', *Journal of Development Economics*, 22, 337–50.

Krueger, A. O., Schiff, M., and Valdes, A. (1988), 'Agricultural incentives in developing countries: measuring the effect of sectoral and economywide policies', *World Bank Economic Review* 2, 255–72.

Lucas, R. E. B. and Stark, O. (1985), 'Motivations to remit: evidence from Botswana', *Journal of Political Economy*, 93, 901–18.

Lustig, N. (1992), 'Mexico: The Social Impact of Adjustment', paper presented at IUSSP and CEDEPLAR Seminar on the Demographic Consequences of Structural Adjustment in Latin America, 29 September–2 October 1992, Belo Horizonte, Brazil.

Maasland, A. and van der Gaag, J. (1992), 'World Bank-supported adjustment programs and living conditions', in Corbo, V., Fischer, S., and Webb, S. (eds.), *Adjustment Lending Revisited: Policies to Restore Growth*, Washington, DC: World Bank, 40–63.

Morales, R., 'The Impact of the Macroeconomic Policy Reform on Poverty, Household Food Security and Nutrition in Bolivia', paper presented at the Workshop on Macroeconomic Crises, Policy Reform and the Poor in Latin America, October 1991, Cali, Colombia.

Musgrove, P. (1991), *Feeding Latin America's Children: An Analytical Survey of Food Programs*, Washington, DC: World Bank.

Pinstrup-Andersen, P. (1993), 'Economic Crises and Policy Reforms During the 1980s and Their Impact on the Poor', *Macroeconomic Environment and Health with Case Studies for Countries in Greatest Need*, Geneva: World Health Organization.

—— Jarmitto, M. and Stewart, F. (1987), 'The impact on government expenditure', in Cornia *et al.* (eds.), *Adjustment with a Human Face*, Oxford: Clarendon Press for UNICEF. 73–89.

Pitt, M. M. and Rosenzweig, M. R. (1985), 'Health and nutrient consumption across and within farm households', *Review of Economics and Statistics*, 67, 212–23.

Ravallion, M. and Dearden, L. (1988), 'Social security in a "moral economy": an empirical analysis for Java', *Review of Economics and Statistics*, 70, 36–44.

Rosenzweig, M. R. (1988), 'Risk, implicit contracts and the family in rural areas of low-income countries', *Economic Journal*, 98, 1148–70.

—— and Stark, O. (1989), 'Consumption smoothing, migration, and marriage: evidence from rural India', *Journal of Political Economy*, 97, 903–26.

Ruel, M. and Garrett, J. (1991), 'Economic Crisis, Health and Nutrition: Evidence from Central America', paper presented at the Workshop on Macroeconomic Crises, Policy Reform and the Poor in Latin America, October 1991, Cali, Colombia.

Stewart, F. (1991), 'Protecting the Poor during Adjustment in Latin America and the Caribbean in the 1980s: How Adequate was the World Bank Response?', paper presented at the Workshop on Macroeconomic Crises, Policy Reform and the Poor in Latin America, October 1991, Cali, Colombia.

Strauss, John (1984), 'Joint determination of food consumption and product in rural Sierra Leone: estimates of a household-firm model', *Journal of Development Economics*, 14, 77–104.

—— and Thomas, Duncan (1992), 'The shape of the calorie expenditure curve', New Haven, CT: Yale University, mimeo.

Thompson, A. (1991), 'Crisis Económica, Reformas de Políticas y su Effecto Sobre Los Pobres en la Argentina en los 80', paper presented at the Workshop on Macroeconomic Crises, Policy Reform and the Poor in Latin America, October 1991, Cali, Colombia.

Townsend, R. (1994), 'Risk and Insurance in Village India', *Econometrica*, 62/3 (May), 539–92.

Trejos, J. D. (1991), 'Crisis, Ajuste y Pobreza: la Experience de Costa Rica en los Ochenta', paper presented at the Workshop on Macroeconomic Crises, Policy Reform and the Poor in Latin America, October 1991, Cali, Colombia.

Williamson-Gray, C. (1982), *Food Consumption Parameters for Brazil and their Application to Food Policy*, Research Report 32, Washington, DC: International Food Policy Research Institute.

World Bank (1981), *World Development Report, 1981*, Washington, DC: World Bank.

Part III

Short-term Fluctuations in Vital Rates

5 The Effects of Economic Changes on Mortality by Age and Cause:

Latin America, 1950–90

ALBERTO PALLONI AND KENNETH HILL

I. Economic Swings and Mortality Changes

A fairly recurrent idea of population theory is that the weakening of frequent and sharp fluctuations in the levels and age patterns of mortality is an important marker distinguishing pre- from post-industrialization mortality trends (Livi-Bacci 1992; Vallin 1991; Flinn 1974; Schofield and Reher 1991). The appearance and disappearance of epidemics, the outbreak and aftermath of wars, and the vagaries of weather left clear if not always durable imprints in the profiles of mortality before the middle of the nineteenth century. With improvements in technology and standards of living, advances in sanitation and public health and, later during the twentieth century, the application of vector eradication and chemotherapy, mortality levels began an apparently irreversible downward trend, while the frequency and duration of oscillations around secular trends were reduced to insignificance or, for all purposes, disappeared altogether.[1]

Although the idea that patterns of mortality of industrialized countries exclude even loose linkages between mortality changes and oscillations of levels of living has been forcefully challenged in the US (Brenner 1983), it is nevertheless well established that the aggregate connection between the two is far from being tight and is undeniably much weaker than it was in the past.[2] The situation in some of

We thank Jorge Bravo, David Lam, Andrew Mason, Samuel Preston, and George Tapinos for useful comments on an earlier draft. The research on which this paper is based was completed while Alberto Palloni was at the Center for Advanced Studies in the Behavioral Sciences, Stanford, California. We gratefully acknowledge support by a grant to the Center by the National Science Foundation (BNS-870084). In addition, research was carried out, in part, using facilities of the Center for Demography and Ecology at the University of Wisconsin-Madison, which receives core support for population research from the National Center for Child Health and Human Development (Grant P30-HD05876).

[1] Although apparently harmless, the idea that the disappearance of crises-mortality can be taken as a marker of modern mortality ought to be carefully qualified since it is by no means clear that their contribution to the high levels of mortality prevailing during pre-industrial times was inordinately high (see Fogel 1989).

[2] We point out at the outset that the evidence regarding the association between economic changes and mortality in pre-industrial societies is murky. Although there is a general pattern reflecting the existence of short-term associations (Galloway 1988; Hammel 1985; Richards 1984; Lee 1981), the strength of such associations is less than impressive. Some have argued that the weak association of short-term fluctuations masks stronger connections that are confounded by the nature of the indicators (Fogel 1989).

today's Third World countries may well be different. Indeed, the context of mortality decline in developing nations differs in many respects from the one that characterized western Europe and North America. The differences are sharp and leave sufficient room for the possibility that 'pre-industrial' short-term connections between mortality and in socio-economic conditions are still operating.

One important feature of patterns of mortality decline in some parts of the developing world decline is the fact that, after experiencing unprecedented gains in survival during the period immediately following the Second World War, changes proceed at a slower pace than expected (Gwatkin 1980); in some cases the downward trend in mortality has flattened prematurely (Palloni 1981), while in others there have been outright reversals (Muller and Accinelli 1978; Romero 1993; Carvalho and Wood 1988). While the evidence corroborating the details of this process is controversial and there is ample room for disagreement (Hill and Pebley 1989), there is less dissension about the fact that the process of mortality decline in developing countries could be on a fragile and vulnerable course, one that is considerably less insulated from exogenous changes in economic conditions.

A second empirical feature of the patterns of demographic changes in at least *some* developing countries is that they indeed have reproduced the connection between economic fluctuations and mortality that was characteristic of pre-industrial Europe. In a brief review of an admittedly short list of available studies R. D. Lee concluded that 'the experience of European populations before the twentieth century is highly consistent with the experience of the poorer Third World countries up to the present' (Lee 1990: 11). He then went on to add that the population patterns of wealthier Third World countries are expected to conform more closely to those of the developed countries (e.g. with a lower influence of economic cycles on mortality). But the evidence that we study in this chapter suggests that, at least in Latin America, this may well not be the case.

Finally, the protracted and severe economic recession that began late in the 1970s and lasted in most Latin American countries until well into the 1980s (although until today it shows only weak signs of loosening its grip on large sections of the Third World) may have had social and economic consequences that set it apart from previous recessions. Some have argued that its severity and duration was such that even the most advanced among developing countries were on the verge of experiencing crushing setbacks in standards of living, in health, and in mortality (Jolly and Cornia 1984; Cornia *et al.* 1987).

The evidence is ambiguous, the data insufficient, and the methodologies applied are not always unassailable and leave ample room for questionable inferences about whether, when, and where the setbacks have occurred. The task of finding relations is made even more difficult for, as we discuss later, the nature of the mortality response in recessionary times is complex and need not always appear in tidy ways that make self-evident the connection between it and the deterioration of the economy. The same applies *mutatis mutandis* to mortality (or health) responses in periods of economic boom and expansion.

Does the available evidence support the idea of any response whatsoever, in periods of relative scarcity as well as in periods of relative abundance, in at least some areas of the developing world? The question that we attempt to answer in this paper concerns the association between economic fluctuations and mortality changes in Latin American countries during the period 1955–90.[3] We are interested in elucidating the existence, magnitude, direction, and trends of linkages during a period that witnessed both sustained (but not continuous) economic prosperity— basically the years between 1949 and 1965—as well as severe economic recession —the period after 1975. We are also interested in determining whether the association between economic oscillations and mortality varies across countries in ways that are consistent with the conjecture that adjudicates similarities between 'poor' Third World countries and pre-industrial Europe, on the one hand, and 'richer' Third World countries and contemporaneous developed countries, on the other (Lee 1990). Admittedly, Latin America is only part of the Third World and may not be representative of trends elsewhere. Yet its experience is directly relevant to the hypotheses for if they fail to be verified there, they become considerably less relevant in explaining contemporary trends in general. If, however, the expected patterns turn out in countries of Asia or Africa, the hypotheses should be redefined and elaborated to account for contingencies that make them relevant in some social and economic contexts but irrelevant in others. A nontrivial advantage of our sample is that we are able to assemble a relatively long series of statistics on death by age and by cause, as well as socioeconomic indicators that enable us to test a broad variety of hypotheses.

It should be emphasized that the nature of the question that we address requires that we focus on short-term changes and associations, not on trends over the long run. The fact that post-1945 mortality trends in Latin America have, with one or two exceptions, followed a consistently downward slope while indices of socioeconomic development have, by and large, been on an upward trajectory, is not in itself immediately relevant for our purposes. Neither is the fact that about 50 per cent of the secular decline in mortality may have been due to changes in socioeconomic conditions (Palloni and Wyrick 1981; Preston 1976). It is on the strength, direction, and variability of associations between *departures* from long-term trends that we focus, since they are the ultimate material to confirm or disprove the hypotheses of linkages between mortality and economic fluctuations. This does not imply that we dismiss the importance of long-term relations between economic conditions and mortality (or even the relevance that short-term oscillations may have for these). But in this chapter we are able only to focus on short-term trends.

Although our work is not completely original either in its substance or its methods,[4] we deal with well-known and less familiar problems using conventional as well as

---

[3] For most countries we have information after 1955 but before 1987 or 1988. For a few countries information stretches back to 1951 and reaches up to 1990.

[4] Bravo (1992) and Bravo and Vargas (1990) have paved the way for the analysis of mortality by causes in Latin America. Hill and Palloni (1992) have suggested procedures and analysed a partial data base on total deaths. Galloway and Lee (1985) and Reher (1989) have pursued similar ideas on the analysis of demographic fluctuations in China and colonial Mexico, respectively.

experimental and untried solutions. Our results suggest that some of the conclusions that we and others have derived from the straightforward application of conventional time series methods may not be as solid as originally believed, that there are some persistent and intriguing regularities in all the countries that we examine, and that there is much more to be discovered with the data already available, provided that appropriate methodologies are judiciously applied.

The plan of the chapter is as follows. In Section II we define alternative mechanisms linking economic fluctuations and mortality, and discuss a series of relevant hypotheses. We emphasize here that the nature of these mechanisms requires investigation of changes in mortality by age and cause, not just in total levels. In Section III we summarize the data and describe the methods applied to generate estimates of the magnitude, direction and variability of effects. In the main, the methods we employ follow closely those developed elsewhere for the analysis of short-term fluctuations (Lee 1981; Galloway 1988; Bravo 1992; Hill and Palloni 1992). However, we introduce a few improvements that enable us to deal with causes of deaths, to generate seemingly stable and robust estimates of elasticities, to estimate changes over time in the magnitudes of the linkages and to control for the influence of fluctuations in the accuracy of reporting of causes of deaths. In Section IV we discuss our results and investigate their implications. In particular, we show that estimates of linkages between economic fluctuations and mortality changes by age and cause can be translated into estimates of changes in the overall level and pattern of mortality.

II. Mechanisms Linking Mortality Changes and Economic Fluctuations

A. The effects on exposure, resistance, and recovery

The relation between deterioration of economic conditions and mortality is mediated by changes in exposure and resistance to diseases and other mortality risks, as well as by the capacity of individuals to recover from ailments produced by illnesses or other health-threatening conditions. A direct, non-mediated relation may be observable only in situations leading to outright starvation or to acute deficiencies in major nutrients (proteins, vitamins, and minerals) and their sequelae. The mechanisms through which exposure, resistance, and recovery are affected by economic conditions are numerous and vary by age and sex.

First, a drop in individual standards of living can translate directly into lowered nutritional intake and this in turn, if sustained long enough, can lead to deteriorated nutritional status. Deficiencies in nutritional status compromise immuno-competence and render the host more susceptible to some infectious diseases, while at the same time weakening its ability to ward off the effects of illness and eroding its capacity for recovery. Nutritional status has been shown to strongly influence susceptibility and resistance to about ten infectious diseases including cholera, bacterial diarrhoea, measles, respiratory tuberculosis, whooping cough, and respiratory diseases. Other infectious diseases show a less clear, more variable relation to nutrition (Lunn 1991; Rotberg and Rabb 1983). Of particular importance are diseases associated with bacterial diarrhoea and dysentery. In this case a synergistic relation exists whereby the infection weakens nutritional status even when nutritional intake is adequate, as the host's ability to absorb nutrients is impaired by the disease (Scrimshaw *et al.* 1968).[5] The population groups that are most vulnerable to nutritional status deficiencies are young children, the elderly, and women of reproductive age. Infants who are fully breastfeeding are better protected by the cleanliness of breastmilk and by the immunities and nutrients transferred from the mother to the child. The benefits of lactation may last for as long as one year. At higher risk are children who are weaned early, and those who begin to be fully exposed to a host of pathogens and must rely on regular food intake to satisfy nutritional requirements. Women of reproductive status experience the burden of pregnancy and child feeding, both of which place heavy demands on their nutritional status. In societies where child spacing is typically short, the maternal health response to falls in levels of living standards will be exacerbated. However, since diseases such as pulmonary tuberculosis are more likely to strike women who experience pregnancy as a result of compromised cell-mediated immunity (Larsen 1983), one would expect deteriorated social and economic conditions to have effects over and above those due to maternal depletion.

The observed connection between nutrition and survival, however, is likely to be exaggerated by the influence of other factors associated with sanitation, personal hygiene, poor housing, etc. In a recent review of the evidence, an author has remarked that while 'we may agree that malnutrition does play its part in worsening the conditions of survival in the presence of other factors which favour the spreading of infections and act against their cessation (poor hygiene, poverty, ignorance) . . . the role of malnutrition is not uniform, being nil for some diseases, uncertain and variable for others, considerable and certain for still others' (Livi-Bacci 1991). This cautionary note is echoed in a review of the relations between nutrition and infection which suggests that 'although nutrition plays a major part, the extent to which other socio-economic variables contribute to disease prevalence and mortality remains to be assessed' (Lunn 1991; see also Martorell and Ho 1984; McKeown 1988). Although spurious effects may be part of the observed relations, it is undoubtedly the case that the negative effects of nutrition on survival are *enhanced* by conditions of poverty. Thus, mortality responses will be more discernible among social groups living in precarious conditions. It is this expected (individual-level) relationship that leads to the conjecture according to which responses to economic crisis are probably attenuated in countries with higher standards of living.[6]

---

[5] There is also evidence that respiratory tuberculosis and enteric diseases may be interrelated in complex synergy (see Szreter 1988).

[6] A different but complementary factor that leads to stronger responses among impoverished groups has been advanced by Fogel to interpret findings from preindustrial societies (Fogel 1989, 1991). In

Second, a lowering of standards of living results in conditions and behaviours that increase exposure to diseases and that minimize the ability to recover from bouts of illness. First, individual or family reactions to the crisis could aggravate crowding, housing and general hygiene conditions, thus providing a strong link between economic conditions and mortality. This is likely to occur, for example, when deterioration of economic conditions leads to rural–urban migration or to massive displacement of people between urban areas. But these factors are only part of the story. In a recent review of the relations between nutrition and health, Livi-Bacci (1991) finds that observations from clinical studies, the historical experience of selected population groups, and the historical record of western Europe all support the idea that the apparent response of mortality to reduced intake of food may be confounded by simultaneous outbreaks of epidemics (see also Braudel 1985). Since the evidence linking malnutrition and incidence of infectious diseases is not strong, the sharp increase in mortality that appears in response to economic crisis can only be explained successfully by social behaviour that, in response to the crisis, augments the *exposure* to diseases. This is an observation which is pertinent in developing countries where the occurrence of significant increases in exposure (and lowered capacity to recover) is likely to require far more than transient reductions in food intake. It probably necessitates serious deterioration or complete breakdown of infrastructure and considerable inaction, or outright paralysis, of national and local governments. Consequently, mortality responses will be magnified if the downturn is sharp and sustained enough to inflict damage on sanitation and public health, the continuity of public work programmes, food assistance and subsidies, and on the integrity of social welfare including preventive and curative health services. The partially protective shield conferred on citizens by centralized institutions is thus of fundamental importance as it may constitute a mechanism through which some of the effects of economic downturns are postponed or are simply never felt. This is not unique to developing countries. Indeed, there is evidence that in pre-industrial societies central governments were often successful in anticipating shortages and, accordingly, smoothed oscillations in food inventories through corrective interventions (Fogel 1989).

The most direct outcome of both individual and family accommodation to the crisis and deterioration of infrastructure is an increased exposure to infectious diseases. Living in crowded and cramped quarters as families double up to cushion the impact of poorer economic conditions, lack of access to uncontaminated water and food, and substandard disposal of refuse and sewage may all multiply exposure to transmittable diseases. First in line to be affected are diseases of the intestinal tract, respiratory ailments, and respiratory tuberculosis.[7] Furthermore, if governments'

economies with highly unequal distribution of assets, particularly land, the propertyless groups tend to have less of a cushion during hard times and their mortality response may be consequently augmented. Substantial group differentials in responses to the crisis of the 1980s for urban areas in Latin America have been documented by Altimir (1984).

[7] Puranen has argued that death rates of pulmonary tuberculosis may be more responsive to exposure than they are to nutritional status. His conclusion, however, is derived from evidence for small populations

ability to support a network of health services delivery is undermined, families' access to vaccination, prevention, and proper medical attention will be compromised, thus simultaneously worsening exposure and threatening individuals' ability to recover from bouts of illness. Under these conditions, increases in respiratory tuberculosis among young adults and older people, in respiratory ailments among the very young, and in the incidence of other infectious diseases (particularly bacterial diarrhoea and dysentery) among young children and the elderly are to be expected. If the impaired ability to deliver health services involves prenatal care, infants are likely to be seriously affected as well.

A less direct effect is on exposure to conditions and behaviours that bolster the risk of noninfectious diseases. Consumption of alcohol and other drugs may increase,[8] adults may become more likely to engage in work conditions that entail higher risks of accident,[9] and added stress will augment susceptibility to chronic ailments, self-injury, homicide, and suicide. These conditions will affect most seriously young male adults and the elderly and should have virtually no effects among the very young, unless increased poverty and lack of access to resources forces families and women to cut down on safe childcare practices.

To conclude this section we remark that the influence of economic downturns and upturns may operate anywhere in the chain from exposure to recovery. It is conceivable though unlikely that, under current conditions in developing countries, bad economic times affect both exposure and resistance but leave unscathed the capacity to provide treatment and aid recovery. This means that we should search for responses not in levels of mortality but in levels of morbidity. A muted response in mortality is ambiguous since it can mean one of two things: either economic crises simply do not affect health status in any significant way, or they affect it significantly but without undermining the capacity to bounce back from episodes of illness and thus without substantially altering mortality risks.[10]

B. Timing and contingencies: who is affected by what and when?

Ages and causes of deaths
Almost all studies of the relation between socio-economic fluctuations and mortality focus on total mortality (for an exception to this see the work by Bravo 1992). It

(Puranen 1991). Cronjè, on the other hand, has studied evidence suggesting that exposure was probably more important in Victorian England (Cronjè 1984). The evidence that pulmonary tuberculosis is linked to nutritional status is strong (see also Barnes 1992). What is unclear, however, is the magnitude of the deterioration in nutritional status that is needed to induce an increase in active cases, and the time lags involved.

[8] We note that the incidence and case fatality of respiratory tuberculosis may be causally related to alcohol consumption (Puranen 1991).

[9] Evidence for the most recent recession in the United States suggests that the rate of accidents associated with work tends to decrease rather than to increase.

[10] It should be noted that for the most part the direct effects of malnutrition, for example, are nowhere very prevalent even though chronic malnutrition could be well entrenched in many places. Under these conditions, economic crises could well lead to changes in the prevalence of certain diseases but it does not follow that case fatality rates will increase proportionately (McKeown 1988).

should be clear from our previous discussion that the effects could vary across age groups and causes of deaths, and that the observed changes in total mortality may mask very different responses by age and causes of deaths. Thus, proper identification of effects calls for separate treatment of mortality by age and cause:

(i) causes of death that are more closely connected to nutritional status (such as malnutrition and avitaminosis, bacterial diarrhoea and dysentery, some infectious diseases such as measles, acute respiratory ailments, and respiratory tuberculosis) are more sensitive to changes in socio-economic conditions and among young children, young adults, and the elderly. Infants should not be affected by this mechanism unless there is severe disruption of feeding patterns or unless the prevailing patterns of breastfeeding are not long and universal;

(ii) accidents, suicides, homicides, and some chronic ailments (such as cirrhosis, ulcers, and ischemic heart disease) are likely to be the responses among adults; and

(iii) in the absence of changes in feeding patterns, infant mortality will be affected to the extent that pre- and postnatal care deteriorate. Paradoxically, as a crisis may increase the incidence of stillbirths, a stronger selection of weaker newborns will operate and neonatal and possibly postneonatal mortality could be *favourably* affected by the crisis, although the effects will be short-lived.

Time lags and direction of effects
The timing and direction of the expected effects are more difficult to pin down with precision. First, effects operating through nutrition should lag by at least one year, except under wretched initial conditions. Shorter lags should be expected for infants if the patterns of breastfeeding are severely disrupted. Second, effects associated with increases in neo and postneonatal mortality are likely to occur within one or at most two years of the initial changes. Increases in respiratory ailments are unlikely to take place before a year and increases in death due to respiratory tuberculosis will not be observed before two years.[11] Finally, effects associated with accidents, suicides and homicides, and chronic ailments are more likely to operate in full force after there has been some time for the consequences of the crisis to be felt at the individual level.

The effects of downward economic swings will not always be in the direction of increasing mortality. We have already noted that the changing composition of births may indeed induce *lower*, not higher, infant mortality as a higher proportion of those whose prenatal health status is substandard are stillbirths. A similar argument applies to young and adult mortality: after the initial response the composition by frailty of the surviving population will lead to lower than normal average mortality risks. Thus, the increase in mortality above normal levels soon after an economic

---

[11] Increases in the death rates due to respiratory tuberculosis can be due to a combination of increased incidence and increased mortality among those already infected. Increased exposure (due to overcrowding, for example) can have increased incidence but not before one or two years. And a reduction in nutritional status is unlikely to have effects that will be felt before a year or two. The expected reaction of respiratory tuberculosis may come early, however, if the occurrence of other infectious diseases weakens the resistance of those already infected with tuberculosis.

downturn should be followed by a decrease below normal levels (Caldwell and Caldwell 1987; Palloni 1988). This is exactly the pattern observed in the majority of the empirical studies that have been carried out so far (Lee 1990): the lag-pattern of effects is wave-like, displaying a sinusoidal profile that alternates negative with positive responses whose magnitude gradually converges toward zero as the lag increases. But the nature of the pattern of effects by lag is partly dependent on the composition by frailty of the *initial* population. Groups at the lower end of the frailty scale will definitely show it, whereas those that are better off may experience multiple (but decreasing) echoes of the mortality increase as people who are weakened during the initial stages of the response are never able to recover fully. We expect that the wave-like pattern will have different profiles by age and by cause of death. Selection effects should be stronger among the very young and the very old than among younger adults. The implication is that the echoes will be more salient for young children and the elderly. Similarly, selection effects should be stronger for wasting diseases such as respiratory tuberculosis than they are for other infectious diseases. Finally, selection may operate in unexpected directions and produce reinforcing rather than offsetting responses, as when an increase in death through violence among the most fit segment of the population increases the average frailty of the subpopulation that is less exposed to violence.

A potentially powerful selection effect could operate indirectly through effects on fertility. It has been shown that both marital fertility and nuptiality respond quite readily to economic fluctuations (Galloway 1988; Lee 1981; Reher 1989; Hill and Palloni 1992; Palloni, Pinto, and Hill 1993). In particular, the number of births drops significantly in response to the initial impact of a recession. Since the composition of births by risk factors such as parity (proportions of first births), mother's age (proportion to younger mothers), and birth interval (proportion born after exceedingly short intervals) is likely to change favourably, infant and even early child mortality will tend to decrease, thus partially offsetting the increases due to other forces directly affecting mortality. As the fertility response wanes and the original composition of births is restored, infant mortality will increase at higher lags.

A general conclusion to be drawn from the discussion in this and the preceding subsection is the following: as conjectured before, one important consequence of the differentials in the timing, direction, and magnitude of responses by causes of deaths and age-groups is that the observed effects of economic fluctuations on total mortality could mask important variability in its components. This holds generally except in cases when there is only one single dominant mechanism producing the mortality response. Indeed, the absence of an observed mortality response may be the result of a perverse pattern of age-cause specific responses by lags. As we show later, our data do reveal the presence of important potentially offsetting effects, though we found no example of the extreme case of fully offsetting effects.

Social and behavioural contingencies

Heterogeneity in the nature and duration of crises, the social and political conditions that prevail in a country during a crisis, and the mixture of social groups and their bargaining power are important sources of variation in the magnitude and even direction of the mortality response (Hill and Palloni 1992).

Not all economic downturns (or upturns) have the same effects even though they may be reflected in similar empirical fluctuations of economic indicators. Recessions that have their origins in international crises and that lead to draconian reorganization of internal consumption patterns, massive loss of purchase power, and substantial cuts in government spending will hit the urban working class and lower white-collar occupational groups more severely than those whose income depends on rural wage labour, subsistence agriculture, or on activities associated with large export sectors. Economic downturns that are more localized, less influenced by international recessions, and associated with sagging demand for selected exports, for example, will have a less serious and immediate impact. As has been shown elsewhere, the recession currently affecting Latin American countries belongs more to the first class and is one of many others of the same type that have hit the continent with some recurrence since the times of independence (Marichal 1989; Altimir 1984; Frieden 1991).

A related though distinct factor that affects the magnitude of the response is the duration of the downturn (or upturn). Protracted crises are more likely to exhaust reserves and inventories or to outlast the shielding effect of public interventions. Longer exposure times are also more likely to trigger effects that require thresholds to lead effectively to heightened mortality (for example, malnutrition). If a long series including the occurrence of multiple crises were available to us, we could test for the effects of crises of different durations. As we show later, however, our data set does not allow detailed tests of this nature and instead we are forced to use an indirect and fairly crude assessment of duration effects: since the analysis covers only a very restricted period of time, we estimate the existence of differential effects over time by modelling the effects of pre-1975 recessions in an attempt to assess the uniqueness of the most recent one.

Given the nature and duration of the crisis, different social groups and economic sectors will be unequally affected by it. Some groups and sectors will be more insulated from its main effects, others will be able to adapt and accommodate using survival strategies of a different calibre and, finally, others will resist erosion of standards of living by mobilizing and successfully applying political pressure on decision makers. Convincing evidence of social differentials in the impact of the most recent crisis in Latin America has been obtained from a series of surveys in selected urban areas and analysed at length elsewhere (Altimir 1984). As Frieden (1991) has forcefully argued, the impact on different social groups and economic sectors is largely a function of their actual position in the national economy and vis-à-vis the state, of their interrelations with elites and of the degree and type of class conflict. The long time series by social groups that are required to assess the nature of these differentials are generally unavailable although glimpses of it and suggestive evidence illustrating their presence can be obtained from case studies (Frieden 1991) or from cross-sectional surveys (Altimir 1984). The issue is important, for just as the observed responses of total death rates conceal the detail of age- and cause-specific processes, so do population-based responses mask group-specific dynamics.[12]

In the absence of information on social groups we test hypotheses at more aggregate levels regarding two possibly important contingencies. *First*, when crises are of roughly comparable magnitudes the response should be more muted in countries where the mortality decline starts earlier, has been more sustained, and is better entrenched, than in others where mortality decline is more recent and more dependent on newer institutions and programmes. This is because the former are more likely to have a more adequate infrastructure for the delivery of services so that health education, sanitation, and public health can efficiently reach a majority of the population. It should be noted that, although the correlation is not perfect, countries of the former type are those that are higher up in a continuum of development. Thus, if empirically verified, the expected differential effects will probably coincide with differentials in the levels of development as well.

Second, the effect on infant mortality was postulated to be mediated by practices of infant feeding. Among groups that rely less on breastfeeding, an economic downturn may have an immediate impact on child morbidity and mortality, whereas among those where there is universal and prolonged breastfeeding (more than one year) the effects will be attenuated. An analogous though admittedly less persuasive contrast can be drawn at the more aggregate levels of countries, namely, in countries where traditional breastfeeding patterns prevail mortality levels will be less affected.[13]

III. Data and Methods

A. Description of the data

Assessing economic fluctuations
In pre-industrial societies annual fluctuations in the price of grain were the most dominant determinants of variations in the real wage and could be taken, with some important qualifications, as good indicators of fluctuations in families' standards of living (Galloway 1988; Lee 1981; Weir 1984; Livi-Bacci 1991; Meuvret 1946; Corradi 1973; Appleby 1979). In contemporaneous Third World countries with fairly diversified and open economies the prices of one or a combination of commodities and the real wages (derived from it and from nominal wages) are unlikely to be a good gauge of individual standards of living. Diversified production and individual consumption renders futile the attempt to single out a combination of price of staples as indicator of household budgetary pressure. Real wages are not always available and, furthermore, they represent the experience of a variable subset of the population. In addition, fluctuations of real wages are heavily influenced

---

[12] The idea of differential impact has been explicitly formalized in the study of responses to economic crisis in pre-industrial times (Fogel 1989).

[13] These relations should hold only when confounding factors are controlled.

by the strength and fortunes of segments of the working class and their political organizations and may trace the movements of the economy only poorly. Elsewhere we have argued that a good indicator of standards of living is the level of personal consumption (Hill and Palloni 1992). Due to the nature of the current crisis which is associated with high levels of international indebtedness, this could be a compelling choice. Yet, as shown in Figure 5.1, the variability of this indicator is less than that of other candidates such as GDP (and GNP) and about the same as that of the ratio of debt servicing to exports.[14] As GNP and GDP do include nonpersonal consumption elements such as investments and exclude borrowing to sustain individual levels of consumption, they may in theory be more weakly related than personal consumption to the mechanisms that trigger a mortality response. But, on the other hand, GNP and GDP include elements intimately related to the maintenance and functioning of infrastructure, sanitation, and public health that are excluded from personal consumption but are central to our argument. In some of our analysis at least we use real GDP per capita and private consumption separately and show that despite some differences, the inferences are quite similar.[15]

Conventional economic indicators may not reflect well the timing and nature of hardships generated by recessions in Latin America. Indeed, either as a response to the protracted current crisis or as a broader and more entrenched adaptation to long-term economic stagnation, many Latin American countries have experienced the growth of an informal sector that absorbs a significant fraction of the labour force, occupies massive amounts of resources and capital, and satisfies a demand for products and services that the formal sector of the economy does not address at all (see DeSoto 1990). For the most part, the indicators of economic activities from national accounts do not reflect transactions and production in the informal sector although, in principle at least, prices and wages should reflect the value of all goods and services. Worse yet, if the activities in the informal economy intensify precisely during pronounced downturns, the indicators we have chosen will lead us astray. This problem is analogous to one faced by historical investigations that focus on price trends of staples when a substantial fraction of food resources is not purchased by means of market transactions but originates in subsistence activities, is bartered, or received in exchange for services and labour.[16]

[14] Private consumption and debt service are affected by potentially damaging measurement errors. The calculus of private consumption in national accounts is often of a residual nature and final estimates are obtained after total GDP and gross investments have been accounted for. The total value of debt servicing can reflect changes in a host of external prices that bear no clear relation to a country's standards of living. In theory at least, the ratio of long-term debts service to the value of exports should be well suited to the task to the extent that crises originate in excessive external borrowing. However, it may be poorly correlated with the actual effects of internal economic policies.

[15] Ideally we would have liked to use both indicators but our series are too short to accommodate more than one independent trend. Real GDP was calculated using national figures on GDP per capita per annum, deflated and expressed in constant US dollars of 1970.

[16] The existence of an informal economy changes the institutional context within which mortality responses may occur. Let us assume that the true relation is as follows: $D = kI^\alpha$, where D is the death rate, k is a constant (that can be standardized to be equal to 1), I is the economic indicator and α is the elasticity of mortality relative to economic conditions (as measured by I). The existence of informal economies can be posited to affect the value of α. If so, the equation above is misspecified and, depending

The data on causes of deaths
Although data on both mortality and morbidity would have been desirable, the available information on the latter is patchy and unreliable. As indices of mortality we use detrended values, namely, the ratio of the observed to the predicted *number* of deaths in the total population and, in age groups 1–4, 5–14, 15–64 and 65+, classified by causes of deaths (see Table 5.A1, Appendix 5.1). As argued elsewhere (Lee 1981) the analysis of short-term fluctuations can omit reference to denominators of rates when these change only gradually over the period of time considered. Detrending also minimizes the effects of gradual changes affecting completeness of death registration.[17] The case of infant mortality is different since the number of infant deaths is a function of the number of births, which itself is responsive to economic oscillations. To reduce the impact of this second order effect we use the ratio of infant deaths in a calendar year to the weighted number of births during that year and the immediately preceding one.

An important problem is that the time series by causes of deaths reveals discontinuities that are the result of changes in the classification of causes, idiosyncracies of practices and routines applied by national statistical offices or, more importantly, empirical variation in the probability that deaths of a given cause will be classified as ill-defined. The groups of causes of deaths that we define in Table 5.A1, Appendix 5.1, are a compromise between what is of substantive interest (see in Section II) and what enables us to minimize distortions.[18] In the section on methods we suggest a procedure that should minimize the effects of distortions due to changes in the propensity to classify deaths in ill-defined categories.

Our final series of mortality and socioeconomic indicators is for nine countries (see Appendix 5.1) and, for the most part, covers the period 1955–90.

B. Methods

The most general form for the model we propose is the following:

$$y_{nk}(t) = \alpha_{nk} + \Sigma_j \beta_{nk.j} x(t-j) + \Sigma_r \Sigma_j \lambda_{nk.jr} z_r(t-j) + \varepsilon_{nk}(t) \tag{1}$$

where $y_{nk}(t)$ and $x(t)$ are, respectively, the detrended values of the indices of mortality for cause k and age group n and of economic levels evaluated at time t, $z_r(t-j)$ is the lagged value of the rth control variable evaluated at time $t-j$, β's and λ's are regression coefficients, and $\varepsilon_{nk}(t)$ is an error term following an autoregressive process to be specified later. Under these conditions, the β's can be interpreted as

---

on the exact role played by the informal economy and its degree of responsiveness to recessions in the formal economy, it will yield a biased estimate of the true mortality response.

[17] This statement is invalid, of course, if the recession itself affects the levels of completeness of death registration. It is quite possible that registration of vital events becomes more inaccurate during recessionary periods. If this is so, we will underestimate the magnitude of the response to the crisis.

[18] Other groupings of causes of deaths were tried. In particular, we estimated effects on deaths due to several infectious diseases, including measles and typhoid. In most cases, however, individual infectious diseases yield unstable results.

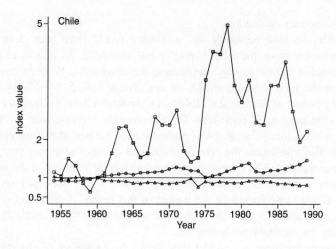

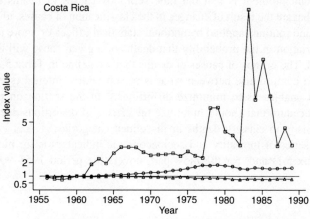

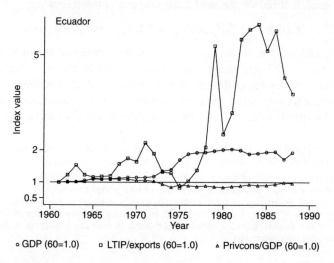

∘ GDP (60=1.0)   □ LTIP/exports (60=1.0)   ▵ Privcons/GDP (60=1.0)

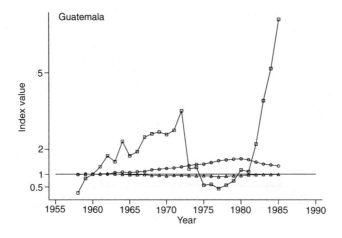

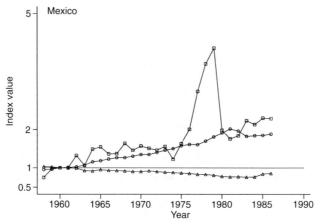

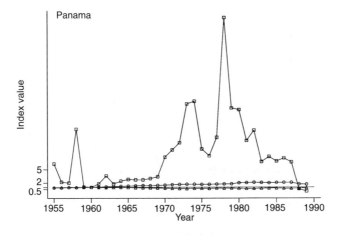

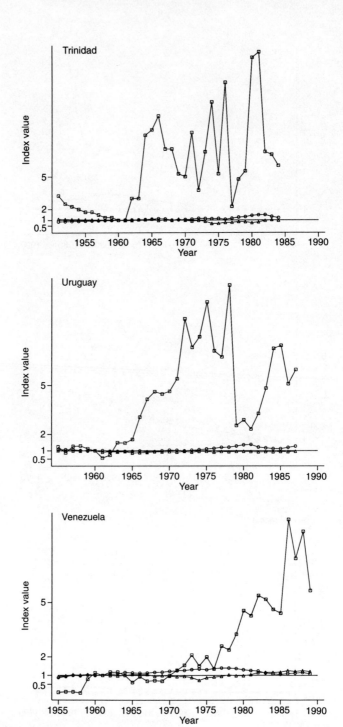

Trinidad

Uruguay

Venezuela

∘ GDP (60=1.0)   □ LTIP/exports (60=1.0)   ▴ Privcons/GDP (60=1.0)

elasticities: for example, they are proportionate changes in the mortality indicator attributable to a proportionate change in the socioeconomic indicator. Adding the β's across all lags yields the total (net) effect generated by a proportionate change in the economic indicator(s).

The model in (1) is not well defined, however. Several factors need to be discussed in order to specify it completely.

Detrending

Although detrending procedures have followed fairly well-established conventions involving the calculation of centred moving averages of variable length (Lee 1981; Galloway 1988; Hill and Palloni 1992), they are quite costly in terms of degrees of freedom, particularly for short series like those available to us, which include at most thirty-five observations. An eleven-year moving average is considered desirable and is perhaps ideally suited for relatively short series (not exceeding, say, 200 hundred years). But it would eliminate ten observations from the outset and if the maximum lag is fixed at 5, we would be left with only twenty-six observations. Reducing the length of the moving average is possible but at the cost of making the detrending procedure more vulnerable to the variability we are trying to remove. An alternative procedure is to fit a trend to the data and then use the predicted values as denominators for detrending (Bravo 1992). However, this requires a functional form for the trends and the choice of functional form is not always empirically obvious or unequivocally dictated by theoretical considerations.

A solution that combines the best of the previous two procedures without being hindered by their respective drawbacks is to use local least squares, a technique that provides a robust fit of the data without imposing a *global* functional form. Indeed, the resulting trend is retrieved by locally fitting robust straight lines to portions of the data (Cleveland 1979). This is an optimal strategy: it utilizes all points without deleting information and, simultaneously, does not force a *single* parametric form to the data.[19]

[19] To implement local least squares it is necessary to define the range of observations that are relevant for fitting any particular point (the so-called 'band-width', or bw for short). Since the aim is to produce a trend that is not affected by sharp deviations from it, we choose to use bw values between 0.90 and 1.00. This means that almost *all* observations are used to fit a particular point, but that the weight given to points that are far removed from the fitted one will be proportionately less than the weight given to points that are close to it. Although we estimated models employing bw values ranging from 0.20 to 1.00, the results that we present here, unless otherwise specified, correspond to bw values equal to 0.90. It is important to emphasize that although the numerical values of the estimates change as we alter bw, the *main inferences* that we draw are very similar.

Fig. 5.1   Index value of three economic indicators for selected Latin American countries

Note: GDP is the value (in 1970 US$) of the real gross domestic product per capita. Privcons is the fraction of GDP represented by private consumption. LTIP/exports is the ration of long-term interest payments to the value of exports.

Source: Palloni and Hill data bank.

Controls
The controls refer to variables that could have an effect on the nature of the response of mortality. In our country-by-country applications $z_r(t)$ refers to either a dummy for time-location that retrieves changing effects over time, or to the detrended value of deaths to ill-defined causes to neutralize possible distortions due to misclassification of deaths by causes.

(i) Retrieving changing effects   To model changes in responses over time we assume that $\beta_{nk.j}$ is time dependent and that its value can be broken down into two components, one that is time-invariant and one that depends on time, that is, $\beta_{nk.j}(t) = \delta_{nk.j} + \phi_{nk.j} \cdot w(t)$, where $w(t)$ is a dummy variable which attains the value 1 if $t < t_o$ and 0 otherwise. Substituting this in expression (1) yields

$$y_{nk}(t) = \alpha_{nk} + \Sigma_j \delta_{nk.j} x(t-j) + \Sigma_j \phi_{nk.j} x(t-j) \cdot w(t) + \varepsilon_{nk}(t) \tag{2}$$

depending on $x(t-j)$ and $z(t-j) = x(t-j) \cdot w(t)$. In this chapter we set t_o to be equal to 1975 in the belief that the recessions that took place after 1975 elicits responses that are different from those that occurred before. This is a simplified representation of another stochastic process—the one generating the effects or 'parameters' being estimated. It should enable us to test the hypothesis that more or less 'normal' cyclical recessions (those occurring before 1975) are conducive to qualitatively different responses than deeper recessions (after 1975).[20]

(ii) Neutralizing the effects of misclassification of deaths   Spurious fluctuations of causes of deaths due to changes in the category of 'ill-defined causes' are likely to occur. In theory at least, the proportionate change in the number of deaths due to ill-defined causes must be totally accounted for by a proportionate change in the frequency of all other causes of deaths. If periods of hardship have a nontrivial effect on the accuracy of recording of cause of deaths, we would expect the ill-defined category to be sensitive to economic downturns, and the estimated response of deaths due to well-defined causes to be underestimated. To partially correct for this we include a control for the (detrended) number of deaths assigned to the category 'ill-defined' at time t. This is not an optimal solution but should, except under warped conditions, produce unbiased estimates of responses. A justification of this is in Appendix 5.2.

The autoregressive process and the lag structure
The nature of the autoregressive process governing the error terms needs to be defined. Two types of processes have been estimated in the literature: a first- and

---

[20] Although other specifications are possible, they are excessively demanding of the data. For example, if recessions of longer durations are likely to elicit stronger responses, we could have introduced a measure of duration of the crisis as a dummy variable and then estimate the 'added' elasticity that accompanies recessions of longer duration.

a second-order autoregressive process. However, we have found no compelling argumentation anywhere that would justify choosing one over the other. For the most part the selection is made to preserve comparability with what others have done rather than to represent processes inherent in the data being analysed. In this chapter we chose a first-order autoregressive model for purely heuristic reasons. Second-order autoregressive processes are more appropriate with data that represent very fine units of time (months or quarters), a situation where in-built dependency is more likely to retain some inertia. Also, our series are not long enough to withstand the data demands required to identify second-order autoregressive processes. Indeed, in most cases where we experimented with the second-order autoregressive process, we were unable consistently to find convergence in the iterative process.

The nature of the lag structure that we estimate is also dictated by a combination of heuristic and theoretical considerations. Although some of the hypothetical responses might take longer, we set the maximum lag to 4 completed (5 exact) years. This is the same lag structure used in previous work in western Europe (Lee 1981; Galloway 1988) and involves one extra lag relative to our previous work (Hill and Palloni 1992). All past research indicates that lags beyond the fifth are of no importance whatever.

Handling multicollinearity

A problem that models with distributed lags encounter frequently is the high level of collinearity between the variables representing the various lags. This is probably more serious in contemporary developing countries than in pre-industrial societies, for the series of economic indicators that we use are quite stable despite sharp fluctuations. The result of this inherent stability is that the detrended values of a series will incorporate a fair degree of cross-lag collinearity. This will result in inefficient and unstable estimates of effects and may lead to the appearance of a pattern of effects with alternating signs as one moves from one lag to the next.

There are many solutions to this problem but none of them is entirely satisfactory (Judge *et al.* 1985). In this chapter we first estimate models with all pertinent lags and then suggest a simplified technique that enables us to reduce the parameter space, increase parsimony, and reduce instability while simultaneously preserving the central features of the lag distribution of effects. In particular, we will assume that responses across lags follow a 'triangular' pattern with effects reaching a maximum at lag 2 and decaying to 0 at lag 0 and 4.[21]

---

[21] This parameterization starts from the assumption that the effect at lag 2 is a maximum (minimum) and that the effects before and after lag 2 decline (increase) linearly:

$$\beta_j = \beta + \text{abs}(j - 2) \cdot \sigma \text{ if } 0 < j < 5,$$

where σ is the rate of decline from the maximum value of the response. We expect that $\sigma > 0$ if $\beta < 0$ and that $\sigma < 0$ if $\beta > 0$. We have not yet experimented with obvious modifications to this model, including consideration of polynomials or trigonometric functions. It should be noted that imposing this structure (or any alternative one) entails a risk of biasing the estimated effects. Whether the magnitude of this bias is larger than the losses of precision due to multicollinearity is an issue that deserves to be investigated.

IV. Analysis

A. Results from basic models

General patterns
The estimated elasticities, adjusted R-Squared, and flags for statistical significance are contained in a very large table containing information on the estimates of effects by lag, by age group, by cause of death, and by country. To save space we have omitted this table but it is available from the authors on request.[22] Table 5.1 is a compact representation of the patterns uncovered from the massive original table. The table shows the frequency of significant coefficients by lag and by groups of causes of deaths. Table 5.2 is a simpler distillation of Table 5.1, and Table 5.3 is a stricter synthesis of results describing the *net* value of the response across lags.[23] Table 5.1 and its summary in Table 5.2 reveal several interesting features.

First, responses that are statistically significant are somewhat infrequent, even with the rather liberal criteria used in the table.[24] Thus, for example, in panel A of Table 5.2 we see that for lag 2 the proportion of estimated responses that were negative ranged between 0.29 and 0.50, and those that were significantly positive ranged from 0.03 to 0.11. Other lags reveal responses that are closer in agreement with our expectations. The age groups where most of the negative and statistically significant responses occur are 0, 1–4, and 65+ (in that order) followed closely by 15–64. Panel B of the same table highlights the patterns of responses by causes of deaths and age regardless of lag. This panel shows that infectious diseases, diseases of the respiratory system, and ill-defined causes respond more frequently in the expected direction. The panel also helps to signal the role of two sets of infectious diseases whose responses stand out above all others: respiratory tuberculosis and diarrhoeas.

Second, there is some evidence in Table 5.3 to support the idea that responses to economic changes do exist and that, by and large, they are in the expected

---

[22] Although we estimated effects for the group of causes associated with heart diseases, we have excluded presentation of the corresponding results to avoid congestion. Without exception, the patterns of responses for this group were erratic and did not conform to what we expected. It is important to note that diarrhoea and respiratory tuberculosis are listed separately but are also included in the group of infectious diseases (see Appendix 5.1).

[23] The *net* value of a given response is the sum of the estimated elasticities across all lags. There are three statistical tests that we perform. The first is an F-test to falsify the null hypothesis that the true model is one with no lagged terms (that is, the best fitting model is one with only a constant term). The second corresponds to the null hypothesis that the sum of effects (the sum of the coefficients) is zero. The third is a test of the null hypothesis that the *sum of the negative coefficients* is zero. The first test simply reveals whether or not oscillations around a trend are explained at all by oscillations of the economic indicator. The second test provides evidence of whether or not the *net* effect—after initial impact and subsequent echoes are taken into account—amounts to something. The third test is designed to draw inferences about the magnitude of the responses that are in the expected direction, *regardless* of the magnitude of echoes that ultimately offset them. To avoid excessive cluttering we only present the results of the tests for all deaths (total) by cause.

[24] Throughout the chapter and unless otherwise noted, we use two-tailed tests and infer significance at levels of 0.05 or less.

Table 5.1 Frequencies of Responses According to Their Direction and Significance, by Lag, Age Group, and Cause of Death

Age group and cause of death	Lag 0 −	Lag 0 +	Lag 1 −	Lag 1 +	Lag 2 −	Lag 2 +	Lag 3 −	Lag 3 +	Lag 4 −	Lag 4 +
All										
All	0	0	1	0	1	0	0	1	1	0
Infections	1	0	1	0	0	0	0	0	0	1
Chronic	0	0	0	1	0	1	0	1	2	0
Respiratory	0	1	1	0	1	1	1	1	2	0
Violence	0	1	0	3	1	1	0	0	2	0
Ill-defined	3	2	3	0	1	1	1	1	0	0
Respiratory TB	0	0	1	0	0	0	1	1	0	0
Diarrhoeas	1	1	2	0	0	0	0	0	0	1
0										
All	1	0	1	0	0	0	1	0	0	1
Infections	2	0	1	0	1	0	1	0	1	0
Respiratory	3	2	1	0	1	0	2	0	0	1
Violence	0	0	0	1	1	0	2	0	0	1
Ill-defined	1	2	1	1	0	1	2	0	2	0
Diseases of infancy	0	0	1	0	0	1	0	0	1	0
Diarrhoeas	1	0	1	0	0	1	1	0	1	1
1–4										
All	0	1	1	0	0	1	0	0	0	0
Infections	0	1	1	0	1	0	1	0	0	1
Respiratory	1	3	2	0	0	2	0	0	1	0
Violence	0	1	2	0	0	0	0	0	0	0
Ill-defined	1	0	1	0	1	1	0	0	2	0
Diarrhoeas	0	1	2	0	0	0	1	0	0	1
5–14										
All	0	1	1	0	0	0	1	0	0	0
Infection	1	0	2	0	0	1	0	0	0	0
Respiratory	1	1	2	0	0	0	0	0	1	0
Violence	1	1	0	0	1	0	2	1	0	0
Ill-defined	2	1	0	1	1	0	1	1	3	0
Diarrhoeas	1	1	0	0	0	0	1	0	0	0
15–64										
All	0	2	2	0	1	0	0	1	1	0
Infections	2	0	1	0	0	0	1	0	1	0
Chronic	0	0	0	1	1	0	0	3	2	0
Respiratory	1	1	0	0	1	1	1	1	1	1
Violence	0	1	1	0	1	2	0	0	1	0
Ill-defined	1	1	1	0	2	0	1	0	1	1
Respiratory TB	1	1	2	0	2	0	2	1	1	0
Diarrhoeas	2	1	1	0	0	1	1	1	0	0

Table 5.1   (cont.)

Age group and cause of death	Lag 0 −	Lag 0 +	Lag 1 −	Lag 1 +	Lag 2 −	Lag 2 +	Lag 3 −	Lag 3 +	Lag 4 −	Lag 4 +
65+										
All	1	4	1	0	1	1	2	0	1	1
Infections	3	0	1	0	1	0	1	1	0	0
Chronic	0	0	1	0	0	1	0	0	1	1
Respiratory	1	1	1	0	1	1	1	1	1	1
Violence	0	3	1	0	0	1	0	0	1	1
Ill-defined	3	1	2	0	2	0	1	1	1	1
Respiratory TB	1	0	0	0	0	6	3	1	0	0
Diarrhoeas	2	1	1	1	0	0	2	0	0	1

direction and follow the anticipated age pattern. Note that, with few exceptions, in all countries and all pertinent age groups the net effects on infectious and respiratory diseases and on diarrhoeas and respiratory tuberculosis are negative and quite substantial. But neither the net effects nor the sum of negative effects reach statistical significance very often. By and large, the sum of negative effects becomes statistically significant only for all infectious diseases, respiratory diseases, and respiratory tuberculosis and diarrhoea.

Also, the age pattern of effects is consistent with expectations. However, although the largest effects take place in the age groups 1–4 and 65+ as we suspected they would, there are also somewhat unexpected strong effects at age 0.

Are the patterns of breastfeeding associated at all with responses at age 0? It should be noted that the effects at age 0 are lowest (or slightly positive) in Guatemala, Ecuador, and Panama. As it turns out, the median length of breastfeeding in Ecuador and Guatemala hovers around 13.0 months whereas in Mexico, Panama, and Costa Rica it is 6.7, 3.7, and 1.8 respectively. Although no national estimates are available for Chile and Uruguay, it is known that they are at the lowest end of the spectrum. Thus, excluding the case of Panama, the conjecture formulated at the outset about the effects of patterns of breastfeeding on the overall responsiveness of infant mortality appears to be borne out by this association. However, as this is only aggregate evidence, its relevance for the testing of the hypothesis should not be overplayed.

Is the conjecture that there is a relation between the magnitude of the responses and the countries' levels of mortality supported by the data? Figure 5.2 shows plots of levels of life expectancy during 1980–5 and the net response for selected causes of deaths. Although in all cases the direction of the association appears to be as expected, none of the graphs exhibit a sufficiently tight association to support robust inferences. Excluding the most deviant cases from each plot leads to somewhat tighter and stronger relations in the cases of all deaths, deaths due to infectious

Table 5.2 Summary of responses according to their direction and significance, by lag, age group, and cause of death

A: Proportion of negative significant effects by lag and age

Age	Lag 0	Lag 1	Lag 2	Lag 3	Lag 4
All	0.52 (0.04)	0.68 (0.13)	0.46 (0.06)	0.54 (0.04)	0.43 (0.10)
0	0.44 (0.11)	0.57 (0.08)	0.43 (0.04)	0.50 (0.13)	0.44 (0.07)
1–4	0.44 (0.03)	0.53 (0.13)	0.26 (0.03)	0.40 (0.03)	0.43 (0.04)
5–14	0.43 (0.08)	0.50 (0.07)	0.29 (0.03)	0.50 (0.07)	0.40 (0.06)
15–64	0.51 (0.10)	0.64 (0.11)	0.50 (0.11)	0.56 (0.08)	0.44 (0.11)
65+	0.51 (0.15)	0.65 (0.11)	0.44 (0.07)	0.60 (0.14)	0.60 (0.07)

B: Proportion of negative significant effects by cause and age

Age	All	Infectious	Chronic	Respiratory	Violence	Ill-defined	Respiratory TB	Diarrhoea
All	0.60 (0.07)	0.64 (0.04)	0.49 (0.07)	0.60 (0.11)	0.33 (0.07)	0.49 (0.18)	0.53 (0.04)	0.64 (0.07)
0	0.58 (0.07)	0.71 (0.38)	0.44 (0.04)[a]	0.64 (0.16)	0.49 (0.07)	0.51 (0.13)	—[b]	0.53 (0.09)
1–4	0.56 (0.02)	0.64 (0.07)	NA	0.60 (0.09)	0.36 (0.02)	0.49 (0.11)	—[b]	0.60 (0.07)
5–14	0.62 (0.04)	0.64 (0.07)	NA	0.47 (0.09)	0.49 (0.09)	0.56 (0.16)	—[b]	0.62 (0.04)
15–64	0.47 (0.09)	0.51 (0.11)	0.53 (0.07)	0.56 (0.09)	0.40 (0.07)	0.56 (0.13)	0.62 (0.18)	0.58 (0.09)
65+	0.47 (0.13)	0.53 (0.13)	0.53 (0.19)	0.58 (0.11)	0.44 (0.04)	0.60 (0.20)	0.67 (0.09)	0.58 (0.11)

[a] Diseases of infancy.
[b] The frequency of deaths due to respiratory TB in the age groups 0, 1–4 and 5–14 was too low and did not yield useful estimates.
NA = not applicable.

Table 5.3 Sum of effects (net response) of lags 0 to 4 by countries, causes of deaths, and age groups

Country	Age Group	Cause of death							
		All	Infections	Chronic[a]	Respiratory	Violence[b]	Ill-defined	Respiratory TB[c]	Diarrhoea
Chile	All	0.29	-0.87	1.13	1.12*‡	1.11	-2.58	-1.62†*‡	-0.75
	0	-0.24	-1.89	-0.43	-0.01	0.66	-3.30	—	-1.72
	1–4	0.37	-0.24	—	0.24	0.53	-2.19	—	-1.57
	5–14	0.16	-0.78	1.46	1.56	1.08	-2.61	-1.29	-0.69
	15–64	0.59	-1.22	0.74	-1.18	1.27	-2.78	-1.45	-1.00
	65+	0.23	-0.41	0.02	1.41	0.72	-2.08	—	-1.32
Costa Rica	All	-0.35	-1.53*‡	-0.51	-0.75	0.63	0.30	-0.07	-1.93‡
	0	-2.17	-5.37	—	-3.36	-4.04	-3.65	—	-5.28
	1–4	-0.95	-1.36	—	-1.13	-0.12	-0.31	—	-1.40
	5–14	-0.25	-2.16	—	-0.58	0.72	0.00	—	-2.85
	15–64	-0.02	-1.42	-0.04	-0.45	0.70	1.44	0.04	-4.52
	65+	-0.29	-1.99	0.11	-0.85	0.72	1.16	-0.16	-5.49
Ecuador	All	-0.24	-0.72	0.19	-0.82	0.40	-0.38	0.19	-0.55
	0	0.08	-0.36	1.64	-0.66	0.70	-0.16	—	-0.13
	1–4	-0.72	-0.91	—	-0.73	0.03	-0.92	—	-0.75
	5–14	-0.63	-0.99	—	-1.00	0.04	-0.88	—	-1.20
	15–64	-0.04	0.07	-0.09	-0.93	0.19	-0.06	0.17	-0.43
	65+	-0.27	0.14	-0.41	-0.64	0.20	-0.19	0.36	-0.21
Uruguay	All	-0.32*‡	-0.88‡	-0.93	-1.13*	0.25	0.52	-0.73	-0.74
	0	-0.36	-1.46	0.05	-1.57	0.88	0.68	—	-0.51
	1–4	0.08	0.67	—	-0.34	0.14	1.01	—	-0.22
	5–14	-0.31	0.75	—	-0.95	-0.42	0.52	—	2.93
	15–64	-0.15	-1.11	-0.90	-0.58	0.24	0.61	-3.10	2.33
	65+	-0.29	0.66	-1.00	-0.81	0.67	0.48	-0.70	3.07
Guatemala	All	-0.70	-1.37	0.13	-1.65	—	-1.01	-1.72	-1.15
	0	-0.15	-0.11	4.20	-2.17	—	-2.89	—	0.62
	1–4	-1.28	-1.33	—	-1.32	—	-0.55	—	-1.34
	5–14	-2.31	-3.06	—	-2.69	—	-1.63	—	-3.09

Mexico	15–64	−0.12	−1.81	0.34	−2.01	—	−3.89	−2.86	−2.28
	65+	−1.45	−1.41	−0.64	−2.09	—	−1.65	−1.71	−2.08
	All	−0.20	−1.03‡	0.68	−1.08	0.52	−1.64	−1.42‡	−0.99‡
	0	−1.11	−1.52	0.60	−1.91	−1.18	−4.76	—	−1.32
	1–4	−0.42	−0.32	—	−0.32	−0.84	−2.69	—	−0.14
	5–14	−0.11	−0.81	—	−0.16	−0.38	−1.94	—	0.66
	15–64	0.27	−0.42	0.96	−1.47	1.13	−1.25	−1.50	0.07
	65+	−0.15	−0.64	−0.07	−1.56	0.10	−0.69	−1.83	−0.23
Panama	All	0.68	0.13	0.43	1.36	−0.33	1.04	0.25*	0.35
	0	0.41	0.26	1.16	2.09	2.29	0.78	—	0.44
	1–4	0.58	0.22	—	−0.19	−1.58	1.75	—	1.10
	5–14	−0.30	−0.12	—	−0.49	−0.38	1.20	—	0.58
	15–64	−0.20	1.10	0.13	2.27	−1.07	1.98	0.69	0.72
	65+	0.94	1.38	0.51	1.73	0.79	1.85	0.54	1.83
Venezuela	All	0.05	−1.40*‡	0.81	−1.25	1.17	0.02	−0.96	−1.58*‡
	0	−0.32	−1.17	0.54	−2.17	−2.38	−2.59	—	−1.21
	1–4	−1.30	−2.65	—	−1.85	−0.29	−1.72	—	−1.69
	5–14	−0.11	−2.19	—	−0.30	0.59	−1.22	—	−3.71
	15–64	0.38	−0.17	0.59	0.94	0.60	−1.10	−0.75	−0.67
	65+	−0.09	−0.11	−0.15	−1.05	−0.42	1.08	−0.67	−0.44
Trinidad	All	−0.12	−2.88*	−1.19	−1.29	−0.17	0.16	−3.19*‡	−4.27
	0	−0.50	−5.89	2.43	−1.75	3.61	4.05	—	−1.46
	1–4	1.07	−4.37	—	2.72	2.86	1.32	—	−4.51
	5–14	−0.43	−0.66	—	1.65	−2.46	−9.52	—	−5.70
	15–64	0.01	0.11	−2.31	−1.22	−0.26	1.45	−1.81	−0.41
	65+	−0.41	−0.26	−1.49	−1.80	0.11	−0.12	−2.28	−2.33

[a] For the age group 0 'chronic' diseases corresponds to 'diseases of infancy'.

[b] In the case of Guatemala estimates of effects on deaths due to 'violence' were deemed to be erratic and unreliable.

[c] Deaths due to respiratory TB in the age groups 0, 1–4 and 5–14 were too sparse and infrequent and yielded unreliable estimates.

† Sum of effects significantly different from 0 at $p < 0.05$

* Sum of negative effects different from 0 at $p < 0.05$

‡ F-statistic for inclusion of all lags (vs model with a constant) significant at $p < 0.05$

Note: For a definition of each of the three statistical tests carried out in the table, see footnote 30.

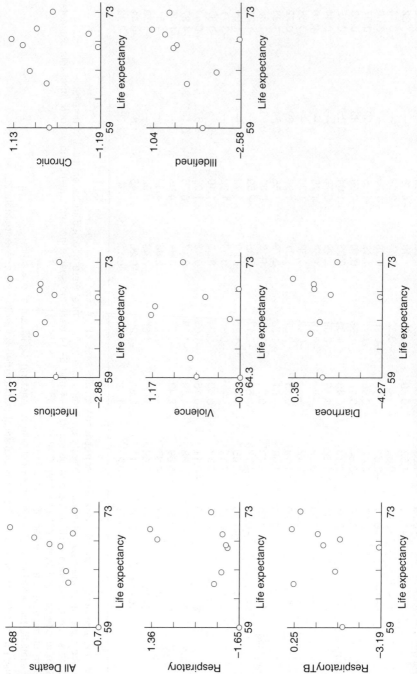

Fig. 5.2 Relations between life expectancy circa 1980–85 and net elasticities by causes of death

Source: Estimates of life expectancy from Palloni (1991); estimates of elasticities from Table 5.A1.

diseases, deaths due to ill-defined causes and, more importantly, deaths due to respiratory tuberculosis.

Is the lack of an overwhelming presence of statistically significant effects decisive for our conclusion? Although the fact that only nearly half of all responses are statistically significant is indeed limiting, the *patterns* we have retrieved and those that we discuss in the following section are simply too regular to be dismissed. It is important to note that during the period under study there is essentially only one important crisis that dominates the historical landscape (Hill and Palloni 1992). As Marichal has pointedly remarked, 'During the three decades that followed World War II, there were numerous economic crises in different Latin American nations, but there was no major financial upheaval that shook the entire region . . .' (Marichal 1989: 231). Recessions may have punctuated the history of countries everywhere during this period but none of them in isolation was a large enough departure from the secular trend to trigger mortality responses of significant relevance and durability. It is only after the mid-1970s that the spectre of genuine economic crisis looms large. Supporting this statement, Figure 5.3 displays for selected countries a plot of detrended GDP and detrended total deaths. The plots show the graphic profile taken by a succession of minor crises followed by a major one. Note that, with the exception of the early part of the 1950s and 1960s for Venezuela, there is a clear negative association between the course followed by the GDP series and the series of total deaths. Note also that, in all cases, the downturn of GDP is considerably more pronounced after 1970.

All cautionary appeals notwithstanding, the fact that we are able to uncover systematic, recurrent patterns of effects that agree broadly with our hypotheses is probably more important than their statistical significance within the confines of a single experiment. We now examine more closely the nature of such patterns.

The lag–age–cause pattern of effects
We begin by studying the box-plot in Figure 5.4 that shows in a synthetic graphic form the same data as contained in Table 5.4. There are three features that deserve to be mentioned. *First*, *regardless* of the age group, the net response of infectious and respiratory diseases is always predominantly negative, as expected. Furthermore, for the last three age groups, the negative response of respiratory TB and diarrhoea is uniformly negative. *Second*, the variability of responses is higher at the lower end of the age spectrum and for deaths due to chronic illnesses, violence, and ill-defined causes. The effects on respiratory TB and diarrhoea exhibit least variability. These two features strongly imply a *third* one, namely, that the observed total net response conceals a considerable amount of age–cause specific heterogeneity in responses.

An important feature of our results is better displayed in Figure 5.5 and its various panels. In this figure we plot the median response by lag and by age groups. In the first panel the median total response (all deaths for the entire population) reveals a topography which is similar to the median from various estimates for developing and developed countries calculated by Lee (1990). To facilitate comparisons,

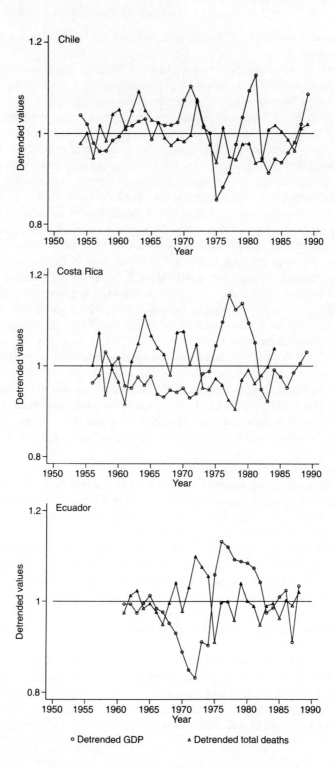

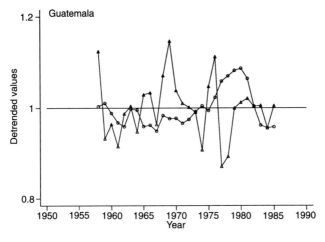

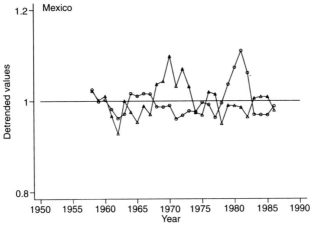

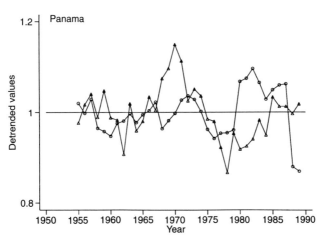

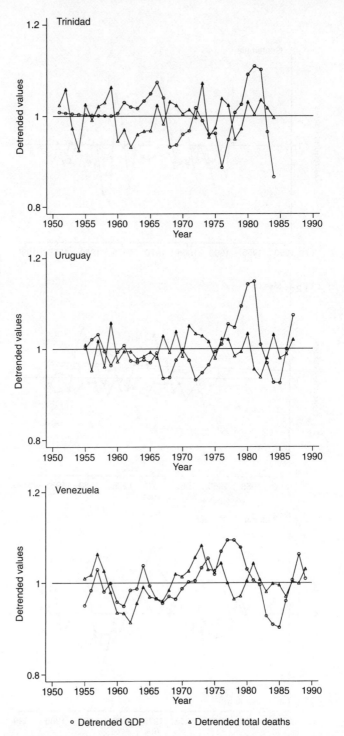

Fig. 5.3 Detrended GDP and detrended total deaths for selected countries
Source: Palloni and Hill data bank.

we show those patterns in the same panel.[25] In Latin America, the response at lag 0 is followed by one of lower magnitude at lag 1, an inverted response at lag 2, and then more muted reactions bearing negative signs and converging to 0 for lags 3 and 4. In the pattern calculated by Lee, the absolute magnitude of the responses is larger, the reversal occurs earlier (lag 1) and, when they subside, the effects change from positive to 0 (instead of from negative to 0 as in Latin America).

The similarity in the profiles of the patterns, particularly in Latin America and pre-industrial Europe, is quite remarkable in view of the fact that the indicators used by us (real GDP) and by Lee (prices) are quite different. Furthermore, it could well be that the differences that remain are due to the relation conjectured before, namely, that societies at the extremes of the mortality spectrum should show different response patterns. To provide a partial test of this we have plotted the median of the total responses in Uruguay, Costa Rica, and Chile—the three countries with the highest levels of life expectancy—and contrasted them with those of Guatemala, Ecuador, and Mexico—the countries with the lowest levels of life expectancy. The plot appears in the second panel of Figure 5.5. If the conjecture were correct we should see that responses in the first group of countries cluster close to the European pattern. The comparison is facilitated by the fact that the pattern in low mortality countries is somewhat flatter (as is the one found in western Europe) than the one for high mortality countries. But despite similarities between the low mortality Latin American countries and western Europe, they remain distinct whereas the patterns of response of low and high mortality are not easy to tell apart.

The third and fourth panels of Figure 5.5 display the median patterns of responses by age, and partially confirm the heterogeneity that was hypothesized before: strong responses are found at ages 1–4 and 65+, and less in the age group 15–64. There is always a wave-like pattern by lag with a maximum response reached at lag 2, reversals at lag 3 and then gradual reductions toward 0. The figures confirm that sharp responses (with similar lag-patterns) also occur at ages 0 and 5–14 and, furthermore, suggest that the strongest reaction takes place between 0 and 5 or between 0 and 15 rather than at the older ages.

The advantages of disaggregating responses by age and causes are made evident in the two panels of Figure 5.6. The graphs display the median response for selected causes of death for each of the age groups considered. The patterns by lags are not the same across causes (holding constant age). Thus, for example, respiratory tuberculosis displays steeper responses than infectious diseases and peaks at lags 2 and 3 rather than at lag 0 as infectious diseases tend to do. By the same token, the patterns by lags are not the same across ages (holding constant cause of death). For example, the elasticities for diarrhoeas are stronger for ages 0 and 1–4 than they are for all other age groups.

---

[25] Since the data used by Lee were on prices and mortality, a positive response was equivalent to a negative response in our data. Thus, to make comparisons easier we have reversed the signs of Lee's graph.

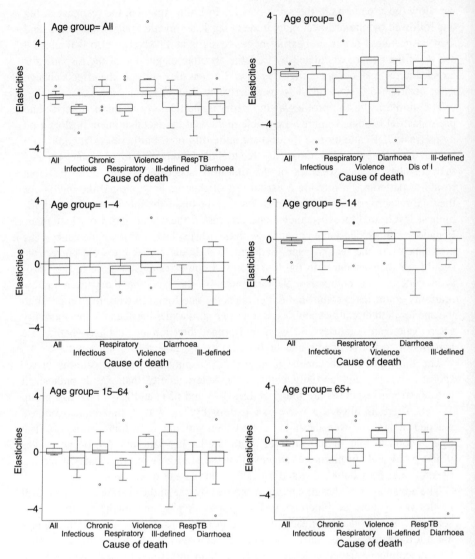

Fig. 5.4 Box plots of net elasticities by causes of death and age group
Source: Table 5.2.

Country	Model		Cause of death							
			All	Infectious	Chronic	Respiratory	Violence	Ill-defined	Respiratory TB	Diarrhoea
Chile	I	Net response	0.29	-0.87	1.13	1.12	1.11	-2.58	-1.62	-0.75
		Adj R²	-0.02	-0.11	-0.13	0.19	0.11	0.23	0.17	-0.17
	II	Net response	-0.09	-0.58	-1.32	-0.98	0.49	-1.02	-1.68	-0.62
		Adj R²	-0.08	-0.08	-0.11	0.11	0.39	-0.07	0.14	-0.13
	III	Net response	-0.15	-0.34	0.07	-0.69	-0.03	-0.12	-0.08	-0.58
		Adj R²	0.06	-0.08	-0.15	0.27	-0.02	-0.16	-0.12	-0.06
Costa Rica	I	Net response	-0.35	-1.53	0.02	-0.75	0.63	0.30	-0.07	-1.93
		Adj R²	0.21	0.75	-0.06	0.06	0.54	-0.01	-0.04	0.62
	II	Net response	-0.33	-1.69	0.23	0.00	0.38	2.08	-0.18	-3.93
		Adj R²	0.36	0.30	-0.10	-0.06	0.40	0.11	0.05	0.37
	III	Net response	0.18	0.74	0.14	0.45	-0.18	-0.22	-0.22	0.73
		Adj R²	0.19	0.37	0.08	0.14	0.27	-0.02	0.08	0.37
Ecuador	I	Net response	-0.24	0.72	0.19	-0.82	0.40	-0.38	0.19	-0.55
		Adj R²	0.06	-0.08	-0.07	0.11	0.04	0.49	0.01	-0.19
	II	Net response	0.90	1.52	0.75	0.85	0.54	0.57	-0.72	1.45
		Adj R²	0.35	0.09	0.05	0.03	0.04	0.19	-0.09	-0.01
	III	Net response	0.05	0.07	0.06	0.06	-0.08	0.18	-0.06	0.04
		Adj R²	-0.12	-0.20	-0.02	-0.22	0.38	0.16	0.20	-0.25
Uruguay	I	Net response	-0.32	-0.88	-0.93	-1.13	0.25	0.52	-0.20	-0.73
		Adj R²	0.28	0.24	0.27	0.14	0.27	0.10	-0.03	0.07
	II	Net response	-0.17	-0.68	0.53	-2.71	0.61	-0.06	-1.79	-0.83
		Adj R²	0.04	0.00	-0.09	-0.06	0.47	0.04	0.07	0.04
	III	Net response	0.02	0.13	-0.02	0.14	-0.01	-0.01	-0.03	0.16
		Adj R²	0.14	0.29	-0.12	0.07	0.20	-0.02	0.01	-0.02

I Results of model with GDP.
II Results of model with private consumption.
III Results with model with debt as proportion of exports.

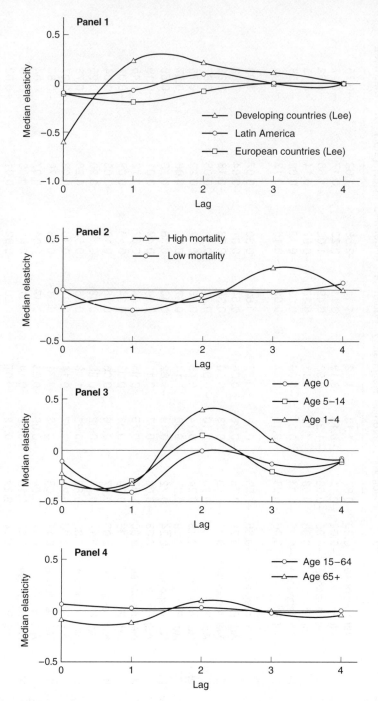

Fig. 5.5 Estimated elasticities by lag in different social contexts and for different age groups

Note: In Panel 1 the curves for 'developing countries' and 'Europe' were taken from Lee (1991) with signs reversed.

Source: Table 5.A1.

The responses of respiratory TB and diarrhoeas

Newberne and Williams (1970) remark that there are four ways in which mal-nutrition influences infection: '(1) by effects on the host which facilitate initial invasion of the infectious agent; (2) through effects on the agent once it is established on the tissues; (3) through effects on secondary infection; or (4) by retarding convalescence from infection'. The groups of causes that we labelled 'diarrhoea' include some of the illnesses that are known to be very sensitive to nutritional status, partly because of suppression of immunocompetence (factors 2 and 3 above) and partly because of synergism that aggravates nutritional deficiencies present at the outset (factors 2 and 4 above). Furthermore, for the most part, the illnesses in this group have proven connections even with *mild states* of malnutrition (McKeown 1988). Although the link forged by nutritional status is strong enough to dominate the relation between diarrhoea and economic downturns, there is an additional source of association: deterioration of hygiene and services (water, sewage, living conditions) can quickly escalate to increase exposure to agents of disease. Acting in conjunction, increased exposure due to breakdowns in services and hygiene and increases in susceptibility with lowered resistance are more than sufficient to explain the response that was estimated from the data.

That the progress of respiratory tuberculosis is associated with nutritional status has been vigorously argued before (McKeown 1988). It is known that although people may harbour the bacterium, they are not necessarily struck by the disease. Whether or not they are depends on their ability to fend off the advances of *Mycobacterium tuberculosis*. And this, in turn, is largely a function of a host of factors including the prevalence of other infectious diseases (Szreter 1988), stress, malnutrition, and vitamin deficiencies (Wingfield 1924; Davies 1985). Suggestive epidemiological evidence comes to us from historical records in the northern and western European countries, where the death rate due to the diseases began a secular decline at around 1870 or 1880 and was broken only by wild spasmodic leaps during the First World War and then again during the Second World War. A sharp decline in food consumption and erosion of a balanced diet has been associated with both interruptions of the secular decline (Puranen 1991; Keers 1978).

Admittedly, the epidemiological evidence is only circumstantial since the effects of other contributory factors are usually not controlled for. But, added to the clinical evidence, it suggests that there is a strong case to bolster the argument that the connection between respiratory tuberculosis and economic downturns is likely to operate through the nutritional status of populations. This evidence helps to shed light on our findings which single out respiratory tuberculosis as a disease with one of the strongest responses to economic indicators.[26]

---

[26] Other infectious diseases strongly linked to nutritional status, such as measles, do not show the same patterns as respiratory TB. Indeed in results not shown we identified only erratic patterns for deaths due to measles. It is likely that vaccination campaigns as well as seasonality conceal some of the fluctuations due to deterioration of nutritional status. Of course, it may also be that some of the deaths attributable to other diseases (particularly diarrhoea) have measles as an underlying cause.

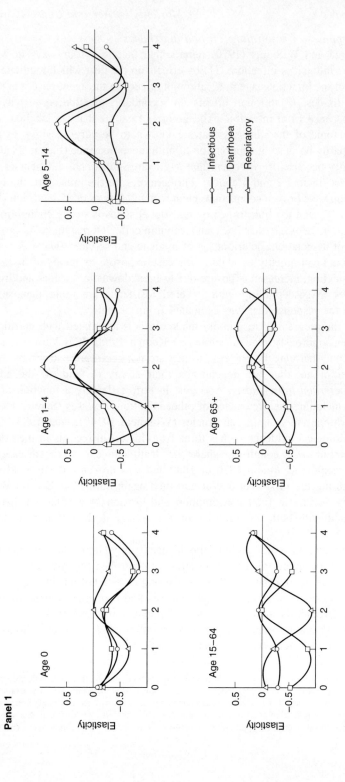

Panel 1

Panel 2

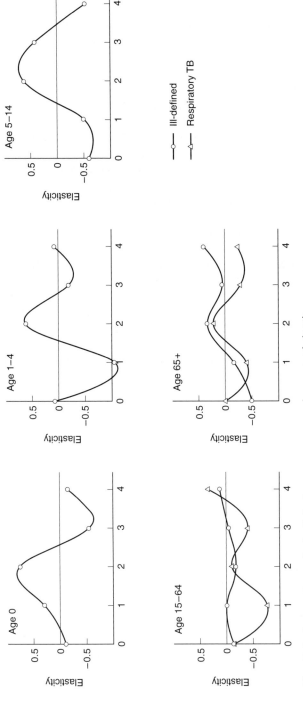

Fig. 5.6 Lag pattern of elasticity by age group and cause of death

Source: Table 5.A1.

B. The robustness of the findings

To test the robustness of our estimates to violations in the assumptions and to changes in model specification we proceed to apply a battery of tests. We will report briefly only the most important of these.

Alternative measures of economic performance

Table 5.4 of the main text summarizes (only) the net responses by cause estimated from models that include alternative independent variables drawn from national accounts: private consumption (model II) and the magnitude of the external debt relative to the value of exports (model III). We contrast these with the results from the model with GDP (model I) for four 'test' countries which span the spectrum of mortality levels.[27] The full table of responses by lags (not shown) indicates that there is a handful of cross-model differences in statistical significance of effects. Table 5.4 reveals some changes in the magnitude and, in a few cases, reversals of signs of coefficients. For example, whereas the total response to GDP in Chile is positive (0.29), the response to private consumption (PC) and debt service as proportion of exports is negative (−0.09 and −0.15 respectively). The main culprit for the reversal appears to be deaths from respiratory illnesses, which show a strong negative response to changes in PC but positive (and high) net responses to changes in GDP. The contrast occurs in Ecuador and, to a lesser extent, in Uruguay. For the most part, however, the conclusions that we drew before regarding the sensitivity of infections diseases, respiratory ailments, respiratory tuberculosis, and diarrhoea stand unaffected when PC is used as an indicator of economic well-being. Instead, the models estimated with the index for the load of external debt fit very poorly and yield the lowest estimates for the responses. This is in keeping with what was anticipated earlier in view of the observed lack of variability and intrinsic information content of the measure.

The lag structure

A more 'favourable' parameter space can be conceived in light of our previous findings. In particular, one could represent the effects with a lag-pattern that follows an *n*-degree polynomial or a sinusoidal function. Allowing for different coefficients for different causes of death and age groups should enable us to replicate the variability detected throughout the analysis. This representation has the advantage of simplicity and provides an escape from the multicollinearity problem that affects the detrended series. In an initial exploration we estimate a lag-pattern with a triangular structure that imposes a maximum effect at lag 2 and then symmetric declines from the maximum to zero (see footnote 23). Since the location of the maximum is fixed a priori, this representation requires only two parameters identifying respectively the magnitude of the maximum effect and the slope of the

[27] Although we obtained results for all countries, we display only those corresponding to four of them to avoid presentation of an excessive number of tables. All the conclusions we reach examining the selected set are confirmed by those not shown.

decline of the effect. For diseases that increase with deterioration in economic conditions our hypotheses suggest that the 'maximum' effect should be highly negative and that the slope should be positive. For diseases that decline with deterioration in economic conditions the situation is reversed: the maximum should be positive and the slope should be negative.

Table 5.5 displays the results for the same four 'test' countries we used in Table 5.4. In the table, b_o refers to the estimated maximum and R to the estimated slope. To facilitate comparisons with the previous models we also display the *net* effects implied by b_o and R over a duration of 5 years. Note first that only in Ecuador do the values of b_o associated with infectious diseases, respiratory ailments, respiratory TB, and diarrhoea take on the 'wrong' sign (positive). This is not surprising since Ecuador also shows anomalous results from the more conventional models. In Chile and Costa Rica the implied net elasticities are 'biased' toward zero when compared to those estimated with a free lag structure (see Table 5.4), whereas those for Uruguay attain much higher (absolute) values.

A few conclusions can be drawn from this handful of experiments. On the one hand, our lag-free model is certainly preferable for it is less restrictive. On the other hand, the problems created by multicollinearity are cleared in the triangular model by imposing more structure. But since none of the coefficients b_o or R in Table 5.5 are statistically significant, our inferences are hardly strengthened. It is likely, however, that a triangular lag-structure is excessively restrictive and should attenuate the estimated net responses in most cases.

Control for changes in the ill-defined category
A third test was performed to assess the possible effects that misclassification of deaths into the category of ill-defined could have on our estimates. As explained above and in Appendix 5.3, the test consists of controlling for the current detrended value of the number of deaths in the ill-defined category. The derivation in Appendix 5.3 suggests that controlling for the non-lagged detrended value of the deaths due to ill-defined causes is an approximation to the correct (but unfeasible) procedure to eliminate the effects of oscillations in misclassifications. We should expect the estimated effects for well-defined diseases to increase (in absolute value) and the estimated effect associated with the control variable to be negative. Table 5.6 displays the results for the same four 'test' countries used before. Model I is the model discussed before and does not include a control. Model II includes a control for deaths due to ill-defined causes. The results obtained are somewhat disappointing, since in two of the four countries (Ecuador and Uruguay) the estimated regression coefficient for the control has a sign opposite to the expected one for all relevant causes (infectious, respiratory, respiratory TB and diarrhoea). In Chile and Costa Rica the estimated coefficient is properly signed but rarely significant. In most cases, the introduction of the control has little or no impact on the net responses.[28]

---

[28] The same applies for the remaining countries in our sample (Guatemala, Mexico, Panama, Venezuela, and Trinidad).

Table 5.5 Estimated net effects and estimated parameters for a model with a triangular structure for the lag pattern of effects

Country	Parameter	Cause of death							
		All	Infectious	Chronic	Respiratory	Violence	Ill-defined	Respiratory TB	Diarrhoea
Chile	b_0	0.033	−0.092	−0.054	0.042	−0.040	−0.092	−0.300	−0.040
	R	−0.002	0.038	0.015	−0.001	0.012	−0.023	0.039	0.035
	Adj R^2	−0.07	−0.03	−0.07	0.08	−0.07	−0.05	0.040	−0.06
	Estimated net response	0.15	−0.23	−0.18	0.20	−0.13	−0.60	−1.27	0.01
Costa Rica	b_0	−0.081	−0.179	0.013	−0.116	−0.195	0.020	−0.071	−0.421
	R	0.023	0.008	−0.032	0.040	0.077	0.143	−0.013	−0.039
	Adj R^2	−0.066	−0.08	−0.08	−0.10	0.04	0.09	−0.10	−0.018
	Estimated net response	−0.27	−0.85	−0.13	−0.34	−0.051	0.96	−0.28	−2.34
Ecuador	b_0	0.118	0.149	0.078	0.107	0.189	0.123	0.000	0.020
	R	−0.031	−0.039	−0.019	−0.017	−0.046	−0.034	−0.028	−0.022
	Adj R^2	0.05	−0.10	−0.02	−0.103	0.050	−0.05	0.059	−0.10
	Estimated net response	0.40	0.72	0.38	0.43	0.67	0.41	−0.01	0.13
Uruguay	b_0	−0.053	−0.575	−0.017	−0.618	0.165	−0.119	−0.602	−0.988
	R	−0.006	−0.049	−0.042	0.014	0.004	0.017	0.033	−0.072
	Adj R^2	−0.05	0.29	−0.01	−0.044	−0.05	−0.08	−0.004	0.26
	Estimated net response	−0.30	−3.17	−0.34	−3.01	0.25	−0.49	−2.81	−5.37

Changes over time

Mortality responses must have been correspondingly weaker during past crises if they were less durable than more recent crises. Testing for this hypothesis is somewhat treacherous for a couple of reasons. First, one should effectively control for the presence (absence) of mechanisms that attenuate the impact of economic downturns, particularly those affecting the most vulnerable groups. If social interventions become more efficient over time in their quest to shield these groups and if we are unable adequately to measure such changes, the estimates of the *differences* in responses attributable to the seriousness of the crises will contain a downward bias and may even have the wrong sign. Second, if, as is likely to happen, the completeness of death registration becomes less affected by economic crises, the estimated response will appear to be larger for the more recent periods. Only if we ignore these two difficulties—which introduce opposite biases—will we be able to model any period effects.[29]

Table 5.6 (mode III) shows the estimates corresponding to a model that controls for the interaction between response and time period. The parameter shown in the table measures the difference in response—assumed constant across all lags—between the years before and after 1975. A positive sign is indicative of *smaller* effects in the past. The results are mixed since they are strongly dependent on country and only a few estimates are statistically significant or properly signed. In Chile and Costa Rica the estimates are positive, but only those associated with infections, diarrhoeas, and respiratory diseases are statistically significant in Chile whereas none of them is in Costa Rica. In Ecuador and Uruguay the coefficients for infections and respiratory diseases are negative whereas those for diarrhoea and respiratory tuberculosis are positive but insignificant. The grouping of countries that emerges from these results is at least consistent with the view held by some authors (Altimir 1984) that the crisis hit harder in Chile and Costa Rica than in some other countries. In summary, it is only for some causes of deaths that the effects are uniformly stronger during the most recent period. Indeed, the estimates for diarrhoea and respiratory tuberculosis are positive in all four countries, but only in one (Chile) are some of these effects statistically significant. If these results are reliable at all, they would partially confirm the conjecture that longer and more intense crises, such as those that took place after 1975, do indeed lead to stronger responses at least for causes of deaths that are highly sensitive to changes in

---

[29] There are two strategies to model period effects. The first is to assume that the lagged effects within one period are proportional to the lagged effects within another period and that a single proportionality factor suffices to capture variability. According to this reasoning the proper model should include a single interaction term corresponding to the sum of the products of the lagged exogenous variables and a dummy for period. The second strategy imposes the less restrictive assumption that the ratios of lagged effects across two periods varies with the lag. Thus, the corresponding model includes one interaction term per lag. Each of these equals the product of the lagged exogenous variable and the dummy for period. This model uses considerably more degrees of freedom and, as it turns out, does not fit the data any better than the model corresponding to the first strategy. To simplify presentation we display the results of the first model only. The results of the more cumbersome model corresponding to the second strategy do not reveal different patterns.

Table 5.6 Estimated net effects in models controlling for ill-defined and time period

Country and model		Cause of death							
		All	Infectious	Chronic	Respiratory	Violence	Ill-defined	Respiratory TB	Diarrhoea
Chile									
I	Net response	0.29	−0.87	1.13	1.12	1.11	−2.58	−1.62	−0.75
	Adj R^2	0.02	−0.11	−0.13	0.19	0.11	0.23	0.17	−0.17
II	Net response	NA	−0.66	1.02	0.94	0.83	NA	−1.47	0.26
	Adj R^2	NA	−0.09	−0.17	0.15	0.10	NA	0.13	0.10
	Coefficient	NA	0.24	−0.04	−0.07	−0.10	NA	0.06	0.52[†]
III	Net response	0.27	−0.66	1.02	1.04	1.20	−2.56	−1.51	−0.32
	Adj R^2	0.13	0.02	−0.13	0.25	0.14	0.21	0.16	0.02
	Coefficient	0.008*	0.035*	0.013	0.022*	−0.007	−0.006	0.027	0.060*
Costa Rica									
I	Net response	−0.35	−1.53	0.02	−0.75	0.63	0.30	−0.07	−1.93
	Adj R^2	0.21	0.75	−0.06	0.06	0.54	−0.01	−0.04	0.62
II	Net response	NA	−1.46	0.10	−1.12	0.65	NA	−0.07	−1.55
	Adj R^2	NA	0.74	−0.04	0.50	0.52	NA	−0.10	0.72
	Coefficient	NA	−0.05	−0.13	0.47*	−0.03	NA	−0.03	−0.46*
III	Net response	−0.54	−1.39	0.05	−0.81	0.67	0.78	0.00	1.73
	Adj R^2	0.24	0.75	−0.12	0.07	0.51	−0.05	−0.10	0.61
	Coefficient	0.0055	0.0064	0.0019	0.0043	0.0014	−0.016	0.0039	0.0092

Group		(1)	(2)	(3)	(4)	(5)	(6)	(7)	(8)
Ecuador									
I	Net response	−0.24	0.72	0.19	−0.82	0.40	−0.38	0.19	−0.55
	Adj R²	0.06	−0.08	−0.07	0.11	0.04	0.49	0.01	−0.19
II	Net response	0.07	−0.04	−0.08	−0.35	0.01	NA	0.12	−0.05
	Adj R²	0.45	0.18	0.05	0.40	0.26	NA	−0.03	−0.11
	Coefficient	0.67†	1.51†	−0.59*	1.13*	−0.59*	NA	0.15	1.28†
III	Net response	−0.27	−0.79	0.24	−0.88	0.41	−0.45	0.20	−0.65
	Adj R²	0.08	−0.08	−0.04	0.15	0.11	0.46	−0.04	−0.08
	Coefficient	−0.0041	−0.0126	0.0079	−0.012	−0.0063	0.0026	0.0032	−0.036
Uruguay									
I	Net response	−0.32	−0.88	−0.93	−1.13	0.25	0.52	−0.20	−0.73
	Adj R²	0.28	0.24	0.27	0.14	0.27	0.10	−0.03	0.07
II	Net response	0.43	−1.05	−0.90	−1.00	0.28	NA	−0.93	−1.28
	Adj R²	0.53	0.22	0.24	0.10	0.23	NA	−0.07	0.15
	Coefficient	0.25*	0.30	−0.09	−0.16	−0.05	NA	0.32	1.04†
III	Net response	−0.40	−1.02	−0.99	−1.45	0.16	0.56	−0.53	−0.62
	Adj R²	0.42	0.25	0.24	0.18	0.26	0.06	−0.05	0.03
	Coefficient	−0.0037*	−0.0064	−0.0024	0.0161	−0.0052	−0.0012	0.0085	0.0056

I Results of model with GDP.
II Results of model with GDP and control for ill-defined.
III Results of model with GDP and control for time dummy.
* In all cases the 'coefficient' refers to the estimated regression coefficient of the control.
* Significant at less than 0.05
† Significant at less than 0.10
NA = Not applicable.

standards of living. Naturally the results we obtain could be affected by violations of the underlying assumption about a unique time marker separating types of crises which holds for all countries. Finally, it could well be that, instead, or in addition to, the shifts in the effects of crises over time different countries adopt different profiles or patterns.

V. Refinements and Extensions

A. Distributed lags on causes of deaths: additivity properties

The estimation procedure we have used is not as efficient as it could be. An optimal strategy is to estimate simultaneously all elasticities in a parameter space that satisfies simple restrictions. In particular, if model (1) is correct for all causes of deaths that we care to recognize, the weighted sum over all k of the $\beta_{nk,j}$'s should equal the co-efficient for the jth lag for all causes combined, $\beta_{nT,j}$. Analogous constraints across ages (and causes) are easily derived from simple additivity rules. Ideally, the result-ing constraints should be imposed a priori and the parameters estimated using con-strained generalized least squares estimators. However, if one does not impose the constraints it is possible to derive a 'measure of fit' of the models. Indeed, the mag-nitude of the difference between $\theta = \sum_k (W_{nk} \cdot \beta_{nk,j})$, where w_{nk} is the proportional distribution of causes of deaths in age n, and $\beta_{nT,j}$, the j-lag response from all causes of deaths combined, is a measure of the degree of fit of the model.

In the interest of brevity we examine only one out of many possible tests of consistency. In particular we calculate the net elasticity by adding the (weighted) total cause-specific elasticities (expected total elasticity) and compare it with the elasticity for total deaths estimated directly (observed total elasticity).[30] Results not

---

[30] The alternative tests are fairly obvious. A first test statistic is the difference between age-specific estimated elasticities and the one that obtains by adding across causes the age-cause-specific estimated elasticities. The second test statistic focuses on the difference between cause-specific estimated elasticities and the one that obtains by adding the age-cause-specific elasticities across ages. These test statistics are easily derived by imposing additivity to the age-by-cause matrix of elasticities. Indeed, by adding the values of $\beta_{nT,j}$ across ages (n) we will obtain estimates of the total mortality response (regardless of age); if model (1) is correct, these estimates should equal the total response estimated directly. Under these conditions, the response distribution of lags-by-cause can be extended to include age as well:

$$\lambda_{nk,j} = \beta_{nk,j} / \sum_n \beta_{nT,-j} \cdot W_n \qquad (A)$$

where W_n is the age-distribution of deaths.

The joint distribution in (A) can be readily converted into a marginal distribution to assess the magnitude of the responses across causes only (regardless of age) or across age only (regardless of cause). These quantities may also be used to test some of the hypotheses put forward before regarding the nature of the effects on some age segments.

Another refinement to investigate the nature of the mortality response is the joint distribution of lags-by-cause:

$$\lambda'_{nk,j} = \beta_{nk,j} / \beta_{nT,j} \qquad (B)$$

or the proportion of the total response that is attributable to cause k in age group n at lag j. These statistics are implicitly used in the next section to check that our expectations regarding the role of different causes is empirically confirmed.

displayed here show that in all countries the values of the expected and estimated responses are remarkably close to each other, thus providing alternative confirmation about the goodness of fit of the models.

B. The effects on the patterns of mortality

The estimated elasticities of mortality by age and causes of deaths provide a first approximation for an assessment of the magnitude of effects of economic oscillations on patterns of mortality. A more refined but also more heuristic appraisal consists of transforming the estimated elasticities into changes in life expectancy at birth (or at any other ages). To accomplish this we utilize Pollard's (1988) expression that translates changes in age-cause-specific forces of mortality into changes in life expectancy:

$$\eta_0 = \sum_k \int_0^\infty (\mu_k(x) - \mu_k'(x)) \cdot \omega(x) dx \qquad (3)$$

where η_0 is the total change in life expectancy, $\mu_k(x)$ and $\mu_k'(x)$ are the forces of mortality at age x due to cause k before and after an economic recession (expansion), and $\omega(x)$ is the average given by:

$$\omega(x) = 0.5 \cdot (p(x)e_x' + p'(x)e_x) \qquad (4)$$

where $p(x)$ and $p'(x)$ are the probabilities of surviving up to age x in the life tables prior to and after the oscillation, and e_x and e_x' are the corresponding life expectancies at age x.

To implement equation (3) we calculate the function $\mu_k'(x)$, taking into account responses at all lags as $\mu_k(x) \cdot (1 + \sum_j \beta_{kn,j})$, and then obtain the corresponding probabilities of survival and life expectancies. Note that, like their counterparts in absolute numbers, all the calculations involved in (3) can be partitioned by lags, ages, and causes. These operations are tantamount to the calculation of the partial derivatives of life expectancy with respect to changes in economic indicators. Table 5.7 shows the result of implementing equation (3) to a 'median' country (with a median age-cause structure of mortality rates) subjected to a 10 per cent drop in GDP and to age-cause-specific elasticities equal to the median of our sample. We examine only the responses and contributions of causes of death that altogether represent about 60 per cent of the total deaths. Of the total change in life expectancy triggered by the downturn (0.70), only a fraction (0.23) can be accounted for in a model that takes into account the causes of death we chose to examine. The difference is due to the lack of fit of the model by cause and also to the contribution of causes that we do not consider in the table. Not surprisingly, the most important contribution corresponds to changes at age 0: about 87 per cent of the total (explained) change can be attributed to worsening conditions at this age. This is simply due to the fact that the figures in Table 5.7 reflect both the responsiveness to the economic changes and the more than proportionate influence exerted by infant deaths in the determination of life expectancy. Infectious diseases account for about

Table 5.7   Decomposition of change in life expectancy induced by drop of 10 per cent in GDP

Age groups	Contribution to the change in life expectancy associated with groups of causes of deaths (in years of life expectancy)					
	I	II	III	IV	V	Total[b]
0	0.1230	0.0760	−0.0050	—	0.0850	0.1940
1–4	0.0070	0.0010	0.0009	—	0.0040	0.0089
5–14	0.0070	0.0011	−0.0007	—	0.0003	0.0074
15–64	0.0007	0.0011	−0.0007	0.0008	0.0003	0.0011
65+	0.0013	0.0072	−0.0008	0.0007	0.0012	0.0077
Total[c]	0.1390	0.0864	−0.0063	0.0015	0.0908	0.2191

Notes:
The life expectancies before and after the drop in GDP are 73.17 and 72.47 or a difference of 0.70. The difference calculated using cause-specific equations is 0.23.
I = Infectious; II = Respiratory; III = Ill-defined; IV = Respiratory TB; V = Diarrhoea.
[a] The figures in this table were calculated using Mexico 1980 as a baseline, the median of the estimated age–cause specific elasticities, and the equation derived by Pollard.
[b] Row totals or total contribution by age. They exclude IV and V which are already included in I.
[c] Column totals or total contribution of a cause.

51 per cent of the (explained) changes, whereas respiratory diseases contribute slightly less (39 per cent). The total contribution of respiratory tuberculosis is small both among infectious diseases (1 per cent) and as a fraction of the total changes (0.7 per cent). Diarrhoeas, on the other hand, are the most influential of infectious diseases and operate mostly at age 0.

C. The effects of periodic crises on excess mortality

A more precise assessment of the consequences of periodic economic downswings is to calculate the average relative excess mortality induced by any number of them during a fixed period of time. The calculations are fairly straightforward: we first estimate the total death rate during the chosen time interval, assume a frequency of crises and their location in time and, for each of them, estimate the excess number of deaths by applying the net total elasticities estimated before (by age and cause of deaths). As an illustration, we use the following initial conditions: i) a 'median' Latin American country that experiences two downturns of GDP equivalent to 10 per cent over a period of twenty-eight years; ii) the crises are centred within the first and last five years of the period. We estimate that such a regime of crises combined with the patterns of median net responses would increase the total death rate by about 3.5 per cent over the 'crises-free' death rate of about 8.9 per thousand. A breakdown of contributions by causes of death again shows that the bulk of the response is attributable to infectious diseases and respiratory ailments and that, of these, an excess of deaths due to diarrhoea explains most of the changes.

VI. Summary and Conclusions

Far from being an arcane feature of preindustrial societies, mortality responses are still noticeable in demographic regimes of developing countries. In Latin America the responses follow a profile by age and cause that is consistent with theoretical expectations. Thus, infectious and respiratory diseases and, in particular, respiratory tuberculosis and diarrhoea are the causes of deaths that are most responsive to economic downturns. Infants and young children as well as youngsters up to the age of fifteen appears to be the most affected.

Less clear than the existence of the responses themselves are the regularities that underlie them. We found some aggregate evidence suggesting that the reactions of the levels of mortality at age 0 are inversely related to the patterns of breastfeeding. This is in agreement with the idea that vulnerability of the very young is maximized in societies where the norm of universal and long breastfeeding has crumbled. Furthermore, although the patterns of response are roughly consistent with those found in other developing societies, there are only weak grounds for suspecting that the magnitude of the mortality upturns have any association at all with levels of development or average levels of mortality. Nor is it evident that there is any systematic relation to the character or nature of the crisis.

Although the empirical evidence for the Latin American countries that we examine does indeed weaken the idea asserting that short-term reactions to economic changes are dissociated from mortality changes, it simply does not reveal very strong associations. This is not just an issue of statistical significance but one of scale of responses. In the last part of the chapter we showed that a moderately large drop of GDP would lead to a comparably small response of mortality both in terms of intrinsic changes in life expectancies (Table 5.7) and in terms of excess deaths. These two characteristics permeating our data—patterned responsiveness and muted scale of the response—are not inconsistent and indeed are a marker of preindustrial patterns as well, when mortality crises supposedly played a more dominant role than they do today. This being said, we emphasize that excess mortality is just the tip of the iceberg, and that wretched conditions of large segments of the population are perfectly compatible with mortality increases of only small magnitudes. The actual deterioration of conditions will probably remain concealed until we refocus our attention to other dimensions of health status.

Lastly, it should be emphasized that the chapter utilizes definitions and a methodology that could be refined in several respects. First, it is clear that one could focus on other causes of death and explore the possibilities of regrouping causes of death in ways that are more consistent with theories linking economic changes and morbidity and mortality. Second, we should enlarge our sample not only to increase the power of some tests but also to do justice to the variability of patterns in the continent. Third, one could explore more thoroughly the alternative economic indicators as gauges of actual changes in standards of living of some or all social classes. A final but equally important issue is designing a procedure of estimation that does not rely on the assumption systematically invoked in our distributed lag models that the magnitude of responses to a booming economy ought to be opposite in sign but equal in magnitude to the responses in recessionary times. This seems to be a fairly restrictive and limiting assumption that if relaxed could lead to different results. Until some or all of these issues are addressed it will be difficult to derive more than tentative conclusions.

REFERENCES

Appleby, A. B. (1979), 'Grain Prices and Subsistence Crises in England and France, 1590–1790', *The Journal of Economic History*, 39/4, 865–87.

Altimir, O. (1984), 'Poverty, Income Distribution and Child Welfare in Latin America: A Comparison of Pre- and Post-Recession Data', *World Development*, 12/3, 261–82.

Barnes, D. S. (1992), 'The Rise and Fall of Tuberculosis in Belle-Epoque France: A Reply to Allan Mitchell', *Social History of Medicine*, 2, 279–96.

Braudel, F. (1985), *The Structures of Everyday Life*, London: Fontana Press.

Bravo, J. (1992), 'Economic Crisis and Mortality: Short and Medium-Term Changes in Latin America', Proceedings of the Conference on the Peopling of the Americas, Veracruz: International Union for the Scientific Study of Population, 439–56.

—— and Vargas, N. (1990), 'Tendencias y Fluctuaciones de la Morbilidad y la Mortalidad por ciertas ecusas de la Actividad Económica: Costa Rica, Chile y Guatemala, 1960–1986', unpublished manuscript, CELADE.

Brenner, M. H. (1983), 'Mortality and Economic Suitability: Detailed Analysis for Britain and Comparative Analysis for Selected Industrialized Countries', *International Journal of Health Services*, 13/4.

Caldwell, J. C. and Caldwell, P. (1987), 'Famine in Africa', paper presented at the IUSSP Seminar on Mortality and Society in Subsaharan Africa, Yaounde, Cameroon.

Carvalho, J. A. Magno de and Wood, C. (1988), *The Demography of Inequality in Brazil*, Cambridge: Cambridge University Press.

Chandra, R. K. and Newberne, P. M. (1977), *Nutrition, Immunity and Infection*, New York: Plenum Press.

Cleveland, W. S. (1979), 'Robust Locally Weighted Regression and Smoothing Scatterplots', *Journal of the American Statistical Association*, 74/368, 829–36.

Cornia, G. A., Jolly, R., and Stewart, F. (eds.) (1987), *Adjustment with a Human Face*, Oxford: Clarendon Press.

Corradi, A. (1973), *Annali delle Epidemè Occorse in Italia dalle prime memorie fino al 1850*, Bologna: Forni (reprint of original edition).

Cronjè, G. (1984), 'Tuberculosis and Mortality Decline in England and Wales, 1851–1910', in Woods, R. I. and Woodward, J. (eds.), *Urban Disease and Morbidity in Nineteenth Century England*, London: Batsford Academic and Educational, Ltd.

Davies, P. D. O. (1985), 'A Possible Link between Vitamin D Deficiency and Impaired Host Defence to Mycobacterium Tuberculosis' *Tubercle*, 66, 301–6.

DeSoto, H. (1990), *The Other Path: The Invisible Revolution in the Third World*, New York: Harper-Row.

Flinn, M. W. (1974), 'The Stabilization of Mortality in Pre-Industrial Western Europe', *Journal of European Economic History*, 3/2, 285–318.

Fogel, R. W. (1986), 'Nutrition and the Decline in Mortality since 1700: Some Preliminary Findings', in Engerman, S. L. and Gallman, R. E. (eds.), *Long-Term Factors in American Economic Growth*, Chicago: University of Chicago Press.

—— (1989), 'Second Thoughts on the European Escape from Hunger: Famines, Price Elasticities, Entitlements, Chronic Malnutrition, and Mortality Rates', Working Paper 1, Working Paper Series on Historical Factors in Long Run Growth, Cambridge, MA: National Bureau of Economic Research.

—— (1990), 'The Conquest of High Mortality and Hunger in Europe and America: Timing and Mechanisms', Working Paper 16, Working Paper Series on Historical Factors in Long Run Growth, Cambridge, MA: National Bureau of Economic Research.

—— (1991), 'New Sources and New Techniques for the Study of Secular Trends in Nutritional Status, Health, Mortality, and the Process of Aging', Working Paper 26, Working Paper Series on Historical Factors in Long Run Growth, Cambridge, MA: National Bureau of Economic Research.

Frieden, J. A. (1991), *Debt, Development, and Democracy: Modern Political Economy and Latin America, 1965–1985*, Princeton: Princeton University Press.

Galloway, P. (1988), 'Basic Patterns in Annual Variation in Fertility, Nuptiality, Mortality, and Prices in Pre-Industrial Europe', *Population Studies*, 42/2.

—— and Lee, R. (1985), 'Some Possibilities for the Analysis of Aggregate Historical Demographic Data from China', paper presented at the Workshop on Qing Population History, Pasadena California, 26–30 August 1985, California Institute of Technology.

Gwatkin, D. (1980), 'Indications of Change in Developing Countries. Mortality Trends: The End of an Era?' *Population and Development Review*, 6/4, 615–44.

Hammel, E. (1985), 'Short-term Demographic Fluctuations in the Croatian Military Border of Austria, 1830–47', *European Journal of Population*, 1/2–3.

Hill, K. and Palloni, A. (1992), 'Demographic Responses to Economic Shocks: The Case of Latin America', paper presented at the Conference on the Peopling of the Americas, Veracruz, Mexico, Session C.131.

Hill, K. and Pebley, A. R. (1989), 'Child Mortality in the Developing World', *Population and Development Review*, 15/4, 657–87.

Jolly, R. and Cornia, G. A. (eds.) (1984), *The Impact of World Recession on Children*, Oxford: Pergamon Press.

Judge, G. G., Griffiths, W. E., Hill, R. C., Lütkepohl, H. and Lee, T. C. (1985), *The Theory and Practice of Econometrics* (2nd ed), New York: John Wiley and Sons.

Keers, R. Y. (1978), *Pulmonary Tuberculosis: A Journey Down the Centuries*, London: Balliere Tindall.

Larsen, B. (1983), 'Host Defensive Mechanisms in Obstetrics and Gynecology', *Clinics in Obstetrics and Gynecology*, 10, 39–51.

Lee, R. (1981), 'Short-Term Variation: Vital Rates, Prices and Weather', in Wrigley, E. A.

and Schofield, R. (eds.), *The Population of England, 1541–1871: A Reconstruction*, Cambridge MA: Howard University Press.

—— (1990), 'The Demographic Response to Economic Crisis in Historical and Contemporary Populations', *Population Bulletin of the United Nations*, 29.

Livi-Bacci, M. (1991), *Population and Nutrition: An Essay on European Demographic History*. Cambridge: Cambridge University Press.

—— (1992), *A Concise History of World Population*, Cambridge, MA: Blackwell.

Lunn, P. G. (1991), 'Nutrition, Immunity, and Infection', in Schofield, R., Reher, D., and Bideau, A. (eds.), *The Decline of Mortality in Europe*, Oxford: Clarendon Press.

Marichal, C. (1989), *A Century of Debt Crises in Latin America: From Independence to the Great Depression, 1820–1930*, Princeton: Princeton University Press.

Martorell, R. and Ho, T. J. (1984), 'Malnutrition, Morbidity and Mortality', *Population and Development Review*, 10 (Supplement), 49–68.

McKeown, T. (1988), *The Origins of Human Disease*, Oxford: Basil Blackwell.

Meuvret, J. (1946), 'Les Crises de Subsistence et la Démographie de la France de l'Ancien Régime', *Population*, 1/4, 643–50.

Muller, M. and Accinelli, M. (1978), 'Un Hecho Inquietante: La Evolución Reciente de la Mortalidad en la Argentina', *Notas de Población*, 6/17.

Newberne, P. M. and Williams, G. (1970), 'Nutritional Influences on the Source of Infection', in Dunlop, R. H. and Moon, H. W. (eds.), *Resistance to Infectious Disease*, Saskatoon: Modern Press.

Palloni, A. (1981), 'Mortality in Latin America: Emerging Patterns', *Population and Development Review*, 7/4, 623–49.

—— (1988), 'On the Role of Crises in Historical Perspectives: An Exchange', *Population and Development Review*, 14, 145–58.

—— (1990), 'Assessing the Levels and Impact of Mortality in Crisis Situations', in Vallin, J., D'Sousa, S., and Palloni, A. (eds.), *Comparative Studies of Mortality and Morbidity: Old and New Approaches*, Oxford: Clarendon Press.

—— and Tienda, M. (1992), 'Demographic Responses to Economic Recession in Latin America Since 1900', *Sociological Inquiry*, 62/2, 247–70.

—— and Wyrick, R. (1981), 'Mortality Decline in Latin America: Changes in the Structures of Causes of Deaths, 1950–1975', *Social Biology*, 28/3–4, 187–216.

——, Pinto, G. and Hill, K. (1993), 'Economic Swings and Demographic Changes in the History of Latin America', paper presented at Population Association of America meetings, Cincinnati, April 1993.

Pollard, J. H. (1988), 'On the Decomposition of Changes in Expectation of Life and Differentials in Life Expectancy', *Demography*, 25/2, 265–76.

Preston, S. H. (1976), *Mortality Patterns in National Populations*, New York: Academic Press (chapter 5).

Puranen, B. (1991), 'Tuberculosis and the Decline of Mortality in Sweden', in Schofield, R., Reher, D., and Bideau, A. (eds.), *The Decline of Mortality in Europe*, Oxford: Clarendon Press.

Reher, D. S. (1989), 'Coyunturas Económicas y Fluctuaciones Demográficas en Mexico durante el Siglo XVIII', paper presented at Conference on the Population History of Latin America, Session 5, Population and Economy, Belo Horizonte, Brazil.

Richards, T. (1984), 'Weather, Nutrition and the Economy: The Analysis of Short-Run Fluctuation in Births, Deaths, and Marriages, France 1740–1909', in Bergtsson, T. *et al.* (eds.), *Pre-Industrial Population Change*, Stockholm: Almquist and Wiksell.

Romero, D. E. (1993), 'La transición de la mortalidad y la evolución económica de Venezuela. El deterioro en la decada de los años ochenta', paper contributed to the Fourth Latin American Conference on Population, Mexico, March 1993.

Rotberg, R. I. and Rabb, T. K. (1983), *Hunger and History*, Cambridge: Cambridge University Press.

Schofield, R. and Reher, D. (1991), 'The Decline of Mortality in Europe', in Schofield, R., Reher, D., and Bideau, A. (eds.), *The Decline of Mortality in Europe*, Oxford: Clarendon Press.

Scrimshaw, N. W., Taylor, C. E., and Gordon, J. E. (1968), *Interaction of Nutrition and Infection*, Geneva: World Health Organization.

Szreter, S. (1988), 'The Importance of Social Intervention in Britain's Mortality Decline c.1850–1914: A Reinterpretation of the Role of Public Health', *Social History of Medicine*, 1/1, 1–38.

Vallin, J. (1991), 'Mortality in Europe from 1720 to 1914: Long term trends and changes in patterns by age and sex', in Schofield, R. and Reher, D. (eds.), *The Decline of Mortality in Europe*, Oxford: Clarendon Press.

Weir, D. (1984), 'Life Under Pressure: France and England, 1670–1870', *Journal of Economic History*, 44, 27–47.

Wingfield, R. C. (1924), *Modern Methods in the Diagnosis and Treatment of Pulmonary Tuberculosis*, New York: Hoeber.

Appendix 5.1

The groups of causes of death in the chapter and the corresponding items in the International Classification of Diseases (ICD) are given in Table 5.A1. The countries and years included are as follows: Uruguay 1955–87; Chile 1954–89; Costa Rica 1956–84; Guatemala 1958–85; Mexico 1956–86; Panama 1955–89; Trinidad 1951–84; Venezuela 1955–89; Ecuador 1961–88.

Table 5.A1   Definition of groups of causes of death (recording to ICD lists)

Title of group [Term used in the text]	ICD 6th and 7th	ICD 8th	ICD 9th
1. Respiratory TB [Respiratory TB]	A001	A006	B020–B021
2. Typhoid (+)	A012–A013	A002–A003	B011
3. Measles	A032	A025	B042
4. Whooping cough	A022	A016	B034
5. Hepatitis (+)	A034	A028	B046
6. Diarrhoeas [Diarrhoeas]	A016; A104; A132	A004; A005	B014–B016
7. Ulcers/cirrhosis [Chronic]	A099–A100; A105	A098; A102	B341; B347
8. Pneumonia, bronchitis and influenza (+) [Respiratory]	A088–A093; A087	A090–A093; A089	B320–B323; B310–B312
9. Heart disease [Heart]	A070; A079–A086	A080–A088	B25–B30
10. Diseases of infancy	A127–A135	A126–A135	B44–B45
11. Avitaminosis (+)	A064	A065	B19
12. All infections [Infectious]	A001–A043; A104; A132	A001–A044	B01–B07
13. Suicide, homicide, and accidents [Violence]	AE138–AE150	AE136–AE137	B47–B56
14. Ill-defined [Ill-defined]	A136–A137	A136–A137	B46

Notes:
1. For some countries and some years it was necessary to establish a correspondence between the observed causes of deaths listed according to the B list and the target A list. The problematic linkages affect a handful of causes of deaths and should have no effects on the analysis presented in the chapter.
2. Note that group 12 (infectious) includes A104 and A132 in the ICD 6th and 7th. These are special diseases of infancy and diarrhoeas of the newborn which were in later versions assigned to well-defined infectious diseases. The problems of correspondence should be minor and, in any case, only affect age 0. Non-inclusion of A104 and A132 leads to irreconcilable trends in infant mortality due to infectious diseases before or after the adoption of the 8th revision.
3. For causes marked with '+' there are discontinuities for some countries before 1955 that we were not able to resolve. In these cases our series start after 1955. In the case of avitaminosis we were not able to resolve discontinuities that are apparent at several points in time and for several countries. For this reason we decided not to include this cause of death separately in our analysis.

Appendix 5.2

1. An informal justification

An informal justification for the introduction of the control is fairly simple to develop. If economic downswings lead to increases in the number of deaths due to cause k that are allocated to the ill-defined category, the estimated response of cause k will be underestimated. Controlling for the detrended values of deaths due to ill-defined enables us to estimate the magnitude of this association and thus purges out the downward bias in the estimated response due to the well-defined cause. If our model is correct the *observed* (absolute) deviation from a trend in the number of deaths due to cause k, δy_k, is given by:

$$\delta y_k(t) = \sum_j \beta_j \delta x(t-j) - \rho k \delta y_{ill}(t),$$

where $\delta x(t-j)$ and $\delta y_{ill}(t)$ refer, respectively, to the observed absolute deviations from trends of the economic indicator and the number of deaths due to ill-defined causes at lags j and 0, β is the unstandardized response to changes in income, and ρ_k is the fraction of ill-defined deaths that should have been allocated to cause k. This equality provides sufficient rationale to include the detrended number of deaths due to ill-defined causes as a control in the equation for the observed detrended number of deaths due to cause k: the estimated coefficients for income will be corrected and should be larger (in absolute value) than the uncorrected ones. The estimate of ρ_k should be less than one in absolute value but must bear a negative coefficient.

2. A more rigorous derivation

We suggest now a more rigorous procedure to correct for the biases introduced by misclassification of causes of deaths. However, the procedure involves a complicated model that we are not able to estimate due to the small number of observations available to us. For simplicity, assume that we only have non-lagged effects so that β_k is the true elasticity of cause of death k to changes in income. If a fraction η_k of deaths due k end up as ill-defined, the observed elasticity will be $\beta_k \cdot \eta_k$. One can show that the correct specification for the deaths due to ill-defined causes is one where the independent variables are all terms constructed as the products of: (a) the ratio of the detrended number of deaths due to cause k to the detrended number of deaths due to ill-defined causes and (b) the detrended value of income, for example, $x(t) \cdot y_k(t)/y_{ill}(t)$. The elasticity with respect to these interaction terms are the products $\beta_k \cdot (1 - \eta_k)$. Consequently if one estimates the equation for cause of death k we obtain the (biased) coefficients $\beta_k - \eta_k$. If we then estimate the equation just specified for the ill-defined we will obtain the estimates $\beta_k(1 - \eta_k)$. These two sets of estimates are sufficient to obtain the correct values of β_k. We can relax the assumption on non-lagged effects and the same algebraic equivalences will follow on a lag-specific basis.

Note that if there are, say, ten causes of deaths we need to estimate an equation for deaths in the ill-defined category that contains 10 *1 number of variables, where 1 is the total number of lags to be considered. Since in our case we set 1 = 5, we would need 50 independent variables, far larger than the actual number of observations available.

6 Short-term Economic Fluctuations and Demographic Behaviour: *Some Examples from Twentieth-Century South America*

JOSÉ ANTONIO ORTEGA-OSONA AND DAVID REHER

Introduction

The relationship between economic realities and demographic behaviour has occupied centre stage in most demographic research since Malthus underlined its importance nearly two centuries ago. For Malthus, the 'invisible hand' whereby population growth was kept in line with economic realities was materialized through the relationships between economic well-being, and fertility and mortality. This has been an ongoing theme in much of the existing historical literature. Malthus set his model in the medium and long term, and in recent years some authors, in particular Ronald Lee, have attempted to specify in a more formal manner the empirical parameters of these relationships.[1]

If Malthus' postulates are correct, the expected relationships should hold in the short run as well. Short-term analysis of fluctuations has certain advantages over other types of analysis because adequate indicators are more readily accessible, have a more straightforward interpretation and enable us to verify statistically the relationship between economic and demographic fluctuations.[2] Some years ago Ronald Lee (1981: 356–401) attempted to estimate systematically the relationship between prices and vital events by means of a distributed lag regression model. His work showed that discernible links between the two did exist, though the overall importance of prices in determining fluctuations was often not excessively great. Lee's pioneering work has been followed by a whole host of scholars who have gone a long way towards consolidating and deepening Lee's original understanding of the problem.[3] All of these authors have used similar distributed lag models, though not all have used the same number of lags, so as best to reflect the structure

We would like to thank Patrick Galloway, Jorge Bravo, and Andrew Mason for their helpful comments on an earlier version of this chapter.

[1] Here the work of Ronald Lee is specially important. See Lee (1981: 356–401; 1985; 1986; 1987; 1992). See also Wrigley and Schofield (1981).

[2] An example of this is the case of twentieth-century Spain where, decomposing demographic and economic time series into trend and deviation from the trend, a linear relationship was observed for the short-term component, but not for the long-term one (del Hoyo and García Ferrer, 1988: 130).

[3] See, for example, Galloway (1985; 1986; 1988; 1992); Bengtsson (1984; 1986); Weir (1984); Richards (1983); Hammel (1985); Bengtsson and Ohlsson (1985); Pérez Moreda (1988); Reher (1990; 1992).

of the effect of prices over a period of time. The results of these studies have been basically similar, showing rather convincingly that in many culturally and economically diverse historical populations, yearly price fluctuations were negatively related to fertility and nuptiality and positively related to mortality.

The extent to which this type of method can be successfully applied to twentieth-century populations remains to be seen. We can plausibly expect that the intensity of the relationship will diminish as general levels of fertility and mortality decline, and as living standards rise above the subsistence minimum often supposed to have been the norm in most historical populations. Yet the extent to which ongoing economic–demographic ties continue to exist is not clear. Furthermore, the present century has had its share of profound economic shocks. Whether or not these have elicited immediate demographic responses is a largely unanswered question.

The relationship between population and economy in historic Mexico has been the object of two recent papers. Reher (1992a) attempted to evaluate the medium- and long-term sensitivity of demographic cycles and economic swings in late colonial Mexico, finding that prolonged economic downswings were accompanied by restrictions in nuptiality and fertility, and increases in mortality. Applying distributed lag models to short-term economic and demographic fluctuations during the same period, Reher (1992b) found all demographic variables to be significantly sensitive to short-term price fluctuations, and that these reactions, especially regarding mortality, varied by ethnicity in the expected direction. On the other hand, recent attempts to apply the same method to twentieth-century Latin American data have indicated that the expected links do seem to hold, although they are, by and large, very moderate and statistically insignificant (Hill and Palloni 1992; Bravo 1990; 1992).

In this chapter we will analyse short-term fluctuations of economic and demographic variables for selected countries of the Latin American region. The rather disappointing results of our initial models will be evaluated in terms of the demographic and economic changes taking place during the present century. Two further methods enabling us to view this relationship more clearly will be proposed. Overall, our analysis will point to the following conclusions: 1) during the present century, the traditional relationship between short-term demographic and economic fluctuations continues to exist but has varied considerably over the century; and 2) the new methods of analysis we have proposed have been found to be adequate for testing the existence and intensity of these relationships.

Methodology and Data

The basic method of analysis follows Lee's distributed lag (DL) model to a great extent, especially using many of the improvements incorporated in the work of Patrick Galloway (1987). It consists basically of a set of linear least squares regressions where vital series (non-infant deaths, births and marriages) of year 0 are modelled as a function of a price index (and other variables) in that same year and in the four preceding ones. Since high prices might well have been accompanied by periods of high mortality often caused by epidemics, their effects on fertility or on nuptiality might be confounded. In the original method, Lee and Galloway made births and marriages a function of fluctuations in both prices and deaths so as to be able to sort out the relative weights of both. The use of a DL model is designed to show delayed effects of the explanatory variable or variables which are likely to be important, as will be argued further ahead. In the original method, second-order autoregressive disturbances are modelled systematically and R^2 and corrected R^2 are calculated for the untransformed variables. To remove the long-term trend Lee (1981) proposed a method whereby all series are divided by an eleven-year centred moving average. This filtering removes the influence of population size and age structure from demographic series and is expected to remove secular changes in prices as well. The series so obtained have a mean close to 1 and the coefficients estimated are elasticities.

When applying Lee's method to twentieth-century Latin America some variations should be introduced. Firstly we have preferred to include only lags 0 to 3, along the same lines as Bravo (1992) and Hill and Palloni (1992). The main reason for doing this is the lack of significance of lag 4 parameters in the vast majority of the literature, meaning that its inclusion may only result in increasing the variance of the parameters. Secondly, we have decided against using both mortality and price fluctuations as independent variables in the equations for births and marriages. This is so because, during the period studied, the importance of exogenously-determined mortality fluctuations among adults was probably quite weak; and if mortality does vary with economic conditions, keeping it in the equation as an independent variable would mask the ultimate effects of economic fluctuations.

The choice of an economic indicator has posed a number of problems. Lee and others have used price fluctuations of basic foodstuffs, arguing convincingly that short-term fluctuations in the price of, say, bread was a good indicator of short-term fluctuations in living standards. While this might be true in pretransitional populations, in twentieth-century Latin America rapid price changes, especially during the 1970s and 1980s, often accompanied by wage indexation, might be largely unrelated to short-term changes in well-being. Because of this we have decided to use estimates of yearly fluctuations in per capita gross domestic product as an additional economic indicator. Here too, there are problems, but not nearly so critical as those posed by the use of prices. By using both, we will be able to evaluate and compare their effects on demographic behaviour.

Moreover, the traditional detrending procedure has proved inadequate when strong and unstable exponential rates of growth are present, as is the case of the consumer price indices here analysed. The problem is that some fictitious medium-term variation is created, so that the detrended series tend to show a valley in the years preceding massive inflations and then track the trend of inflation without actually capturing its short-term variation at all. That is why an alternative must be used. We have chosen the standard stationarity transformations of combining Box-Cox transformations and differencing (Box and Jenkins 1976). For the demographic and the GDP time series, first differences of the logs were taken, obtaining stationary series which can be interpreted as percentage changes of the series of events. For prices, two differences of the logs were taken in order to induce stationarity. This is the transformation that makes sense for twentieth-century data when high inflation is prevalent and where some kind of indexation is used to discount its effects. This is particularly true for the great inflations from the 1960s onwards, where wages are revised even within the year, on a monthly or even weekly basis.

Denoting the first-difference operator by ∇, we can write the proposed models as:

$$\nabla\ln(Rate_t) = c_1 + \sum_{k=0}^{3} b_{1k}\nabla\ln\left(\frac{CPI_{t-k}}{CPI_{t-k-1}}\right) + e_{1t},$$

$$\nabla\ln(Rate_t) = c_2 + \sum_{k=0}^{3} b_{2k}\nabla\ln\left(\frac{GDP}{POP}\right)_{t-k} + e_{2t},$$

where $Rate_t$ is the demographic rate in moment t (adult crude death rate, marriage and birth rates); CPI_t is the Consumer Price Index in time t; $(GDP/POP)_t$ is the per capita Gross Domestic Product in year t; $k = \{0,1,2,3\}$ is the number of lag, in years; c_i, b_{ik} are time-independent parameters; and e_{it} are Error terms. Standard ARMA methods are used on a case-by-case basis (Box and Jenkins 1976) so as to obtain zero mean constant variance uncorrelated residuals as postulated by least squares regression.

We can interpret the c_i parameters as allowing for a deterministic exponential rate of change. The b_{1k} are elasticities in the ratio of prices, that is, the percentage change in demographic series induced by a 1 per cent rise in the *rate of change* of prices. For instance, if b_{10} equals 0.2 that means that whenever the ratio of the price index in one year over that of the preceding one rises by 10 per cent (for example, from a December to December inflation rate of 50 per cent to a rate of 65 per cent as $1.65/1.55 = 1.1$), the demographic rate will increase by 2 per cent. As we see, in this model it is the increase or decrease in the yearly inflation rate that determines increases or decreases in demographic time series and not the variation of the price index as in the original DL model. In our model, the variation of the Consumer Price Index is an indicator of economic welfare[4], the expectation being that when inflation increases, real wages decrease. In the second equation, the regression coefficients b_{2k} can be interpreted as standard elasticities: a given percentage change in real GDP will cause a percentage change in demographic variables. When real GDP increases, we can expect living standards to increase. Over the period under study, our two economic indicators are loosely and negatively correlated.

Decreases in living standards (increase in inflation or decrease in real GDP) can be expected to depress fertility levels in a number of different manners. Any form of conscious birth control, or decreases in fecundability due to other reasons (coital

---

[4] The key importance of price control for the economic system has made of it one of the focal points of economic policy during the second half of the century (Foxley 1983: 9; Behrman 1977: chapter 2).

frequency, decreased libido, nutrition, etc.) during periods of crisis, should have a delayed effect on fertility. We can expect a negative or even positive effect for lags 0 and 1, with smaller effects for further lags after the crisis. As general levels of fertility decline, and fertility control becomes more widespread, deliberate attempts to control or delay fertility in the face of adversity should tend to become much more important relative to other factors. In present-day Argentina and Chile, which are at a relatively advanced stage of the demographic transitions and where people enjoy living standards noticeably higher than in many other countries of Latin America, we can expect the links between changes of living standards and fertility to be generally weak and decreasing, especially when responding to non-critical fluctuations in economic variables. During the period of economic hardship which characterized the 1970s and the early part of the 1980s, however, the sensitivity of fertility to economic fluctuations could well have increased, especially within marriage.

We can expect that economic realities will affect marriage in a temporary way, either delaying or accelerating it, and that lasting cumulative effects will be neg-ligible.[5] Since over much of the period under study in both Argentina and Chile women did not need to maximize their fertility within marriage in order to achieve the desired number of surviving children, delaying marriage was entirely possible and had few lasting demographic implications. Determining the best moment to marry thus acquired key importance for young couples, and these decisions were plausibly quite sensitive to the economic conjuncture. As living standards increased, however, as they did over much of the century, the importance of economic fluctuations probably diminished. The result is that clearly discernible effects should be present, but plausibly diminishing in importance over much of the century. Contrary to what occurs with fertility, real GDP and inflation need not necessarily affect marriage in the same way. Increases in real GDP will lead to an acceleration of marriages, as couples strive to take advantage of propitious economic moments, though these effects will be compensated, at least in part, by rebound effects at higher lags as the poor of persons of marrying age diminishes. Periods of inflation, however, especially when not accompanied by high levels of unemployment, need not necessarily lead to decreasing marriage opportunities because under certain circumstances they may induce people to go into debt, especially considering that purchases of consumer durables and housing often accompanies marriage.

Difficult economic times can be expected to be positively linked to mortality levels because mortality has traditionally been influenced by living conditions, nutritional status, vulnerability, and access to adequate medical care; and all of these are very sensitive to economic conditions. These effects, however, are likely to be attenuated by a number of factors. It is well known that links between living standards and mortality are closest in very poor, high mortality populations.[6] The

---

[5] Only if the situation persists over a prolonged period of time may an increase in celibacy be expected. We are unable to assess this possibility with the type of statistical analysis used in this chapter.

[6] For the relationship between living standards and mortality, see McKeown (1976), Preston (1976), and Schofield and Reher (1991). Applying this method of analysis to certain historical populations,

transition from high to moderate mortality can be achieved with relatively small gains in living standards and knowledge of public health and infant hygiene. Once moderate levels of morality have been reached, the links to living conditions are not nearly so clear. Both Argentina and Chile are moderate to low mortality populations throughout much of the twentieth century, and living standards are well above subsistence levels for a large proportion of their populations. Therefore we expect any links between economic and mortality fluctuations to be weak. Furthermore, as the century advances, intervening variables such as the improvement of the quality of public health and parental education should further mitigate these effects. Even in more recent years, when economic hardship has accompanied periods of structural adjustment, links between economic performance and mortality have probably continued to diminish. Significant effects are likely to be noticeable only for certain diseases and among certain age groups (the very young and the aged).[7]

To test some of these hypothesis we have estimated the corresponding equations for twentieth century Chile and Argentina. Differencing, error modelling and the lag structure imply that some observations are lost at the beginning of the sample. The data for Argentina goes from 1914 to 1986.[8] The price index used is the Cost of Living Index in Buenos Aires.[9] GDP figures for Argentina begin in 1900 and are taken from Hofman (1992). In the case of Chile, all demographic series begin in 1899 and refer to the whole country.[10] Between 1928 and 1986, prices refer to the entire country, and between 1899 and 1927 they apply to Santiago.[11] GDP figures for Chile before 1910 were not used since they are not reliable.

The application of the traditional distributed lag regression models to these twentieth century Latin American populations has led to disappointing but not entirely unexpected results (Table 6.1, showing regression results). Few of the regression coefficients have been significant, and the variance explained by the regression equations has been very low. When using gross domestic product as our economic variable in the fertility and nuptiality equations, some of the parameters become statistically significant, and are of the expected sign. With inflation this has not been the case, and the results have been very weak. Both economic variables have performed poorly in explaining mortality fluctuations, and some of the results have been contrary to expectations. These results are similar to those found by other authors using the same method during the present century, and contrast with

mortality has been shown to be most closely linked to short-term changes in living standards among the poorer than among richer populations. For national comparisons, see, for example, Galloway (1988: 290–8). With respect to social groups, see Reher (1991: 1199–201) for late colonial Mexico, and Reher (1990: 143–8) for pretransitional urban Spain. For contradictory urban results, see Galloway (1986).

[7] Any disaggregation of mortality either by age or cause is beyond the scope of this chapter.

[8] Before 1930 we have used the Anuario Geográfico Argentino. From 1930 to 1951 data comes from Ministerio de Asuntos Técnicos (1952). The period 1970–86 contains data taken from Anuario Estadístico de la República Argentina. The rest is completed through the Demographic Yearbook.

[9] Banco de Análisis y Computación (1982; 1987).

[10] Instituto Nacional de Estadísticas. See also Mamalakis (1980).

[11] Before 1928 prices are taken from Sala (1986), and after that date they come from the Instituto Nacional de Estadísticas, Indice de Precios al Consumo.

Table 6.1 Yearly regression results for Argentina and Chile

Dep.	Sample	Constant	Lag 0	Lag 1	Lag 2	Lag 3	AR (1)	MA (1)	R^2	Durbin–Watson
(a) Independent variable: GDP per capita (Logarithm, 1 difference)										
Chile										
CBR	1910–88	–1.04**	0.13***	0.07*	0.02	0.06	0.25**	—	0.20	2.05
CMR	1910–88	–0.34	0.54***	–0.04	0.07	0.06	—	—	0.29	2.07
ADR	1910–88	–1.51*	–0.01	0.03	–0.29***	0.15*	—	–0.27**	0.21	1.95
Argentina										
CBR	1911–86	–0.99***	0.08	0.13	0.03	0.09	—	—	0.09	2.26
CMR	1911–81	–1.08**	0.71***	0.18*	–0.04	–0.03	—	—	0.48	2.25
ADR	1913–86	–0.33	0.16*	–0.12	–0.31**	0.02	–0.52***	—	0.38	2.05
(b) Independent variable: Consumer Price Index (Logarithm, 2 differences)										
Chile										
CBR	1904–88	–0.61	0.01	–0.01	0.00	–0.02	0.29***	—	0.13	1.99
CMR	1903–88	0.46	0.04	–0.00	–0.05	0.02	—	—	0.03	1.89
ADR	1904–88	–1.71	–0.03	–0.00	–0.00	–0.04	0.54**	–0.89***	0.21	2.12
Argentina										
CBR	1918–86	–0.63*	–0.00	0.00	0.01	–0.56	—	—	0.01	2.14
CMR	1918–81	0.18	0.00	–0.03	–0.00	–0.05*	—	—	0.04	1.62
ADR	1919–86	–0.82	–0.02	0.03	–0.02	0.03	–0.47***	—	0.25	2.11

* Significant at 20% level.
** Significant at 5% level.
*** Significant at 1% level.

Notes:
CBR = Crude Birth Rate; CMR = Crude Marriage Rate; ADR = Adult Death Rate.

the strong links shown by eighteenth-century Mexican data. We see little room for the guarded optimism shown by Hill and Palloni (1992: 425), since few statistically significant relations seem to emerge.

This may be due to a combination of factors:

(1) There may be problems of data quality.
(2) While demographic dynamics may be sensitive to economic changes, this sensitivity might not remain constant over the period. By using only one equation we may not be able to detect covariation adequately.
(3) The expected relationships might exist but are not captured when data analysis is carried out within a yearly time frame.
(4) The lack of significance may be induced by a problem of multicollinearity which could cause the appearance of some wrong signs.
(5) There may be no covariance whatsoever between economic fluctuations and demographic dynamics.

We consider the first factor to be unlikely in the cases of Argentina and Chile. Points (2), (3), and (4) will be taken up in subsequent sections of this chapter. The possibility of a sharply diminished or even non-existent effect of short-term economic fluctuations on population dynamics deserves serious consideration, basically because the prevailing demographic and economic regimes in Chile and Argentina underwent pronounced changes during the course of the nineteenth century. After the early years of the century, fertility and mortality levels were considerably below their peaks and fertility limitation was a viable option for a considerable proportion of the population. Furthermore, for a good part of the period public health mechanisms and medical treatment were sufficiently effective to be a real check on the 'natural' fluctuations of mortality.[12] Finally, most people in these countries did not live near the subsistence minimum, a plausible threshold beyond which links between economic fluctuations and demographic behaviour decrease rapidly.

Recursive Analysis: Estimating Change over Time

There is a strong possibility that the basic relationship between economic and demographic variables changed in the course of the present century. When the series of prices and vital events commenced, declines in fertility and mortality had just begun to occur in Argentina and were still two or three decades away in Chile. The twentieth century has been one of profound demographic change in both of these countries, and the use of a single straightforward OLS regression equation, which assumes parametric constancy, might obscure changes in this pattern, making them unrecognizable. This is a hypothesis worth testing.

---

[12] Argentina was a pioneer in reducing levels of fertility and mortality. Chile, while initiating this process somewhat later, nevertheless underwent a demographic transition before the majority of the countries of the region.

One plausible solution to this problem is recursive analysis, a sequential technique of estimation where estimates are updated continuously, working serially through the data in temporal order. With it we can not only check the constancy of parameters but also track the parametric variations. The algorithm we use here has been called by different authors *exponential weighting into the past* (*EWP*) (Young 1984: 60–6) or *discounted recursive least squares* (*DLS*) (Harvey 1981: 194–5). In this algorithm the weight given to each observation decays exponentially over time at a constant rate. After some experimenting, we have chosen a rate of 0.97.[13] This shapes the memory of the estimator as fading exponentially at a rate of 0.97, implying that the contemporary observation has a unit weight, the observations from 5, 10, and 20 years before receive weights 0.85, 0.74, and 0.54, and that the contribution to the residual sum of squares is in proportion to the weights 0.74, 0.54, and 0.30 respectively. The advantage of discounting is that the estimates respond more quickly to a change in the structure of the model. A problem is the increasing parameter instability. This is the reason for choosing a discounting factor close to 1, which would mean not discounting at all; that is, ordinary recursive least squares. To start, the algorithm requires some initial parameters and variances which, after some iterations, tend to converge. The great initial variation is the reason why we have not displayed the estimates for the beginning of the sample in the figures. Starting from these initial estimates, the recursive algorithm operates sequentially, updating firstly the variance-covariance matrix using the one-step ahead forecast error, and afterwards the parameters in a measure proportional to the said forecast error and the estimated variance-covariance matrix. The residual corresponding to each observation can then be obtained from the updated parameters.

Recursive analysis gives us several tools to track the evolution of the parameters governing the relationships. If these are not stable, the hypothesis of constant parameters will be rejected. Under these conditions, we must abandon the idea of estimating a constant relationship for the entire sample, since ordinary least squares regression may give misleading results. Recursive estimation is a good alternative as it lets us track changes in the relationship. The problem is that it may be difficult to interpret the plot of estimated parameters, especially when some or most of them are not highly significant. There is a chance of interpreting spurious variations if there is a high correlation among parameters. Estimation constitutes a whole, and trying to interpret parameters individually is risky. The basic logic of our method is in line with some of the recent changes proposed by Galloway (1992). An advantage of our approach is that it may prove useful when centuries-long series of observations are not available; it also gives a more precise view of the timing and intensity of changes in parameters.

Bearing these problems in mind, our presentation of recursive estimates will be limited to the price and GDP parameters corresponding to lags 0 and 1 and to the

---

[13] What we call the decay constant refers to the weight given to each observation of a^{n-t}. In most references this name is given to the constant, b, that weights the residual sum of squares. The relationship between them is $b = a^2$.

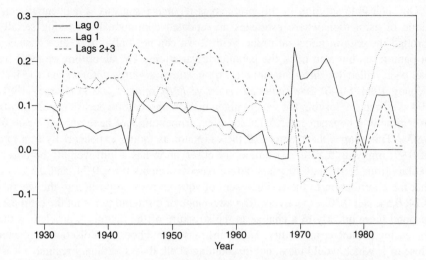

Fig. 6.1   Recursive parameters, GDP per capita on birth rate, Argentina

sum of lags 2 and 3. Some of the results are presented in Figures 6.1–6.6. We see wide fluctuations in the different parameters, as well as an appreciable correlation among them. A first conclusion to be derived from these results suggests that at least during the twentieth century the relation between economic and demographic fluctuations did not remain constant. In situations like this, the application of a single OLS regression equation is not an adequate tool of analysis.

Despite wide changes in the different estimates, some interesting consistencies can be observed. When looking at the recursive parameters of income (that is, per capita GDP) on births, we see that patterns in both Chile and Argentina are similar: there is a gradual decline in the positive effect (more so in Chile than in Argentina) until the early 1970s when this relationship increases substantially (Figures 6.1 and 6.2). This increase is clearer in Chile—where all lags show the same tendency—than in Argentina, where it is mostly visible at lag 1. In both countries, the original decline over much of the century and the subsequent increase are quite visible. Inflation affects fertility in the expected way in Argentina only until the 1960s or 1975 and in Chile only until 1955. After 1975 in both countries the effects diminish to near 0. For an important part of the period under analysis, then, inflation and income have a similar effect on fertility, though in more recent years (corresponding to the period of greatest inflation and economic hardship) inflation has lost all influence on fertility, while real GDP has strengthened its influence.

Real GDP has been found to be very strongly and positively related to marriage fluctuations at lag 0 in both Chile and Argentina, while net effects at other lags have been quite weak (Figures 6.3 and 6.4). It is interesting to note how in both cases, the contemporary effect declines until the decade of the 1960s, and increases steadily thereafter. Until 1960 in Argentina and 1970 in Chile, price tend to be

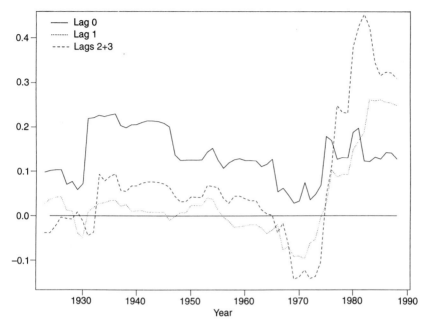

Fig. 6.2 Recursive parameters, GDP per capita on birth rate, Chile

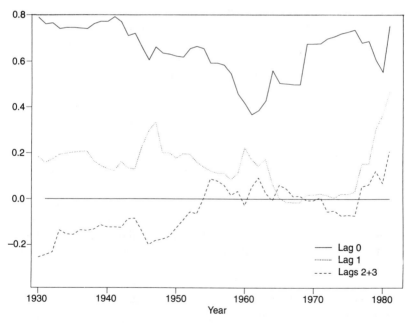

Fig. 6.3 Recursive parameters, GDP per capita on marriage rate, Argentina

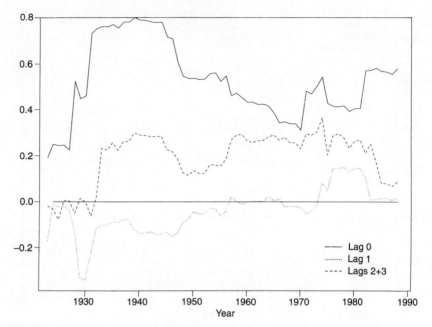

Fig. 6.4 Recursive parameters, GDP per capita on marriage rate, Chile

positively related to marriage fluctuations. This counterintuitive result may well be due to the stimulating effect on marriage which moderate levels of inflation may have had. During the period of drastic inflation of the 1970s and 1980s, these effects disappear and in some cases become even modestly negative.

The results of the mortality equations have been disappointing but not surprising. At lags 0 and 1, the effects of income on mortality are either contrary to expectations (higher incomes lead to higher mortality) or non-existent (Figures 6.5 and 6.6). We find the expected result only at higher lags, indicating delayed negative effects of income on mortality. Before the late 1950s, the effect of inflation on mortality differs greatly in Argentina and in Chile. As was hypothesized originally, in all cases the cumulative effect of income and inflation on mortality in both countries tend to converge towards 0 after approximately 1960.

This part of our analysis enables us to establish some tentative conclusions. First, during the twentieth century, there have been important changes in the relations between economic and demographic fluctuations, and this suggests that traditional distributed lag models applied to the entire period will lead to spurious results. Second, in situations such as this, the technique of discounted recursive estimation seems to be a useful analytical tool. It is, however, subject to some shortcomings, the most important of which is the fact that when we attempt to estimate equations with a relatively small number of data points, coefficients can vary widely, often making them difficult to interpret. Third, at least in some of the cases analysed, the

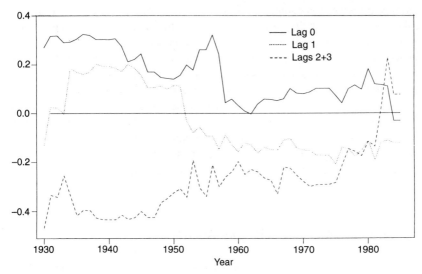

Fig. 6.5 Recursive parameters, GDP per capita on adult death rate, Argentina

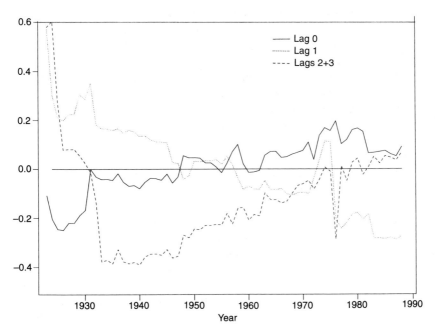

Fig. 6.6 Recursive parameters, GDP per capita on adult death rate, Chile

relationship between economic oscillations and demographic behaviour appears to weaken over much of the period, especially before the 1960s. During the subsequent period corresponding to intense inflation and declining living standards, however, there has been some indication that income has increased its effects on those demographic variables mediated by conscious choice (nuptiality and fertility), but not on mortality. Fourth, income has proven to be a more useful indicator of economic activity than inflation, but during much of the period, especially before 1970, their effects have not been entirely dissimilar. During the period of most intense inflation, price variations seem to become less meaningful for demographic behaviour (and as an indicator of economic well-being), though the extent to which effects continue to exist but are not captured by annual fluctuations remains to be seen.

A Different Time Frame: Monthly Analysis

Earlier it was suggested that there may be a relationship between economic fluctuations and demographic behaviour which is not reflected when yearly data are used. These would be rather immediate reactions and adjustments whose final impact was diminished or even eliminated by compensating effects taking place within a year. In other words, during a period in which the overall demographic responses to economic stimuli were relatively weak, a yearly framework of analysis might not be the most appropriate to capture certain types of effects. By using a monthly perspective, we may be able to assess some of these ties more precisely.

We are able to test this possibility for Chile. Monthly numbers of births, non-infant deaths, marriages, and CPI are available from the National Statistical Institute (INE) which cover the period from January 1945 to December 1988, adding up to more than 500 observations. In order to model monthly variation some changes have been introduced in the equation for price. These changes refer to the inclusion of a set of seasonal dummy variables, and modifications in the lag structure. Impulse dummy variables have also been included in order to model some atypical observations.

Monthly dummies come as a necessary addition to the original model in order that seasonality may be taken into account. Were this not done, the model would be mis-specified, because important variables such as weather effects (Larsen 1990a, 1990b; Lee 1981, 1993) or certain short-term labour market cycles—which may have a pronounced seasonality—would be ignored. Besides, there is a whole set of cultural factors which determine a well-established pattern of seasonal variations in births and marriages. Deaths also show important seasonal effects which reflect the combination of the characteristic seasonality of different causes of death. A set of eleven dummies referring to the percentage change in each month with respect to January has been included. From the estimates it is possible to reconstruct the monthly distribution of demographic events net of economic effects by means of simple calculations. This seasonal schedule is computed in such a way that 100 would mean a uniform distribution of events during the year. The higher the value of the dummy coefficient, the more concentrated the events are in a calendar month.

The modified approach to model dynamics has been the following. In a first run, lags from 0 to 11 for marriages and deaths, and from 0 to 15 for births, were included. This lag structure should cover most of the very short-term demographic response to economic changes. At a second stage lags that were far from significant in every moment were excluded in order to reduce the variance of the parameters and to facilitate interpretation. This process was done several times both through OLS and recursive estimation until the final lag structure was decided upon.

The last change in the model was the incorporation of atypical intervention through differenced impulse dummies. Working with monthly data, variability increases considerably, and sometimes extraordinary events can determine a temporal change in the variables. Examples may be, say, a political crisis or a change in the vital registration system. The most important changes of this kind were modelled through the inclusion of dummy variables which measure the percentage increase over the expected figure for that month.

The modified model can be thus expressed as follows:

$$\nabla \ln(Events_t) = c + \sum_k b_k \nabla \ln\left(\frac{CPI_{t-k}}{CPI_{t-k-1}}\right) + \sum_{k=1}^{11} d_k \nabla S_k + \sum_k f_k \nabla I_{tk} + e_t,$$

where $Events_t$ are non-infant deaths, marriages, and births in month t, or monthly infant mortality rate computed as the ratio of infant deaths in month t to the number of newborns in the preceding 12 months; CPI_t is the Consumer Price Index in month t; S_k is the seasonal dummy (1 in month k, 0 elsewhere); I_{tk} is the impulse dummy (1 for $t = k$, 0 elsewhere); c, b_k, d_k, f_k are time-independent parameters; and e_{it} are error terms.

While a monthly framework of analysis may enable us to pinpoint certain types of behavioural responses to very short-term economic change, it is generally not useful for ascertaining cumulative effects over any prolonged period of time. Monthly effects may be neutralized over the year with the resulting global effect being quite small, as we have already seen in the preceding section of this chapter. In other words, rather than estimating the net implications of economic fluctuations for society as a whole, what we are looking at are temporary behavioural responses, often the product of individual decisions (at least in the case of fertility and nuptiality). Short-term variation in inflation rates is the only economic indicator available on a monthly basis for the period studied. Given the time frame used in an analysis in which the sensitivity of people's demographic response to very short-term economic change is evaluated, price fluctuations might be a more useful economic indicator. Price changes have an immediate effect on people's purchasing power; an effect which is diminished over the longer run by wage adjustments and other compensating mechanisms. For a monthly analysis, however, its advantages would seem to outweigh its defects.

Any effect the acceleration of price changes may have on fertility should be most clearly visible at lags between 8 and 11 months, corresponding to those births not occurring because of women who consciously limited their fertility during difficult times. A more contemporary covariation of both indices due to foetal loss, parental death, or other extreme situations is less likely because during the period under study considerable economic and demographic modernization has taken place, and people generally do not live at a level of subsistence. We expect price fluctuations to have a negative and rather immediate impact on marriages, as couples put off weddings during difficult economic times, or get married when times are good. Postponing however, is by definition only temporary and we might observe a rebound at higher lags.

We can posit a positive link between inflation and mortality which should be visible immediately after, or in the months following, pronounced price changes. The extent to which the quality of and access to public health institutions was affected by fluctuating inflation rates could end up influencing mortality patterns in all age groups. Deaths among the very young, however, probably related to their nutritional status and to deficiencies in general hygiene accompanying difficult economic periods, might well stand out. An example of this situation might be the relative neglect of children, a by-product of the fact that in times of sharp increases in inflation many family member may be out of the home attempting to find additional sources of income. Purchases of food would occupy ever greater proportions of the family budgets, at the expense of clothing, health care, and hygienic aids. In this monthly analysis we will separate adult and infant mortality so as to evaluate the possibly different effects of inflation more clearly. Even though generally negative effects may be discernible for both groups, we expect them to be fairly weak as public health institutions, no matter how sensitive they might be to inflation, are likely to compensate many of the immediate implications of fluctuations in living standards for mortality patterns. The extent to which these links diminish as we approach the present remains to be seen.

The results derived from our monthly analysis have normally conformed to expectations (Table 6.2). Applying the ordinary least squares regression using fertility as the dependent variable, and price fluctuations and seasonality as independent variables, we found that prices at lags 8, 9 and 11 had significant effects ($p < 2$ per cent) in the expected negative direction on monthly fertility fluctuations (Table 6.2). Lag 14 (in the expected direction) and lag 15 (a rebound) also show non-negligible effects, though their statistical significance is somewhat lower. The cumulative effect of price changes (lags 8–14) is quite negative. The change of sign at lag 15 and higher suggests that very short-term price increases tended to make people postpone conceptions for only a few months.

If in the annual regression we found that ordinary least squares (OLS) estimation for the whole period violated a number of implicit assumptions, especially the one referring to the constancy of parameters, the monthly regression for the whole period should reflect these same problems to an even greater degree. The lack of constancy in the seasonal pattern of births and infant deaths increases the inadequacy of the original procedure, which leads to seasonal autocorrelation in the

Table 6.2 Monthly regression results for Chile

Independent variables	Dependent variables (log and 1 difference)			
	Births	Marriages	Adult deaths	Monthly IMR
(a) Log of prices (2 differences)				
Number of lags:				
0		-0.02	0.23*	0.05
1		-0.23*	0.27**	-0.13
2		0.07	0.13	
3			0.10	0.10
4			0.18*	0.23*
5			0.32***	0.36**
6		0.11		
7			0.10	
8	-0.32***	0.01		
9	-0.17***			
10	-0.05			
11	-0.16*			
12	0.05			
13	0.02			
14				
15	0.15**			
(b) Seasonal dummies (1 difference) and seasonal schedule in parentheses				
Jan	4.5*** (104)	-21.5*** (104)	-0.6 (99)	2.6* (125)
Feb	-10.0*** (89)	-24.5*** (100)	-16.7*** (83)	-17.0*** (101)
Mar	-1.5* (98)	-14.6*** (113)	-9.7*** (90)	-20.3*** (97)
Apr	-7.2*** (92)	-15.0*** (112)	-8.5*** (91)	-30.1*** (85)
May	-3.7*** (96)	-23.5*** (101)	0.8 (101)	-25.8*** (91)
Jun	-2.0** (97)	-30.8*** (91)	7.7*** (107)	-25.0*** (92)
Jul	1.9* (101)	-31.9*** (90)	15.7*** (115)	-16.0*** (103)

Table 6.2 (cont.)

Independent variables	Dependent variables (log and 1 difference)			
	Births	Marriages	Adult deaths	Monthly IMR
Aug	4.7*** (104)	−36.8*** (83)	9.6*** (109)	−21.6*** (96)
Sep	8.3*** (107)	−23.2*** (101)	6.3*** (106)	−25.3*** (91)
Oct	10.5*** (110)	−31.5*** (90)	2.6** (102)	−22.3*** (95)
Nov	3.6*** (103)	−37.8*** (82)	−3.9*** (96)	−16.7*** (102)
Dec	Ref. (99)	Ref. (132)	Ref. (100)	Ref. (122)
(c) Other dummies (all significant***)				
Aug 1957			54.1	
May 1962	−11.0			
Oct 1962		−27.9		
Oct 1969		−57.7		
Mar 1971	−10.7			
Sep 1973		−29.1		
May 1976			39.2	
Constant	0.07	0.17	−0.04	−0.47
R²	73.16	79.08	67.00	52.07
Durbin–Watson	2.13	2.89	2.15	1.63
Q(24)	298.68	598.80	48.90	667.45

* Significant at 20% level.
** Significant at 5% level.
*** Significant at 1% level.

Notes:

Seasonal schedule: vital events in a standard month, controlling for inflation, using 1,200 events a year (100 a month) as reference.

Ref.: Month of reference in the estimation.

Q(24): Box-Pierce Q test for overall residual autocorrelation. 24 lags.

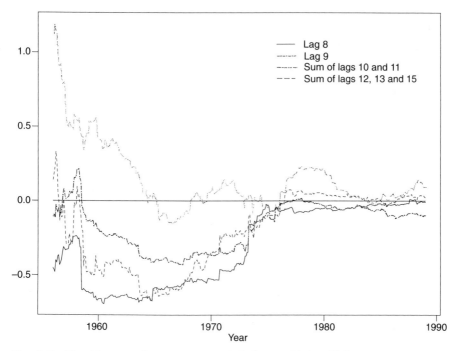

Fig. 6.7 Monthly recursive parameters, inflation on births, Chile

residuals of the OLS model. Once again recursive analysis will be used to tackle this problem, as it will enable us to analyse the temporary evolution of the parameter sets. In this case the discounting parameter is 0.995, which is chosen to make the monthly parameters cover a time period equivalent to that of the annual parameters.

If we plot the lag sum[14] as well as a number of different lag coefficients derived from using recursive parameter estimates (Figures 6.7 and 6.8), we can evaluate the changes over time of the global effect of prices acting through mechanisms of conscious birth control.[15] From the early 1950s the effect is negative and quite strong, with significant coefficients ($p < 20$ per cent) holding for lags 8, 9, 10, and 11 between the middle 1950s and 1970–3) (Table 6.3). Lag 8 shows the most highly significant parameters. After 1972–3 the negative effect of all lags tends quite quickly towards 0, suggesting that after that date there was a sharp decline in conscious birth control in response to very short-term price fluctuations.

Between 1950 and 1970, price fluctuations affect marriages negatively at lags 0 and 1 (Figure 6.9). This initial effect is weak and the coefficients are not significant.

---

[14] In this sum, we have included a lag of 15 months which is always positive and shows a very strong rebound effect.

[15] In order to simplify the very complicated tabular and graphic results from these equations, we have decided to keep graphic representation to a minimum, showing only the most salient results of the study.

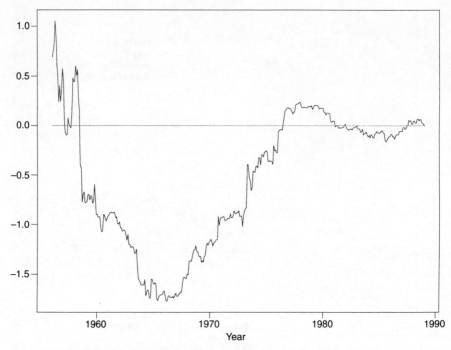

Fig. 6.8 Monthly recursive parameters, inflation on births, Chile, sum of lags 8–15

At higher lags there are rebounds, with the global result being that monthly price fluctuations are positively related to marriages, much as they were in our annual equations. After the mid-1970s the influence of prices on marriages disappears almost completely.

As expected, price fluctuations are positively related to adult mortality, with lags 0, 1, 4, and 5 having significant coefficients (Table 6.2). Using recursive techniques, however, we can see that this pattern is not uniform over the period studied. Effects are strongest before the 1970s, and diminish considerably thereafter (Figure 6.10). By the end of the period under study, while price fluctuations continue to affect mortality patterns, the link is much weaker than in earlier decades.

In order to test for greater sensitivity to price fluctuations among the very young, we have estimated regressions for monthly infant mortality rates. The results suggest that the coefficients are roughly similar to those shown by adult mortality (Table 6.2). Recursive results show how the parameters are specially high during the 1960s, decreasing thereafter (Figure 6.11). Over the period there are important changes in the seasonal pattern of mortality, from a schedule where deaths were concentrated in the summertime, probably associated with diarrhoeal diseases, to one where winter deaths prevail.

A monthly perspective has enabled us to see some of the effects that heretofore

Table 6.3 Periods of significant lagged inflation coefficients estimated in monthly recursive equations, Chile

Variables	Level of significance		
	20%		5%
Births			
Lag 8	(−)	1948–73	1958–72
Lag 9	(−)	1961–73	1964–67
Lag 10	(−)	1964–7	—
Lag 11	(−)	1957–69	1959
Lag 12	(+)	1952–9	1952–5
Lag 13	(+)	1948–56	1951–5
Lag 15	(+)	1948–53, 1961	1951
Marriages			
Lag 0	(−)	1950–1	—
Lag 1	(−)	1950–3, 1964–73	1972
Lag 2	(+)	1958–64, 1968–9, 1975;	—
	(−)	1975	
Lag 6	(+)	1974–82	1974–5
Lag 8	(+)	1950–3; (−) 1973–5	1951–3
Adult Deaths			
Lag 0	(+)	1958–64, 1974–9	1960–1
Lag 1	(+)	1972–9	1973–4
Lag 2	(+)	1974–7	—
Lag 3	(+)	1968–72	—
Lag 4	(+)	1963–72	1969
Lag 5	(+)	1953–8, 1965–79	1974–7
Lag 7	(+)	1965–74	—
Monthly IMR			
Lag 0	(+)	1949	—
Lag 1	(−)	1950, 1986–8	1950
Lag 3	(+)	1966–72	1969–71
Lag 4	(+)	1951, 1965–72	1969
Lag 5	(+)	1969–73	—

Note: (+)/(−) refer to the signs of the regression coefficients.

were not clear. The delayed negative ties of prices to births is a convincing indication that there was conscious restriction of births in negative economic situations. A similar interpretation can be given to the nearly contemporary reaction of nuptiality to price fluctuations, since there is some evidence that the timing of marriages was in part subject to the very short-term swings in the economy. Here, however, the results are weak and somewhat contradictory. The sensitivity of mortality to price

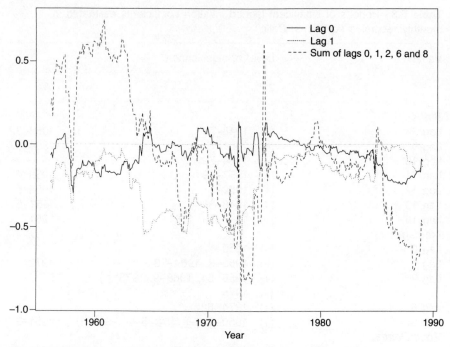

Fig. 6.9 Monthly recursive parameters, prices on marriages, Chile

fluctuations is a strong indication that the economy had implications for people's health. In all cases, however, the effects were neutralized by rebounds in the surrounding lags. In other words, the effects were short-lived, and would not have been picked up had we used a yearly perspective.

Another important conclusion is that the coefficients did not remain constant over the period under study, suggesting, once again, that in a nonstable demographic regime, the use of general OLS estimates is not an adequate way of representing the changing nature of the relations between the economy and demographic behaviour.

Finally, we have been able to observe an appreciable decrease in the importance of economic fluctuations over the period under study. The key moment for all of the variables appears to have come in the early to mid-1970s when, despite strong inflation and economic crisis, the parameter estimates begin to converge towards 0. This is quite different from patterns appearing in historical populations where the economic and demographic ties were, if anything, even more intense during times of crisis. This may be a by-product of using inflation rates as an economic indicator in times of hyperinflation and wage indexation. It may, however, also be an indirect measure of the modernization taking place within Chilean society during the past twenty years.

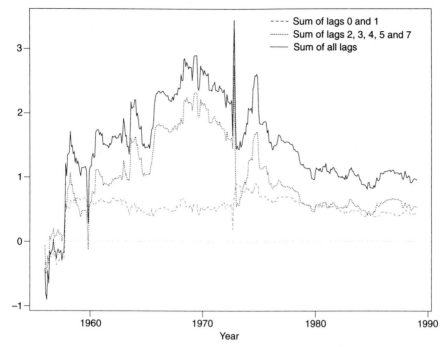

Fig. 6.10   Monthly recursive parameters, inflation on adult deaths, Chile

Conclusions

Our examination of short-term fluctuations of demographic and economic variables in two countries of Latin America has led to some interesting conclusions. From a methodological standpoint, we have seen how using a single OLS regression equation during a period of important demographic and economic transformations has led to spurious results. Monthly data analysis and the use of recursive para-meter estimates have both been proposed to tackle some methodological problems. Both have proved useful, though the interpretation of parameter results has not always been a simple affair.

A still more important finding has been that links between fluctuations in eco-nomic variables and demographic behaviour have proven to be rather tenuous. In our original application of a single regression equation based on annual data, there were few significant results, and the signs of coefficients were not always in agree-ment with the hypothesized relationship. Increased real GDP tended to stimulate fertility and nuptiality initially, but other economic indicators and lags showed contradictory effects. When applying more sophisticated analytical techniques, we were able to perceive the expected ties with considerably greater clarity. Prices had a depressing effect on fertility, especially with an 8–14 month lag. Increased inflation depressed marriages immediately and increased them later, and tended to raise death rates over a period of 6–7 months. In all cases, we found ample, though not conclusive, evidence that some time between the middle of the 1960s and the middle of the 1970s these relations started to converge towards 0.

Real GDP and inflation rates did not always exert a similar influence on demographic behaviour. When we were dealing with demographic variables which are mediated by conscious choice (fertility and nuptiality), patterns were similar before the late 1960s and early 1970s, after which the importance of GDP tended to increase as opposed to that of inflation which diminished drastically. Clearly the value of real GDP as an indicator of living standards, or people's perception of their living standards, is greater than prices, especially in times of strong inflation. With regard to mortality, however, the situation was somewhat different. With yearly equations, both prices and GDP showed unexpected results, and over time the effect of both tended to diminish. When monthly analysis was used, however, price fluctuations proved to have strong positive implications for mortality over a period of at least 6 months. Here too, effects diminished appreciably after the mid-1970s, but were still visible up until very recent times.

Is this a case of modernization, or one of an ill-conceived economic indicator? Here it would seem useful to distinguish between people's perception of their economic situation, and the amount of work and flexibility they must show in order to cope with certain economic realities. We can reasonably expect decision-oriented demographic variables to be based on people's perception of their economic situation, whereas mortality is more directly related to material living conditions, family labour patterns, and the effectiveness of institutional interventions. In the first case, as suggested by our regression results, before the late 1960s both prices and real GDP affected people's perception of their economic well-being in a similar and traditional manner. After that period, however, economic instability tended to render price changes less meaningful for people, as opposed to real GDP (income) whose influence increased. With mortality, prices continued to be a moderately useful indicator because all price changes required certain adaptive mechanisms which affected the wellbeing of families. In other words, even though these adaptive mechanisms may have been successful and people's perception of their economic situation hardly affected, their very existence ended up having implications for very short-term mortality patterns.

Even when a relationship between economic and demographic variables has been shown empirically, the coefficients have been weak and have often not been statistically significant. By the end of the 1970s and during the past decade, a time of ongoing economic instability and of widely changing economic conjunctures, decision-oriented demographic variables showed a modest increase in their sensitivity to fluctuations in income, but not in prices. On the other hand, economic fluctuations showed a noticeable but weak and ever-decreasing influence for mortality. This is a major result, but not a surprising one.

Strong short-term links between economic and demographic fluctuations have appeared in pretransitional populations in which people lived more or less close to subsistence and demographic rates were high. In those societies, strong economic checks on demographic behaviour were essential to the stability of the society. This was not the case in Chile and Argentina during much of the twentieth century. Fertility and mortality were far lower than their pretransitional highs, and average living conditions were relatively satisfactory. As the century advanced, these societies crossed those critical thresholds prevalent in historic societies. In this process of modernization, the degree to which nuptiality and especially fertility were the direct consequence of personal choice was always appreciable and increased substantially. As might well be expected, then, during the past twenty years of economic uncertainty, there has been an increase in the frequency with which people timed their demographic behaviour in order to make it coincide with propitious economic times. Even so, over a period of two or three years, these effects were compensated, and normally ended up having quite small permanent effects. In other words, it was a question of the timing of reproduction rather than its level.

Mortality, however, behaved differently. It too was sensitive to economic realities, but here the element of personal decision was conspicuously absent. Results from the yearly analysis were weak and contradictory; monthly equations showed a strong and expected link over the first few months which has tended to weaken in more recent times. The fact that these links were visible only in the very short term and tended to decline over time is fitting testimony to the fact that living conditions in twentieth-century Argentina and Chile were not extreme by historical standards, and that institutional interventions in favour of public health, parental education, and medical knowledge were more than offsetting with respect to setbacks in living standards. Economic instability and recession may have led to suffering, undernourishment, and poverty, but very seldom to death.

REFERENCES

Banco de Análisis y Computación (1982), *Relevamiento Estadístico de la Economía Argentina (1900–1980)*, Buenos Aires.

—— (1987), *Relevamiento Estadístico de la Economía Argentina (1981–1986)*, Buenos Aires.

Behrman, J. R. (1977), *Macroeconomic Policy in a Developing Country. The Chilean Experience*, Amsterdam: Elsevier-North Holland Press.

Bengtsson, T. and Ohlsson, R. (1985), 'Age-specific mortality and short term changes in the standard of living; Sweden, 1751–1859', *European Journal of Population*, 1/4, 309–26.

Bengtsson, T. (1984), 'Harvest fluctuations and demographic response: Southern Sweden, 1751–1859', in Bengtsson, T., Fridlizius, G., and Ohlsson, R. (eds.), *Preindustrial Population Change*, Stockholm: Almquist and Wiksell, 329–55.

—— (1986), 'Comparisons of population cycles and trends in England, France and Sweden 1751–1860', paper given at the Ninth International Economic History Congress, Bern.

Bravo, J. (1990), 'Fluctuaciones en los indicadores de salud y en la economía chilena, 1960–1986', *Estudios de Economía*, 17/1, Universidad de Chile, Facultad de Ciencias Económicas y Administrativas, Departamento de Economía.

Bravo, J. (1992), 'Economic Crises and Mortality: Short and Medium Term Changes in Latin America', Proceedings of the Conference on the Peopling of the Americas, 3, Veracruz: International Union for the Scientific Study of Population, 439–56.

Box, G. E. P. and Jenkins, G. M. (1976), Time series analysis. Forecasting and control (2nd edition), San Francisco: Holden-Day.

Foxley, A. (1983), Latin American Experiments in Neoconservative Economics, Berkeley: University of California Press.

Galloway, P. R. (1985), 'Annual variations in deaths by age, deaths by cause, prices, and weather in London 1670 to 1830', Population Studies, 39, 487–505.

—— (1986), 'Differentials in demographic responses to annual price variations in pre-revolutionary France. A comparison of rich and poor areas in Rouen, 1681 to 1787', European Journal of Population, 2, 269–305.

—— (1987), Population, Prices, and Weather in Preindustrial Europe, PhD dissertation, Graduate Group in Demography, University of California, Berkeley.

—— (1988), 'Basic patterns in annual variations in fertility, nuptiality, mortality, and prices in pre-industrial Europe', Population Studies, 42, 275–302.

—— (1992), 'Changements séculaires dans la croissance démographique de court terme en Europe, de 1640 à 1909: frein préventif, frein positif et frein de température', in Blanchet, D., Blum, A., and Bonneuil, N. (eds.), Dynamiques et reconstitutions des populations du passé, Paris: Institut National d'Etudes Démographiques/Presses Universitaires de France, 193–240.

Hammel, E. A. (1985), 'Short-term demographic fluctuations in the Croatian military border of Austria, 1830–1847', European Journal of Population, 1/2–3, 265–90.

Harvey, A. C. (1981), Time Series Models, London: Phillip Allan.

Hill, K. and Palloni, A. (1992), 'Demographic responses to economic shocks: The case of Latin America', Proceedings of the Conference on the Peopling of the Americas, 3, Veracruz: International Union for the Scientific Study of Population, 411–38.

Hofman, A. A. (1992), 'International estimates of capital: a 1950–1989 comparison of Latin America and the USA', The Review of Income and Wealth.

Hoyo, J. del and García Ferrer, A. (1988), Análisis y predicción de la población española (1910–2000), Madrid: Fundación de Estudios de Economía Aplicada.

Instituto Nacional de Estadísticas (1981), Series Estadísticas, Santiago de Chile.

Larsen, U. (1990a), 'Short term fluctuations in death by cause, temperature and income in the United States, 1930–1985', Social Biology, 37/3–4, 172–87.

Larsen, U. (1990b), 'The effects of monthly temperature fluctuations on mortality in the United States from 1921 to 1985', International Journal of Biometeorology, 34, 136–45.

Lee, R. D. (1981), 'Short-term variation: vital rates, prices and weather', in Wrigley, E. A. and Schofield, R. S., The Population History of England 1541–1871: A Reconstruction, Cambridge MA: Harvard University Press, 356–401.

—— (1985), 'Population Homeostasis and English Demographic History', Journal of Interdisciplinary History, 15/4, 635–60.

—— (1986), 'Malthus and Boserup: a Dynamic Synthesis', in Coleman, D. and Schofield, R., The State of Population Theory. Forward from Malthus, Oxford: Basil Blackwell, 96–130.

—— (1987), 'Population dynamics of humans and other animals', Demography, 24/2, 443–65.

—— (1992), 'L'autorégulation de la population: systèmes malthusiens en environnement stochastique' in Blanchet, D., Blum, A., and Bonneuil, N. (eds.), Dynamiques et recon-

stitutions des populations du passé, Paris: Institut National d'Etudes Démographiques/ Presses Universitaires de France, 149–74.

—— (1993), 'Methods and models in Macro-Demographic history: An update and assessment', in Reher, D. S. and Schofield, R. S. (eds.), *Old and New Methods in Historical Demography*, Oxford: Oxford University Press.

Livi Bacci, M. (1987), *Popolazione e alimentazione. Saggio sulla storia demográfica europea*, Bologna: Il Mulino.

Mamalakis, N. H. (1980), *Historical Statistics of Chile*. Vol. 2: *Demography and the Labor Force*, Westport, Conn.: Greenwood Press.

McKeown, T. (1976), *The Modern Rise of Population*, London: Edward Arnold.

Ministerio de Asuntos Técnicos (1952), *Síntesis Estadística Mensual de la República Argentina*, Buenos Aires.

Pérez Moreda, V. (1988), 'Respuestas demográficas ante la coyuntura económica en la España rural del Antiguo Régimen', *Boletín de la Asociación de Demografía Histórica*, 6/3.

Post, J. D. (1977), *The Last Great Subsistence Crisis in the Western World*, Baltimore and London: The Johns Hopkins University Press.

Preston, S. (1976), *Mortality Patterns in National Populations with Special Reference to Recorded Causes of Death*, New York: Academic Press.

Reher, D. S. (1990), *Town and Country in Preindustrial Spain. Cuenca, 1550–1870*, Cambridge: Cambridge University Press.

—— (1992a), 'Population et économie dans le Mexique du XVIIIe siècle: Une analyse des fluctuations annuelles', *Population*, 5, 1185–207.

—— (1992b), 'Population Pressure and Living Standards in Late Colonial Mexico', Proceedings of the Conference on the Peopling of the Americas, Veracruz: 1, International Union for the Scientific Study of Population, 447–76.

Richards, T. (1983), 'Weather, nutrition, and the economy: Short-run fluctuations in births, deaths and marriages, France 1740–1909', *Demography*, 20/2, 197–212.

Schofield, R. S. and Reher, D. S., 'The Decline of Mortality in Europe' in Schofield, R., Reher, D., and Bideau, A. (eds.), *The Decline of Mortality in Europe*, Oxford: Oxford University Press, 1–17.

Weir, D. R. (1984), 'Life under pressure: France and England, 1680–1870', *Journal of Economic History*, 44/1, 27–47.

Wilkie, J. W. (ed.) (1974), 'Statistics and National Policy', Supplement 3 to *Statistical Abstract of Latin America (SALA)*, Los Angeles, UCLA Latin America Center.

—— (ed.) (1986), *Statistical Abstract of Latin America (SALA)*, 24, Los Angeles, UCLA Latin America Center.

Wrigley, E. A. and Schofield, R. S., *The Population History of England 1541–1871: A Reconstruction*, Cambridge MA: Harvard University Press.

Young, P. (1984), *Recursive Estimation and Time-Series Analysis. An introduction*, Berlin: Springer-Verlag.

7 Demographic Consequences of Economic Adjustment in Chile

JORGE BRAVO

Introduction

Chile's relatively small population, of some 13 million at around 1990, has somewhat slightly better aggregate economic and social indicators than the average of the Latin American countries. Its per capita GDP in 1990, nearly US$ 2,600,[1] was the fourth largest in the region, and similar to that of Argentina and Mexico. The service sector currently accounts for approximately 60 per cent of the total economic activity, and agriculture for less than 10 per cent. Copper is still a major component of total exports, but the very rapid growth of nontraditional exports since 1984 has reduced to some extent the reliance on mining production as a source of foreign exchange. Well below 10 per cent of the adult population is illiterate, and the country is, together with Argentina, Uruguay, and Venezuela, among the four most highly urbanized in the region. Inequality, however, is no less severe than in Latin America generally: the proportion of the population living in conditions of poverty in 1990 was about 35 per cent (higher than in Argentina, Uruguay and Venezuela), and income distribution became more regressive over the 1970s and 1980s. Demographic indicators display some of the same 'dual' behaviour: moderately low aggregate rates (annual population growth of 1.6 per cent; a TFR of 2.7 children per woman, an infant mortality rate of 17 per one thousand births, life expectancy of 72 years), but significant socio-economic differentials in all of these.

Chile's macroeconomic adjustment process during the last two decades has been widely reviewed, discussed, praised, and criticised by national and foreign scholars, policy makers, and multilateral lending agencies. Detailed studies of this period are found, for example, in Arellano (1988), Corbo *et al.* (1986), Edwards (1986), Foxley (1986), Ffrench-Davis and Raczynski (1987), Ffrench-Davis and Muñoz (1990), Meller (1990, 1991), and Ritter (1990), among others. I will draw heavily from these studies for all discussion on adjustment generally. Like most other countries in the region, Chile has experienced marked macroeconomic swings during the last two decades, associated in part with the international oil crisis in the early

I would like to thank Ricardo Ffrench-Davis, Francisco León, Andrew Mason, and participants at the Ouro Preto Seminar for helpful comments on an earlier draft.

[1] Figure at 1980 prices. *Source*: CEPAL estimates.

to mid-1970s and world recession-*cum*-debt crisis in the early 1980s. These episodes of economic setback were characterized by a deep recession, high unemployment, low wages, high indebtedness levels, and onerous debt servicing. Along with
the other Southern Cone countries Chile made a notable effort to implement structural reforms from around 1974, while authoritarian military regimes were in place,
and, at least on the face of it, was initially successful during the second half of the
1970s, although experiencing a severe crash in 1982. Unlike many other countries,
since the 1982–3 recession Chile has stabilized and experienced persistent overall
economic recovery characterized by rapid export expansion, and currently encoun-
ters no serious external restrictions to future growth. Other distinctive features of
the Chilean adjustment are the intensity and persistency of reforms and policies
oriented toward economic liberalization, deregulation and an outward-looking growth
strategy, which have nonetheless not always been consistently applied. Extraordin-
arily sharp economic fluctuations, and exceedingly high adjustment costs in terms
of aggregate austerity, unemployment and regressive income distribution, are elements that serve to complete the overall macroeconomic picture.

The social consequences of adjustment, including the changes in social policies,
have been studied in a less prolific, but equally interesting literature (see, for
example Arellano 1985; Foxley and Raczynski 1984; Meller 1991; Raczynski 1987).
In addition to the broad macroeconomic reforms, there have been institutional
changes in the country during the last couple of decades that have affected both
the level and the allocation of public and private expenditures in social services:
per capita public expenditures in health, education, and housing have behaved
pro-cyclically and have remained below the 1970 level during most of the last two
decades. This, together with the privatization of a significant part of the health
services and the pension system may have contributed to reinforcing the regressivity
of income distribution within the population. On the other hand, relatively sharp
and increasing focalization of certain public programmes, particularly those related
to child nutrition and health, have had a compensatory effect, and have provided
a partial buffer to the acute economic fluctuations over the last two decades.

Chile is an interesting case to consider from the general economic viewpoint as
carried out a rather extreme experiment in neoliberal transformation, as well as
from the demographic perspective, regarding the behavioural and policy responses
that affect these variables. As discussed in some detail in the remainder of the
chapter, nuptiality has responded quickly and sensitively to economic fluctuations
while fertility, though generally responding to short-term economic changes in the
expected fashion, has done so less pronouncedly, in any case not strongly enough
to reverse the broad declining long-term trend. Nutritional levels, and infant and
adult mortality have on the whole been less sensitive to economic fluctuations, but
some studies have identified specific time periods, diseases and causes of death that
display negative short-term responses. Little is known about the effects on internal
migration patterns and the spatial distribution of the population, mostly because of
the scarcity of appropriate data. Although in general one might expect adjustment
to lead to reduced internal migration because of the overall restriction in job

opportunities, the Chilean adjustment process may have contributed indirectly to increase internal mobility in response to localized job opportunities, as will be explained later.

The remainder of the chapter is organized as follows. A brief overview of the adjustment process is given, highlighting its major phases during the last twenty years. Economic changes, including the evolution of the principal social policies, are then linked to demographic fluctuations, separate sections being devoted to changes in nuptiality, fertility, health conditions and mortality, migration, and spatial distribution. The chapter ends with a summary and conclusion.

Structural Adjustment 1973–90

The military *junta* which seized power in 1973 aimed, in the first place, to reverse many aspects of the Unidad Popular government's strategy of 'transition to social-ism', which had included land reform and the enlargement of the state sector through nationalizations. It also attempted to neutralize the macroeconomic instab-ility that had built up as a consequence of expansionary fiscal and monetary policies, which was aggravated by intense strike activity, disruptions in production, and general political upheaval. A third general orientation that soon emerged from the military government was a switch to externally oriented development, relying internally on a radical version of a free-market, monetarist approach to economic adjustment. Thus commenced one of the most persistent experiments in neoliberal economic transformation within the region, both with respect to the reliance on automatic mechanisms and shock treatments to achieve adjustment, and the struc-tural and institutional changes, including privatization, deregulation of goods and financial markets, opening up to international trade, changes in labour legislation, and major reforms to the social security system and health services.

Analysts generally distinguish three main phases under the military government. The first, 1973–9, defined some of the global economic rules of the new strategy: restoration of market mechanisms by reversing state controls and regulations, reduction of the size of the state by cutting public expenditures, and varied policies aimed at preparing the ground for long-term structural changes, such as the return of expropriated mining companies, agrarian counter-reform, liberalization of im-ports, relaxation of controls on foreign investment, suppression of collective bar-gaining, and curtailment of trade union activities. During the second phase, 1979–82, the open-economy, monetarist approach was followed through more fully. Tariff reductions were completed in 1979, lowered to 10 per cent except for cars, and the nominal exchange rate was fixed, while restrictions to capital flows were reduced substantially. In this context, the exchange rate rose by about 30 per cent between 1979 and 1981 as a result of greater domestic than international inflation. A tem-porary production and consumption boom took place—made possible in part by cheap imports—but finally the cumulative loss of competitiveness combined with external shocks and policy mismanagement led to the 1982–3 recession, one of the

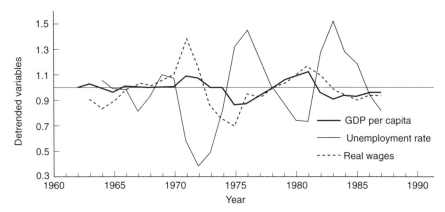

Fig. 7.1 Economic fluctuations, Chile, 1960–90

Note: Detrending is achieved by dividing each obervation point by a 9-year centred moving average.

Source: Table 7.1.

worst crises in Chilean history. Important reforms to the social security system, to expand private health and educational services were launched within this period. The third phase, 1983–9, was a period of adjustment and recovery aided by three multilateral adjustment programmes supported mainly by the IMF and the World Bank. Loans from multilateral lending agencies represented 3–4 per cent of GDP over a period of five years, and provided a consistent and orderly macroeconomic programme, which was a clear improvement on the chaotic policies of 1982. Subsequently the economy recovered, but the adjustment process during the 1980s imposed heavy costs in terms of high unemployment, salary contraction, and worsening income distribution.

How macro adjustment and the associated policies translated into some basic economic indicators is illustrated in Figure 7.1, where the short-term fluctuations[2] of per capita GDP, the unemployment rate and real wages are displayed. They show the main economic cycles during the period under study: sharp real wage reduction and increase in unemployment from the early 1970s until one year after the severe 1975 recession; and a reversal of these trends during the period of the 'economic miracle' (1976–81). Real wages fall again together with per capita GDP during the 1982–3 recession while unemployment climbs again, to reach 30 per cent of the labour force (see Table 7.1). Gradual but persistent recovery sets in after 1983.

Throughout the entire period, social policies generally evolved in the direction of cutting back the total volume of public expenditures, while concentrating these

[2] Short-term fluctuations in Figures 7.1 and 7.2 are represented by the value of each observation point divided by a nine-year centred moving average.

Table 7.1 Economic and demographic time series, Chile, 1960–91

Year	GDP per capita (1980 US$)	Unemployment rate (%)	Real wages (1970 = 100)	Public expenditure per capita (1970 = 100) Health	Education	Crude marriage rate	Crude birth rate	Infant Mortality rate	Live births by order 1	2	3	4
1960	1.768	7.1	64.5			7.3	37.5	119.5	60,772	45,515	38,983	113,108
1961	1.791	8.0	69.0			7.4	38.0	106.4	61,737	47,196	39,872	118,995
1962	1.844	7.9	69.0			6.9	37.9	109.2	63,532	48,198	40,582	120,444
1963	1.937	7.5	61.3			6.9	37.4	100.3	62,987	49,073	39,422	123,676
1964	1.909	7.0	59.6			7.2	36.2	103.7	62,767	49,966	39,240	121,480
1965	1.888	6.4	66.5			7.6	35.2	97.3	66,414	49,815	38,659	119,021
1966	2.024	6.1	77.2			7.5	33.6	98.5	68,194	50,470	37,227	111,931
1967	2.052	4.7	86.3			7.3	30.5	94.7	70,437	50,490	35,312	102,994
1968	2.086	4.9	88.9			7.2	28.7	87.0	70,402	50,915	34,349	93,067
1969	2.116	5.5	94.1			7.2	27.0	83.1	71,663	51,429	33,565	82,832
1970	2.121	5.7	100.0	100.0	100.0	7.5	26.4	82.2	74,183	53,232	33,870	76,866
1971	2.266	3.8	122.9			8.8	27.0	73.9	78,795	56,191	35,852	75,499
1972	2.203	3.1	102.5			8.7	27.4	72.7	85,320	59,659	36,935	72,622
1973	2.052	4.8	76.5			8.3	26.8	65.8	87,931	60,760	36,703	68,167
1974	2.052	9.2	66.3	86.6	79.9	7.8	25.9	65.2	85,164	62,231	36,833	64,890

1975	1.769	16.4	60.2	67.1	63.2	7.4	24.2	57.6	84,135	59,768	35,051	57,516
1976	1.806	19.9	81.5	62.7	67.6	7.0	23.0	56.6	83,974	57,822	34,021	51,759
1977	1.939	18.6	81.7	67.8	78.9	7.0	21.4	50.1	83,188	56,261	31,831	44,006
1978	2.059	17.9	90.4	75.0	83.0	7.2	21.3	40.1	87,585	58,207	31,369	39,866
1979	2.188	17.7	98.0	73.8	90.8	7.3	21.4	37.9	90,116	60,574	32,551	38,103
1980	2.315	15.7	108.9	82.4	88.7	7.7	22.2	33.0	95,289	65,100	35,197	37,221
1981	2.411	15.6	119.3	74.8	96.7	8.0	23.4	27.0	101,068	70,909	38,939	39,221
1982	2.073	26.4	114.7	80.1	114.8	7.0	23.8	23.6	99,468	74,446	41,659	40,930
1983	2.012	30.4	102.9	63.8	99.2	7.0	22.2	21.9	93,634	71,797	40,284	37,997
1984	2.089	24.4	101.8	67.2	94.5	7.3	22.2	19.6	98,111	75,425	40,966	37,263
1985	2.100	21.4	96.6	64.7	92.0	7.5	21.6	19.5	99,053	72,689	40,990	34,598
1986	2.184	16.0	99.5	63.4	89.4	7.6	22.1	19.1	105,803	74,932	42,219	34,841
1987	2.270	12.2	100.3	68.8	86.8	7.6	22.3	18.5	108,916	78,073	42,980	34,225
1988	2.399	9.0	106.1			8.1	23.3	18.9	115,675	83,346	46,018	35,250
1989	2.590	6.3	109.6			8.0	23.4	17.1	118,413	86,489	47,467	34,841
1990	2.598	6.0	111.6			7.5	23.3	16.0				
1991	2.754	6.5	117.1				23.3					

Sources: Per capita GDP: estimates by ECLAC; unemployment rate, real wages, per capita public expenditures: CIEPLAN, Resultados Económicos de Cuatro Gobiernos Chilenos, 1958–1989. Apuntes CIEPLAN No. 89, Octubre 1990, updated with data from CIEPLAN, Set de Estadísticas Económicas No. 93, July de 1992; crude marriage rate, birth rate, infant mortality rate, live births by order: Instituto Nacional de Estadísticas, Anuario Demografía, several years.

reduced funds in particular programmes. This occurred, however, after significant advances in social policies originating early in the century had already been achieved, which meant that there was broad coverage of many social services, such as basic education, housing, social security, and access to basic health care. By 1970, Chile had one of the least unequal income distributions in the Latin American region; public social expenditures represented nearly 20 per cent of GDP and continued to grow under the Unidad Popular government. This initial base, together with the expenditure reallocation, provided an effective—though partial—insulation against economic downturns. At the same time, during the military regime legislation was enacted which gave the private sector a much more important role in the provision of health, social security, and education. Privatization in this sphere had counter-acting effects on the strength of the social service buffer: it has relieved some of the state's burden of providing these services, but has created a transitional public deficit due to the continuation of public pension outlays coinciding with the drastic reduction of public social security contributions induced by the reform. Far from leading to greater equity with regard to access to social services, privatization has accentuated the segregation of the middle–low and the low-income segments of the population.

Data and Method of Analysis

The following sections discuss the relationships between the changes in some basic demographic variables and economic fluctuations. The possible effects of structural adjustment, including the mediating role of social policies, are examined. The demographic data consist of the annual series of nuptiality, births (total and by birth order), and infant mortality rates from civil registration records, from 1956 to 1991. The real GDP data cover the same time period while the unemployment series starts in 1960. The data sources are noted at the bottom of Table 7.1. The choice of the period of the last three and a half decades is a compromise between: 1) focusing attention on the recent past, during which structural adjustment has taken place; 2) fixing a time period in which the underlying structure of the statistical models is likely to be reasonably stable and during which the economic indicators are consistently measured; and 3) the requirement of a sample size sufficient to make statistical inferences.

The statistical method used is of the type developed by Lee (1981; 1990) and Galloway (1988), which have been widely applied to the analysis of short-term demographic fluctuations. Most of these applications have been for countries out-side the region, though recently a number studies using Latin American data have been carried out (for example, Reher 1989; Ortega-Orsona and Reher, Chapter 6 above; Bravo 1992; Hill and Palloni, 1992; Palloni and Hill, Chapter 5 below).[3]

---

[3] Raúl Prebisch pioneered demographic short-term analyses in the Latin American region with a study published in 1927, which of course did not make use of modern statistical methods. However, he employed the currently standard detrending procedure, and used graphical analysis to examine the responses (see the Special Issue of *Notas de Población*, 19/54, 1991).

Among the many possible variations of the basic method, I have specified one of the simplest versions of a distributed lag model with lags from 0 to 3 years, including a correction for first-order serial correlation. The nine-year [centred] moving average used for detrending is sufficiently flexible and coincides closely with other parametric functions that may be used instead (such as logistics, polynomials of time) over the time range in which they overlap. For some variables, like infant mortality, the deviations from the moving average differ somewhat at the end of the time period from those obtained on the basis of a logistic trend, but the effect on the regression results is minimal. Dummy variables were introduced at a later stage to distinguish two main sub-periods as well as crisis episodes, and to allow for possible asymmetries in the demographic responses. Table 7.2 contains precise expressions of the estimated models.

Marriage Patterns

The annual marriage rate is the variable that has displayed the greatest variability of all crude rates shown in Figure 7.2. Also, it is the one that shows the most consistent and close association with economic fluctuations, as measured by any of the variables represented in Figure 7.1. Table 7.2 reports the distributed lag elasticities; the estimates are based on relatively few observations (between thirty-two and thirty-six, minus those required by detrending and lagging), but are none the less sufficient to make statistical inferences. The response of nuptiality to economic swings has been immediate, and the sharpest among the dependent demographic variables, with lag 0 elasticity of 0.64 with respect to GDP and −0.21 with respect to unemployment. It is noteworthy that in certain cases, the movements in nuptiality have *anticipated* economic changes; for example, in the late 1960s marriages started to increase one year earlier than per capita income. This may well be related to the favourable expectations of young couples regarding improvements in employment opportunities, salaries, and social benefits, which were conspicuous in the political manifestos for the 1970 presidential elections, and in fact materialized to a large extent during the first couple of years of the Unidad Popular government. The marriage rate then started to fall sharply in 1973, well before the 1975 recession. This is likely to have been affected by the environment of political upheaval, repression, and uncertainty that followed the military coup, and possibly also by the reversal of the aforementioned expectations of the previous period. The immediate reaction of nuptiality to the 1982 recession and to recovery, starting in 1984, is also striking.

Since all age groups reacted in a similar fashion, the age composition of those who married remained fairly constant, and therefore no large fluctuations are detected in the period mean age at first marriage, which remains around 23.5 for women and 25.8 for men.[4] It seems that couples do postpone the timing of marriage

---

[4] Slightly different estimates are obtained by applying Hajnal's singulate mean age method to census data, but both sources coincide in showing the relative stability of age at first marriage.

Table 7.2 Basic regression results, Chile, 1960–91

	NUP	CBR	IMR	$BORD_1$	$BORD_2$	$BORD_3$	$BORD_4$

Model A: $Y_t = C + \sum\limits_{i=0}^{3}\alpha_i GDP_{t-1} + \phi \cdot \mu_{t-1} + \varepsilon_t$

	NUP	CBR	IMR	$BORD_1$	$BORD_2$	$BORD_3$	$BORD_4$
Constant	0.29	0.17	1.22**	0.36*	0.05	0.05	0.06
Lag: 0	0.64**	0.16	0.02	0.22*	0.13	0.07	−0.01
1	0.06	0.27**	−0.20	0.32**	0.33**	0.28**	0.23*
2	0.05	0.24**	−0.06	0.09	0.16*	0.30**	0.32**
3	−0.04	0.16	−0.03	0.00	0.33**	0.30**	0.38**
ø	0.48**	0.66**	0.57**	0.45*	0.41	0.56**	0.67**
R^2	0.63	0.77	0.38	0.71	0.85	0.83	0.81
Adj R^2	0.52	0.70	0.20	0.62	0.80	0.77	0.74
Durbin–Watson	1.37	1.53	2.15	1.74	2.08	1.54	1.85

Model B: $Y_t = C + \sum\limits_{i=0}^{3}\alpha_i UR_{t-1} + \phi \cdot \mu_{t-1} + \varepsilon_t$

	NUP	CBR	IMR	$BORD_1$	$BORD_2$	$BORD_3$	$BORD_4$
Constant	1.23	1.23**	0.97	1.18**	1.23**	1.24**	1.20**
Lag: 0	−0.21**	−0.08**	0.02	−0.11**	−0.07**	−0.06**	−0.05
1	0.02	−0.05**	−0.02	−0.03**	−0.06**	−0.05**	−0.04
2	0.00	−0.03	0.01	−0.02	−0.03	−0.05*	−0.05
3	−0.04	−0.07**	−0.01	0.02	−0.07**	−0.08**	−0.08**
φ	0.17	0.67**	0.60**	0.51**	0.67	0.70**	0.61**
R^2	0.77	0.79	0.36	0.80	0.80	0.79	0.75
Adj R^2	0.70	0.74	0.17	0.74	0.74	0.72	0.67
Durbin–Watson	1.10	1.39	2.13	2.00	2.01	1.52	1.52

* $5\% < p \le 10\%$.

** $p \le 5\%$

Variables: NUP = nuptiality (crude marriage rate); CBR = crude birth rate; IMR = infant mortality rate; BORD*i* = births of order *i* (*i* = 1, 2, 3, 4+); GDP = per capita GDP (1980 US$); UR = unemployment rate; W = real wages (constant 1970 pesos).

Note: For the data sources, see Table 7.1. In all models, Y_t represents the dependent variables at time *t*, the α's the elasticity coefficients, u_t a first-order, serially correlated error term, and ε_t a constant variance, serially uncorrelated disturbance. The estimation used the Cochrane-Orcutt iterative procedure.

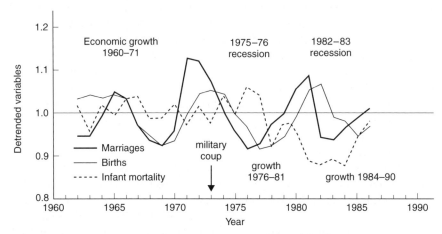

Fig. 7.2 Fluctuations in marriages, births, and infant mortality, Chile, 1960–90
Note: Detrending is achieved by dividing each obervation point by a 9-year centred moving average.
Source: Table 7.1.

in response to adverse economic conditions, but since marriage rates rise quickly once signs of economic recovery are perceived, the ultimate life cycle effect of the observed short-term changes is likely to be small. The overall extent and the age patterns of celibacy observed in census data have remained stable since the 1950s.

Fertility

The crude birth rate (births per thousand persons) has also changed in close association with economic cycles, although its response seems more delayed and less acute by comparison with that of nuptiality. The first large drop in the crude birth rate occurred during the 1960s, was interrupted temporarily during the years that the Unidad Popular government was in power, and has fluctuated below 25 per thousand since. The estimated lag structure suggests that births tend to respond positively to changes in GDP with 1–2 years of lag, and negatively to the unemployment rate with lags of 0–1 year. First births react more quickly (0–1 year lag) than higher order births, whose response is more evenly spread out over the 3-year lag period. This is likely to be in part a reflection of a genuine volitional reaction—couples respond more slowly to economic changes when deciding on higher order births—and partly a reflection of the fact that it takes some time before an increase in first order births translates into a larger number of women likely to give birth to higher order children.

  Might these types of 'denominator effects' be so strong as to distort the interpretation of the foregoing results?[5] These kinds of effects arise in the analysis of all demographic events, but in the case of births by order they are likely to be more important than when *total* births, deaths, and marriages are analysed (where they are generally negligible), because the denominators themselves are relatively small and are comparatively more sensitive to changes in births by order. In the present context, the absence of 'rebounds' in the value of elasticities across lags suggests that denominator effects are not of great quantitative import. A much more direct indication of this is the fact that parity progression ratios—estimated on the basis of the same data for the more limited period 1960–1984 (Solsona 1985)—are highly correlated with births by order.[6] Also, the responses of the progression ratios are qualitatively similar to those of the birth counts (results not shown).

The behaviour of first births is associated, in part, with the contemporary response of first marriages, but such a concentrated response at lag 0 can be fully explained only if premarital conceptions and births are considered. In fact, illegitimacy—a phenomenon highly concentrated in first births—has increased substantially in Chile over the last twenty years and represents now about one third of all births, this percentage being larger among adolescents and young adult mothers. As in the case of the age at first marriage, the average age of women at first birth has remained fairly constant (around 23.5 years) over the last few decades, but spacing is now more spread out: whereas in the 1960s second and third births followed after an average of two years, currently the spacing has increased to about three years. This is associated not only with postponement behaviour, but also with stopping at lower average parities than before; as seen in Figure 7.3, fourth and higher order births have declined even in absolute terms over the last thirty years.

Nutrition and Mortality

Chile's history of governmental intervention in the health sector stretches back to the 1920s. Programmes for the control and maintenance of minimum nutritional levels among infants and young children have been particularly successful, both in terms of reducing the prevalence of undernutrition among children under six years of age and as an effective buffer against extreme economic fluctuations and adjustment. These programmes are among the most frequently cited examples of successful focalization (World Bank 1988: 28–32). As shown in a previous study (Bravo 1990), the short-term fluctuations in infant nutrition and mortality have been linked to short-term economic changes during periods of economic crisis, though their

---

[5] In general, the changes of births of a given order k at any time t are determined not only by the contemporaneous behavioural relation between births and economic fluctuations, but also by the variations in the number of women at risk of bearing k-order births, i.e. the number of fecund women of parity $k - 1$ at t. This is, in turn, a function of births of order $\leq k$ at instants prior to t. For example, an increase in first births reduces the pool of women likely to bear a first child immediately and increases the number of women likely to bear a second child subsequently.

[6] The correlation coefficients between detrended births of order 1, 2, 3, and 4+ and the detrended progression ratios to those parities are 0.99, 0.67, 0.89, and 0.67, respectively.

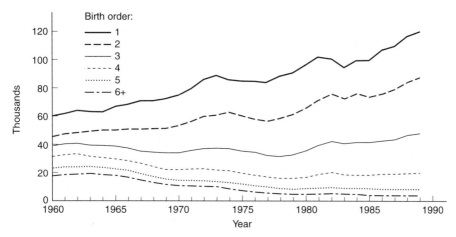

Fig. 7.3 Live births by order, Chile, 1960–90
Source: Table 7.1.

absolute variations have been very moderate by any standard. Table 7.2 confirms the result of small and nonsignificant effects of either GDP or the unemployment rate on infant mortality. The coefficients have the expected signs, although they differ with respect to previous findings on non-infant mortality in that no clear evidence of rebound effects is found here; in fact, the lag distribution is more like the European median pattern (Lee 1990: Figure I). Health checkups and food provided through the national programme of complementary feeding (PNAC) together constitute one of the few items of social public expenditure that has not been permitted to change passively in a procyclical fashion. This programme has therefore lessened the intensity of infant and child mortality responses, and has probably affected the shape of the lag pattern as well.

The insulation of infant mortality to the severe recent crises has been a subject of much debate; the conclusions that have emerged suggest that improved access to primary health care, the effective focalization of resources in these programmes, increasingly broad access to basic sanitary services, including piped water and sewerage, as well as better education of mothers and behavioural demographic responses (that is, reductions in high-risk births) are all factors that contribute to insulation (see Bravo 1990; 1992; and references therein).

The effects on morbidity and mortality are not easy to detect since some of the factors associated with health risks do not change significantly during crisis episodes (education, basic sanitary infrastructure, and hygienic conditions), and therefore only large fluctuations in income are likely to have an effect on mortality. One recent study (Bravo and Vargas 1991) found that while most diseases and causes of death continued their historical declining trend during the 1980s, there were some that displayed significant decelerations in their mortality rates, such as certain diseases related to the digestive tract (enteritis, typhoid fever, hepatitis) and some respiratory infections such as pneumonia, a very frequent cause of death by comparison with other countries with similar levels of life expectancy. Influenza, hepatitis, and whooping cough mortality rates have responded moderately but negatively to economic fluctuations.

Discussion

The total response (measured by the lag sum of the estimated elasticities) of the demographic variables examined thus far, provide a means of summarizing and comparing the results discussed in greater detail in the previous sections. Figure 7.4 displays the lag sum of the elasticities of marriages, births, and infant mortality with respect to per capita GDP and the unemployment rate, that is, the predicted cumulative effect on a dependent variable of a permanent 1 per cent change in each independent variable.

The general conclusion that infant mortality is more immune to economic fluctuations than are nuptiality and fertility is confirmed once more in these graphs. The three variables seem to have become less sensitive with respect to changes in unemployment from 1975 onwards (the 'adjustment' period), although the difference is statistically significant only in the case of nuptiality. On the other hand, the overall magnitude of the response to GDP fluctuations remains the same for marriages and births, and becomes more negative in the case of infant mortality. This is also in agreement with the regression results reported in Table 7.2. But how may the differential demographic reaction to the two economic variables be accounted for? One possible—and admittedly partial—explanation of these results takes into account the fact that the fluctuations in GDP not only reflect current income but also affect overall expectations about the future evolution of the economy, which are likely to be important for decision-making about marriage and fertility; some evidence indicative of this phenomenon was presented in previous sections with regard to nuptiality. In the case of Chile, fluctuations in GDP are also closely related to the provision of social services, which have an effect on living standards beyond that of labour earnings, as proxied by the unemployment rate. With reference to infant mortality, structural adjustment strategies induced a retrenchment of governmental intervention in the health sector, and pro-cyclical behaviour in terms of health expenditure, which tends to intensify any effect that recessions have on labour income. Although the *quantum* of food and health services provided through the public health system did not suffer in the same proportion, there are unequivocal indications that their quality deteriorated during a significant portion of the adjustment period.

Finally, dummy variables were introduced in the basic regression equations to explore the possible differences of elasticities during economic upswings and during downswings, and to test whether the two most acute recessionary episodes (those of 1975–6 and 1982–3) implied responses different from those of less extraordinary fluctuations (regression results not shown). The total responses turn out

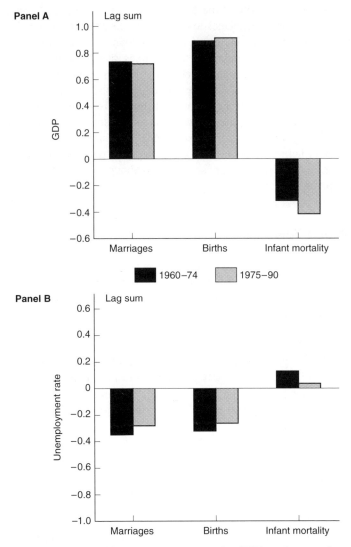

Fig. 7.4 Total response with respect to per capita GDP and unemployment rate
* indicates that the differences in coefficients for 1960–74 and 1975–90 is statistically significant at the 5 per cent level.

Source: Author's calculations, on the basis of data in Table 7.1.

to be fairly symmetrical—the same for economic expansions and contractions—except for the reaction of marriages to declines in unemployment, which is slightly larger than the response to increases in unemployment. An informal, common-sense interpretation of this finding is that couples seem slightly more optimistic when reacting to positive economic changes than they are pessimistic in their reaction to unfavourable ones. The demographic responses during the aforementioned crisis episodes are not significantly different from those during non-crisis periods, again with one exception, namely the total response of infant mortality to GDP, which is slightly larger for crisis periods. This finding is consistent with—and may in fact help to explain—the larger negative response of the infant mortality rate during the adjustment phase discussed above, since both crises took place within this period.

Migration and Spatial Distribution

No time series comparable to those of marriages and vital events that come from civil registers are available to follow through year by year the evolution of migration and the spatial distribution of the population; the available data in this case come from population censuses and special purpose studies. Despite the fragmentary nature of the evidence, some general observations can be made on this topic: available studies (for example, Raczynski 1986; Chang and Garrido 1989; Szasz 1992) coincide in suggesting that (a) there are signs of increasing internal mobility; (b) given that Chile is already highly urbanized, most of the recent migration flows occur between cities; and (c) the historical female dominance of migration to Santiago has given way to a virtual balance in the sex ratio of migrants, who are now more frequently of urban origin.

Structural adjustment may have affected migration and spatial distribution patterns in two main ways. First, economic downturns and the reductions in government spending and employment led to 'terciarization' and informalization of the labour market, especially among women and secondary income earners. Since fluctuations in open unemployment were more acute in large cities, particularly in Santiago, these have lost some of their traditional attractive force, and migration between intermediate-sized cities has been revitalized in response to local economic conditions. Short-term movements associated with seasonal and other temporary phenomena, such as those that followed the recent mining boom in the north or the increasing importance of temporary agricultural workers residing in cities (León 1991), have apparently become more common. These types of movement are facilitated by the improved overall communications (mainly television, telephone, air travel, and to a lesser extent, roads), stimulated in no small part by the growth of primary and semi-manufactured exports starting around the mid-1980s, which were (and continue to be) a key component of adjustment and growth strategies.

Secondly, the regional distribution of per capita social public expenditures favoured systematically the extreme northern and extreme southern regions, and to a lesser extent, the metropolitan region of Santiago. At the same time, the extreme regions have gained population and have experienced the largest positive in-migration flows. The association between the two is not casual: per capita public expenditure emerges as one of the most consistent attraction factors of interregional migration, in both bivariate and multivariate analyses (Chang and Garrido 1989). On the other hand, intraregional inequality has been lessened to some extent by a reorientation of resources toward basic education and primary health care (Raczynski 1986), mirroring the focalization of certain social programmes at the national level.

Summary and Conclusion

Although adjustment in Chile can be judged as successful in terms of some basic macro-indicators, the burden of the external adjustment during the last two decades was supported internally by a prolonged pressure on the labour market, leading to increasing inequality, instability, depressed real wages, and high open unemployment rates. The costs of adjustment during the 1980s were high, exceeding the requirements for closing the gap between aggregate income and expenditures and for accommoding the needed external transfers. Social expenditures, instead of being compensatory, in general behaved in a pro-cyclical fashion, and remained below the real per capita levels that prevailed at the beginning of the 1970s and throughout most of the adjustment period.

The repercussions on demographic variables have been most noticeable regarding nuptiality and fertility. Marriages tend to react contemporaneously with—and sometimes even in anticipation of—economic changes, but no important long-term effects on celibacy are detected. The fluctuations in births are mainly due to variations in first to third order births, since higher order births show a smooth declining trend during the last two decades. Health conditions, as represented by nutrition, morbidity, and mortality statistics have been less affected by the aggregate economic fluctuations and adjustment, partly due to the existence of nutritional programmes for children, and the focalization of governmental policies regarding mother and child health care. On the other hand, infant mortality and deaths due to specific causes have been negatively affected in the short term during some periods of economic setback, specially the crises episodes that occurred during the more recent 'adjustment' period. As regards internal migration and spatial distribution, fragmentary evidence suggests that short-term movements associated with seasonal and other temporary phenomena may have been facilitated by the improved overall communications, which was stimulated in part by the growth of nontraditional exports starting around the 1980s. There are some potentially important longer-term consequences of structural adjustment reforms, such as changes in the social security system, and the privatization of health and education, which have not been analysed here.

The Chilean experience suggests that the heavy costs of unemployment and increasing inequality could have been lessened, both at the level of macro-stabilization policies and of economic reforms, and via compensatory social policies and programmes. The few public programmes that were not allowed to contract passively during adjustment (nutritional and maternal and child health care) serve to illustrate the point. Furthermore, the favourable starting point helped to attenuate the demographic responses: the country initiated structural reforms and adjustment at a time when there was a broad coverage of many basic social services. In the future, however, continued improvement in living conditions will require a recovery of investment in the social sectors, which deteriorated substantially during the adjustment period.

REFERENCES

Arellano, J. P. (1985), *Políticas Sociales y Desarrollo. Chile 1924–1984*, Santiago: CIEPLAN.

Arellano, J. P. (1988), 'Crisis y recuperación económica en Chile en los años 80', *Colección Estudios CIEPLAN*, 24, 5–26.

Bravo, J. (1990), 'Fluctuaciones en los indicadores de salud y en la economía chilena, 1960–1986', *Estudios de Economía*, 17/1, University of Chile, Faculty of Economic and Administrative Sciences, Department of Economics.

—— (1992), 'Economic Crises and Mortality: Short and Medium Term Changes in Latin America', Proceedings of the Conference on the Peopling of the Americas, 3, Veracruz: International Union for the Scientific Study of Population, 439–56.

—— and Vargas, N. (1991), 'Trends and fluctuations in morbidity and mortality by certain causes and in economic activity: Costa Rica, Chile and Guatemala, 1960–1986', *Notas de Población*, 19/53, 117–46, Santiago.

Chang, I. and Garrido, S. (1989), *Migración y desigualdades especiales: el caso chileno*, Santiago: CELADE.

Corbo, V. *et al.* (1986), 'What went wrong with the recent reforms in the southern cone?' *Economic Development and Cultural Change*, 34/3 (April 1986), 607–40.

Edwards, S. (1986), 'Monetarism in Chile, 1973–1983: some economic puzzles', *Economic Development and Cultural Change*, 34/3 (April 1986), 535–60.

Ffrench-Davis, R. and Raczynski, D. (1987), 'The impact of global recession on living standards', *Notas Técnicas*, 97 (3rd edition), CIEPLAN.

—— and Muñoz, O. (1990) 'Desarrollo económico, inestabilidad y desiquilibrios políticos en Chile: 1950–89', *Colección Estudios CIEPLAN*, 28 (June 1990).

Foxley, A. (1986), 'The neoconservative economic experiment in Chile', in Valenzuela, S. and Valenzuela, A. (eds.), *Military rule in Chile: dictatorship and opposition*, Baltimore: John Hopkins University Press, 13–50.

—— and Raczynski, D. (1984), 'Los grupos vulnerables en la recesión: la situación de la infancia y la juventud en Chile', in Jolly, R. and Cornia, G. (eds.), *Efectos de la recesión mundial sobre la infancia*, Siglo XXI Editores, 97–133.

Galloway, P. (1988), 'Basic patterns in annual variations in fertility, nuptiality, mortality and prices in pre-industrial Europe', *Population Studies*, 24/2, 275–303.

Hill, K. and Palloni, A. (1992), 'Demographic Responses to Economic Shocks: The Case of Latin America', Proceedings of the Conference on the Peopling of the Americas, 3, Veracruz: International Union for the Scientific Study of Population, 411–38.

INE (1989), *La transición de la fecundidad en Chile, 1950–1985*, Facsimile F/CHI.7, Instituto Nacional de Estadísticas, Santiago.

Lee, R. D. (1981), 'Short-run fluctuations of vital rates, prices and weather in England, 1539 to 1840', in Wrigley, E. A. and Schofield, R. (eds.), *The Population History of England, 1541–1871: A Reconstruction*, Cambridge, Mass: Harvard University Press, 356–401.

—— (1990), 'La reacción demográfica ante las crisis económicas en poblaciones históricas y contemporáneas', *Boletín de Población de las Naciones Unidas*, 29, ST/ESA/SER.N/29, New York: United Nations.

León, F. (1991), *El empleo temporal en la agricultura chilena, 1976–1990: síntesis y conclusiones*, Santiago: CELADE.

Meller, P. (1990), 'Revisión del proceso de Ajuste Chileno de la década del 80', *Colección Estudios CIEPLAN*, 30 (December), 5–54.

—— (1991), 'Adjustment and social costs in Chile during the 1980s', *World Development*, 19/11 (Special issue, November) 1545–661.

Ortega-Orsona, J. and Reher, D. (1992), 'Short-term Economic Fluctuations and Demographic Behaviour: Some Examples from Twentieth-Century South America', Chapter 6, above.

Palloni, A. and Hill, K., 'The Effect of Economic Changes on Mortality by Age and Cause: Latin America, 1950–90', Chapter 5 above.

Prebisch, R. (1991), 'Anotaciones Demográficas', in *Notas de Población*, Special issue in honour of Dr Raúl Prebisch, 19/45, Santiago: CELADE.

Raczynski, D. (1986), 'La regionalización y la política económico-social del régimen militar: el impacto regional', *Notas Técnicas*, 84 (July), CIEPLAN.

—— (1987), 'Política social, pobreza y grupos vulnerables: La infancia en Chile', in Cornia, G. *et al.* (eds.), *Ajuste con Rostro Humano*, 2, Siglo XXI Editores, 69–118.

Reher, D. (1989), 'Coyuntaras económicas y fluctuaciones, demográficas en México durante el siglo XVIII', in História e População, São Pauto: ABEP, 276–88.

Ritter, A. (1990), 'Development strategy and structural adjustment in Chile, 1973–90', *Canadian Journal of Latin American and Caribbean Studies*, 15/30, 159–96.

Solsona, M. (1985), *Fecundidad y tamaño de familia en Chile, 1960–1984*, Masters thesis, Programa de Maestría, CELADE, Santiago.

Szasz, I. (1992), *Mujeres inmigrantes en el mercado de trabajo de Santiago: El impacto de la transformación productiva*, unpublished manuscript, CELADE, Santiago.

Taucher, E. (1989), 'Behavioural factors in demographic responses to economic crises', paper presented at the 21st IUSSP International Conference, New Delhi, 20–27 September, 1989.

World Bank (1988), *Targeted Programs for the poor during structural adjustment. A summary of a symposium on Poverty and Adjustment*, April 1988, Washington, DC.

8 Demographic Consequences of Structural Adjustment: *The Case of Brazil*

EDUARDO RIOS-NETO AND JOSÉ ALBERTO MAGNO DE CARVALHO

Introduction

The Brazilian economy has experienced numerous economic cycles during this century. These have occurred in the larger context of an expansionary secular trend marked by different phases of industrialization and economic development. Although the century has witnessed several periods of 'stabilization crises'—the slowdown of economic activity induced by anti-inflationary policies—it has been, on the whole, a century characterized by industrialization and economic development.

Although the interactions between population and the economy can be studied both in the short and in the long run, the short-term analysis pursued here has the advantage that the relations can be evaluated without ambiguity with respect to the possibility of reverse causality, something that cannot be controlled for in the long-term studies. One classical theoretical framework, well suited to the analysis of the impact of annual fluctuations in the vital rates, is the Malthusian model. This framework postulates a positive check whereby real wages and mortality are negatively associated, and a preventive check that implies a positive correlation between real wages and fertility. The Malthusian framework was first applied to the study of short-term fluctuations in pre-industrial Europe (Lee 1981; Galloway 1985; 1986; 1988; and others). This chapter intends to apply the Malthusian framework to the study of short-term fluctuations in the contemporary reality of a developing country, in order to assess the demographic consequences of crises and structural adjustments in modern Brazil. In this contemporary context, other economic variables in addition to price fluctuations are included in the model, such as aggregate production and the unemployment rate.

An important confounding factor in assessing the impact on annual variations of demographic variables is the fact that several authors fail to distinguish trends from deviations around the trend. The demographic literature deals with short-term and cyclical fluctuations in at least three different contexts: the pre-industrial era, the demographic transition, and the post-transitional context where cyclical fluctuations such as the one found in the post-war baby boom are examined. In transitional

The authors gratefully acknowledge the editorial assistance of Franklin Goza, and the technical support of Marcelo Pianetti, Bruno Golgher, Letícia Marteleto, and Felipe Pianetti. Antônio Marangoni kindly provided us with the vital registration data for São Paulo.

societies such as twentieth-century Brazil, it is particularly important to implement an appropriate detrending procedure to isolate the short-term responses.

In this chapter, we study the case of twentieth-century Brazil, focusing on the impact of economic variables on the annual variations of vital rates. We give particular attention to the impact of post-war stabilization policies and structural adjustment on the fluctuations of marriages, births, and deaths. In the next section we review the literature dealing with the evolution of vital rates in Brazil and São Paulo, with special emphasis on the historical process and the structural adjustment of the 1980s. In the third section we review the literature on the determinants of short-term fluctuation on vital rates in the pre-industrial and Latin American settings. In the final section, we use time series analyses to evaluate the impact of annual variations in real minimum wages, and real gross domestic product on vital rates (marriages, births, and deaths).

We conclude that the empirical analysis derived from the Malthusian framework can be applied to the study of short-term fluctuations in Brazil, with some qualifications. The impact of variations in real minimum wages on vital rates are of the expected order, although the magnitude of these impacts tends to be more important for infant mortality than for marriages and births. The impacts on vital rates caused by annual variations in gross domestic product (GDP) are of much larger magnitude. GDP affects marriages and births in a procyclical direction, which is coherent with the Malthusian preventive check framework. Unexpectedly, though, GDP also affects infant mortality rate and adult deaths positively in some specifications, which is not coherent with the Malthusian positive check framework.

Economic Performance and Vital Rates in Brazil: A Review

We examine the impact on vital rates caused by the short-term economic fluctuations observed in the city of São Paulo during the twentieth century, focusing on the economic cycles during the most recent period of structural adjustment. As happens in other Latin American countries, many of the analyses that stress the impact of social and economic development on vital rates fail to separate the determinants of trends from those of fluctuations around these trends. Our empirical work is on the *deviations* of vital rates from their medium-term trends for the reasons to be explained shortly.

In the next section we review the literature that deals with the evolution of vital rates in Brazil and in São Paulo during this century in relation to trends in the patterns of development. We then present our empirical analysis, focusing on the study of short-term fluctuations, applying the historical demographic methodology already referred to.

We divide the literature reviewed into two broad groups. The first is focused on the long-term historical trend of vital rates, breaking the socioeconomic process down into a number of periods. The second is more centred on the structural adjustment crisis of the 1980s, contrasting it with the economic performance observed in

Brazil during the so-called economic 'miracle' of the 1970s. We make reference to vital rates only, although there is much more material available on other measures of mortality, fertility, and nuptiality.

The historical process and vital rates

In this review we rely mainly on the work of Sawyer (1980). She has thoroughly examined mortality, fertility, and nuptiality in the city of São Paulo from the nineteenth century to 1973. She divides the economic performance of Brazil in the twentieth century, up until 1973, into three phases: the agrarian export phase (1900–30), the import substitution phase (1930–64), and the phase of 'associated development' (1964–73). Associated development was a term used by some authors during the latter period to define a process of capitalist expansion associated with foreign investments and multinational corporations.

During the agrarian export phase, mortality in the city of São Paulo was as high as it was in England during the early eighteenth century. The crude death rate (CDR) was 17.1 per thousand in 1900–4 and the infant mortality rate (IMR) was 183.1 per thousand live births in 1910–14. The CDR rose by 8 per cent between the first years (1900–4) and the last years (1925–9) of the agrarian export phase, although it had declined by 36 per cent with respect to the last five years of the previous century. IMR declined by 9 per cent between 1910–14 and the end of this period. During this period social and health policies were of limited scope. Governmental public health efforts were directed mainly towards the insulation of the upper socio-economic strata from communicable diseases. Examples of health policy were vaccinations to protect the population from smallpox, and vector control projects, as in the case of yellow fewer. Diseases that did not spread easily and were expensive to control, such as respiratory and gastrointestinal infections, persisted with a high prevalence among the poor.

The impart substitution phase is marked by a steady decline in CDR and IMR in the city of São Paulo. CDR declined by 57.6 per cent from 13.9 per thousand in 1930–4 to 7.8 per thousand in 1960–4. IMR declined by 65 per cent from 152.7 per thousand live births in 1930–4 to 59.3 at the end of the period. The share of deaths due to infectious and parasitic diseases in the total number of infant deaths declined from 60 per cent in 1940 to 23 per cent in 1965, while those caused by perinatal problems as a proportion of the total number of infant deaths increased from somewhat below 40 to 47 per cent over the same period. During this phase infectious diseases were checked to a large extent, although infectious and digestive system diseases were not completely eliminated. Access to health care was still precarious but there was some improvement in the area of immunization. Wood and Carvalho (1988) note a decline in mortality in Brazil during this period, as life expectancy at birth increased from 41.2 years during 1930–40 to 50 years during 1950–60.

The phase classified by Sawyer (1980) as associated development (1964–73) comprises a period of excellent economic performance. Part of this period is the so-called Brazilian 'economic miracle,' from 1968 to 1973, during which Brazilian GDP grew by around 10 per cent a year. Nowadays we define the period between 1964 and 1980 as the military regime period, in order to differentiate it from the 1980s. In 1964 there was a coup d'état after which the military remained in power until the 1980s. Afterwards, there was a gradual opening-up politically with the transition to democracy. This transition was accompanied by successive stabilization policies and by the debt crisis, leading to a period of economic stagnation. From the Brazilian post-war period until the early 1980s there had been some economic fluctuation in GDP, related in part to policy adjustments, but economic growth was generally positive as GDP grew at the average historical rate of 7 per cent a year. It was only in the 1980s that a lengthy period of structural adjustment came into place, characterizing the so-called 'lost decade'.

The best economic performance in the post-war period occurred during the so-called 'economic miracle' (1968–73). Paradoxically, IMR in the city of São Paulo increased by 46.5 per cent between 1960–4 and 1970–3, rising from 59.3 per thousand live births to 86.9. The percentage of deaths due to infectious and parasitic diseases rose from 22.5 per cent of all deaths in 1965 to 34 per cent in 1973, while that due to respiratory diseases rose from 16.2 to 24 per cent. Malnutrition became a very important associated cause of death during this period. The increases in death rates were related to individual living conditions (low income) and local living conditions (poor housing, poor sanitation, and limited access to health care). Thus high death rates were most concentrated in the socially unprotected and economically vulnerable segments of the population (Sawyer 1980). The so-called 'economic miracle' was characterized by a combination of economic growth and widening income inequality, but there was also the trickle-down of economic growth with the absolute improvement of per capita income. Also important was the increase of in-migration to São Paulo, when employment opportunities in the city were increasing rapidly. These factors may be linked to some extent with the paradox of rising IMR in the face of vigorous economic growth during this period.

Wood and Carvalho (1988) have documented the mortality decline in Brazil between 1960–70 and 1970–80, during which life expectancy at birth rose from 53.4 to 61.6 years. During this period of fast economic growth, there was a debate on the linkage between wage policy and infant mortality rate trends. After the military coup a wage containment policy formed part of the governmental development strategy. This curtailed the power of trade unions and led to a deterioration in the real value of the minimum wage. An inverse relationship between the infant mortality rate in São Paulo and a real minimum wage index during the 1963–79 period is unequivocal. The issue is whether or not there is a causal relationship between these two variables. Authors became more cautions about being confined by the conventional debate on the determinants of mortality decline (standard of living versus technological innovation), as the debate on the causal links between real minimum wage and IMR could be confounded with the trend in other factors that influenced IMR. These factors included rural–urban migration, income distribution, coverage of services, investment in public health measures, quality of health care services, and urban infrastructure investments affecting the environment such as water supply and sanitation (including the supply of modern sewerage). A detailed discussion of this issue by Wood and Carvalho (1988) suggests a causal link between minimum real wages and IMR in the 1963–79 period, but they predicted a declining importance of real wages by the end of this period with the implementation of a series of publicly financed programmes targeting the poor.

With regard to fertility, Sawyer (1980) has examined changes in the crude birth rate (CBR) in the city of São Paulo. The CBR fluctuated during the agrarian export phase, but overall declined by only around 2 per cent, from 35.5 per thousand during 1900–4 to 34.8 during 1925–9. The first decade of import substitution (the 1930s) was marked by a marked decline in the CBR, which fell by about 28.4 per cent from 34.8 per thousand at the beginning of the decade to 24.9 during 1935–9. The post-war period was characterized by a recovery in the CBR, which reached 31.6 per thousand in 1960–4. After the military coup in 1964, the new development pattern implemented was accompanied by a steady decline in the CBR.

The total fertility rate (TFR) in Brazil was relatively stable during the import substitution phase, moving from 6.5 in 1930–40 to 5.8 in 1960–70. Brazil's fertility transition, which began in the 1970s, declined from a TFR of 4.3 in 1975–80 to 3.4 in 1981–6. Although we are interested in this chapter in *short-term* fluctuations, it is important to note that these have occurred in the context of a steady fertility decline since the 1970s. The prevalence of the use of contraceptives by women of reproductive age increased from 32 per cent in 1970 to 66 per cent in 1986.

The 'lost decade' and stabilization policies in the 1980s

The impact of adjustment policies and the crisis of the early 1980s on vital rates and childhood in Brazil has been the subject of several recent studies. Chahad and Macedo (1988) focused their study on the social impact of economic adjustment during the post-miracle period (1973–81), defined by the authors as a period of debt-led growth. During the 1973–5 period, following the first oil shock, Brazilian external debt grew by 68 per cent. In the second half of the 1970s the Brazilian government initiated the implementation of an ambitious programme of import substitution industrialization in capital goods and intermediate inputs. This project required large and concentrated investments that were financed by external debt. Thanks to this project GDP grew at 7.1 per cent per year in the 1975–80 period. In 1979, the second oil shock and the rises in interest rates contributed to a large increase in the financial component of the country's external debt. The Brazilian economic situation in the early 1980s was such that a stabilization policy was inescapable.

The 1981–4 period was a period of recessionary adjustment. The adjustment, implemented through fiscal and monetary policies and aimed at the stabilization of inflation and the improvement of trade imbalances, was needed in order to pay the current account deficits. Real GDP declined by 3.4 per cent in 1981; it recovered slightly in 1982 (growing by 0.9 per cent), but in 1983 there was another decline, of 2.5 per cent. In the 1984–6 period real GDP grew again, by 5.7 per cent in 1984 and around 8 per cent in 1985–6. After 1987, real GDP declined again and the inflationary process accelerated (Chahad and Macedo 1988). On average, the 1980s were marked by sharp short-term fluctuations in economic variables, which resulted in a decline of 1.7 per cent of real GDP per capita between 1980 and 1988.

Chahad and Macedo (1988) noticed that the net tax revenue declined during the recessionary period of the first half of the 1980s, leading to a decline in federal government social expenditures. Social expenditures in health and education also showed a pro-cyclical pattern at both state and municipality level.

Goldani *et al.* (1989) have presented an important paper discussing the demographic consequences of the economic crisis in Brazil during the first half of the 1980s. They inquired about the extent to which the basic demographic variables departed from observed trends due to the economic crisis. They relied on the 1984 National Household Survey to identify shifts in trends during the period between 1977 and 1984.

Marriage has been a relatively stable institution in Brazil during this century. According to Goldani *et al.* (1989) women's age at first marriage was about 22 years until 1960, without any trend. A first-marriage rate constructed from longitudinal data indicates that first unions increased in the 1977–80 period from 0.82 to 0.89, and then declined steeply from 0.83 in 1981 to 0.64 in 1984. Regional differences in the rate of first marriage were observed, the decline after 1980 lasting longer in the Northeast than in São Paulo (Goldani *et al.* 1989).

The total fertility rate declined by 6.3 per cent, from 4.2 in 1977 to 3.9 in 1980. This is a smaller decline than the 20 per cent observed between 1980 and 1984, when TFR reached 3.1. Trends in total marital fertility rate showed a similar pattern (Goldani *et al.* 1989).

The authors also estimated the relative risk of dying by age 1 of all children born between 1970 and 1983. These rates indicated no clear impact of the economic crisis on infant mortality rate. However, they do suggest that the dampening of the decline of the IMR might have been a demographic consequence of the crisis. In conclusion, these authors suggest that the economic crisis implied a decline in the rate of first marriage and the acceleration of the TFR decline, while the impact on the IMR was less pronounced (Goldani *et al.* 1989).

In summary, the literature reviewed above suggests that both fertility and marriage are positively correlated with economic performance, while the evidence on infant mortality is less clear. The IMR rose during the economic miracle period when GDP was growing fast and declined during the 1980s when GDP growth was sluggish. This finding suggests that Brazil is like Chile and other Latin American countries, where mortality shows more attenuated responses in comparison with other demographic rates. As will be pointed out below, mortality during the European pre-industrial period showed a very substantial structural shift, whereby an increased level of economic development led to a loss of significance for the Malthusian positive check.

The declining trend of infant mortality during the 1980s has been documented by Simões and Ortiz (1988). Their estimates, based on national demographic censuses and household surveys, indicate that the IMR went from 113.8 per thousand live births in 1940, to 68.1 per thousand live births in 1984, a relatively high rate for Latin America. They also found large regional disparities: the IMR in the Southeast declined from 98.3 in 1970 to 71.6 in 1980, showing an even faster decline in the early 1980s when it reached 49.1 in 1984. This is surprising if we remember that Brazil was affected by an acute economic crisis during the first four years of the 1980s. Based on vital registration data, the same authors calculated yearly IMRs from 1980 to 1986. These rates declined from 1980 to 1986, but this decline was neither monotonic nor uniform, as IMRs increased in practically all regions between 1983 and 1984. The national IMR rose from 63.8 in 1983 to 68.2 in 1984, while in the metropolitan area of São Paulo it increased from 44.7 in 1983 to 50.6 in 1984. It is surprising that in 1985 the national IMR declined substantially again, reaching a level below that of 1983.

Overall, these authors conclude that the impact of structural adjustment in the first half of the 1980s was not enough to countervail the causes underlying the declining trend in infant mortality. These causes were the sharp increase in the number of households with access to piped water and sewerage—which led to a decline in deaths caused by diarrhoea—an increase in vaccination campaigns and in hospital coverage, publicly financed programmes targeting the poor (such as the Maternal and Child Health Programme and the Health and Nutrition Programme), and the fertility decline among poor women (Simões and Ortiz 1988).

Simões (1992) also pointed to the role of environmental conditions and sanitation. He indicated that although the national level IMR in the 1985–9 period was 59.7 per thousand live births, the rate dropped to 29.0 in households with proper sewerage and water supply conditions. It was as high as 78.4 in households with poor conditions, and 50.6 in households with proper water but inadequate sewerage supply conditions. Simões' most important finding concerned the impact of household per capita income on the IMR, as well as that of sanitation conditions. Among poor households earning less than one minimum wage per capita the IMR was 75.2 in 1985–9, while the rate dropped to 35.3 among households earning more than one minimum wage per capita. Poor households with improper sanitation conditions had an IMR 2.8 times higher than those with proper sanitation, while households earning more than one minimum wage per capita but with improper sanitation conditions had an IMR twice as high as those with proper sanitation.

Monteiro *et al.* (1989) compared the nutritional status of Brazilian children between 1975 and 1989. The prevalence of malnourished children under five years of age was measured by the proportion of children below two z-scores of the weight-for-height anthropometric standard used by the National Child Health Survey and the World Health Organization. This prevalence declined substantially, from 18.4 per cent in 1975 to 7.1 per cent in 1989, an absolute decline of more than one million children. This sharp decline in the prevalence of malnourished children parallels the decline in the IMR and the corresponding debate about its causes.

Two hypotheses for this decline are advanced: one that stresses the improvement in economic conditions and the other that holds the increase in social programmes and services to be more important. The economic hypothesis is not plausible since most of the improvement in GDP per capita and decline in poverty occurred before 1975. After that time—and for most of the 1980s—per capita income was stagnant and the share of people below the poverty line increased. The second hypothesis seems more plausible, since several social and health policies performed well during the 1980s: the share of households covered by piped water and sewerage increased substantially, the coverage of vaccinations also increased, and there was an increase in the coverage and number of nutrition programmes.

We concur with the idea that the social programmes and expenditures observed in the 1980s had an important role in the continuation of the declining trend in IMR, a fact consistent with the decline in the share of malnourished children. It remains to be seen whether this declining IMR trend can be sustained without further improvements in economic conditions. The answer may be no for two reasons: first, because the funding of social programmes cannot be sustained in the long run without the recovery of economic growth; second, because there seems to be a limit to the decline in IMR caused by sanitation policy and the extension of coverage. Above a certain threshold, improvements in the quality of health services and household income will be needed to obtain further declines in infant mortality.

Short-term variation on vital rates: past and present

Looking at the case of pre-industrial Europe, we find a large bibliography on short-term variations on vital rates, examining the impact of annual harvest variations, and fluctuations in prices and weather. The development of investigations applying statistical and econometric techniques to this subject started with an important work by Lee (1981), which examined the economic, demographic, and meteorological factors associated with short-term fluctuations in English vital rates from 1540 to 1840. Other works followed this approach, dealing with the same subject in other pre-industrial European countries (see Richards 1983; Galloway 1984; 1985; 1988).

Demographic variation can be studied both in the long and in the short term. The studies of long-term variation on vital rates deal with the impact of economic fluctuation and technological progress on population, and also consider the reverse causality of population dynamics affecting economic variables such as technological progress. The studies of short-term variation of vital rates examine the impact of fluctuations in (exogenous) economic variables such as price and weather (Galloway 1988), and do not present the problem of reverse causality between vital rates and economic fluctuation. This is so because short-term fluctuations of vital rates mostly capture variations on the numerator of the demographic variables since the denominator, which is affected by population size and age structure, tends to move slowly.

In the case of pre-industrial countries, fluctuation in wheat prices and weather temperature were the basic exogenous variables included on the right-hand side of the regression models. Prices are included in the model in order to represent short-term variation in real wage, which is a proxy for workers' welfare. The sign expected from the Malthusian theory suggests a positive relationship between wheat price and mortality (positive check) and a negative relationship between prices and the birth rate (preventive check). The relationship between wheat price and nuptiality is expected to be negative as well (preventive check).

The empirical estimation uses current and lagged prices including lags up to 5 years (lags 0, 1, 2, 3, and 4 years). Empirical results from the analysis of several European pre-industrial countries confirmed the expected signs for the impact of price fluctuation on vital rates. The pattern of fertility response to price increase indicated the expected negative sign on lags 0, 1, and 3, and a positive rebound on lags 2 and 4. The fertility response to price increases cumulated over 5 years was negative, as expected. This negative impact seemed to increase with the countries' level of development. The pattern of nuptiality response to price increase indicated great variation on the strength of this association. The strongest negative effect was observed at lag 0, and although the cumulated response to price increases was also negative, it was relatively independent of the countries' level of development. The non-infant mortality response to price increase also confirmed the expected sign predicted by Malthusian theory. A positive sign was observed in lags 0, 1, and 2, and almost no response in the two following lags. The strength of this positive response of non-infant mortality to price increase decreased with the level of economic development, to the point that the impact became negative in the case of England between 1756 and 1870 (Galloway 1988). A declining positive response of mortality to price increase was also found by Lee (1981).

Reher (1990) applied the same type of methodology in examining short-term variation on vital rates in eighteenth-century Mexico. This application to Mexico during colonial times is an important initial attempt to extend this type of model to other contexts. The vital rates in the time series analyses were divided according to socioethnic groups. The impact of the price of corn on fertility was negative at almost all lags, with some rebounds in the case of lag 2. The cumulative negative impact of the corn price on fertility was larger in the case of ethnic groups of lower socio-economic status, although not significantly so. The impact of corn prices on nuptiality was also negative, as in the case of fertility. The main impact was observed at lag 0 and to a lesser extent at lag 1. This impact was also stronger in the case of ethnic groups of lower socioeconomic status. The cumulative impact of corn price on the Mexican nuptiality pattern is quite similar to the one observed in European pre-industrial countries, as positive checks also operated strongly in Mexico. There was a strong positive impact at lag 0 with a smaller negative effect at other lags. The demographic regime in these societies tended to be more un-stable, with larger fluctuations in death rates. Reher concluded that the Malthusian mechanism operated in eighteenth-century Mexico both through positive and preventive checks.

The studies just reviewed are all on short-term fluctuations of vital rates in the past. Several Latin American social scientists dealing with the contemporary period have been concerned with the short-term effects of the recent economic crises, specially in the case of mortality. We review next the few works that have tried to use a time series methodology to analyse the impact of crisis and structural adjustment on vital rates in contemporary Latin American countries.

Taucher's (1989) work is an example in this direction. She focused her work on the role of behavioural factors in the demographic response to economic fluctuations in Chile, between 1967 and 1987. The main issue dealt with in her paper is the relationship between the steady infant mortality decline in the period between the mid-1970s and mid-1980s with the impact of the economic crisis which showed a declining trend in per capita income coupled with major short-term fluctuations. This is opposed to the traditional explanation based on the impact of mother and child health, family planning, and nutritional programmes that were implemented before and lasted throughout this period. The empirical evidence showed a decline in infant mortality rates during the crisis period. Taucher suggested a behavioural mechanism affecting this decline which is associated with the correlation between fertility and infant mortality. The basic tenet is that couples regulate their fertility in direct response to economic fluctuation, and that this response is larger among poor families, those most affected by the crisis. She suggested that this fertility behaviour in response to economic fluctuations plays a stabilizing role in infant mortality trends, by favouring birth spacing and preventing birth from taking place during bad times.

The empirical evidence presented by Taucher suggests a direct correlation between infant mortality rates and real per capita gross domestic product (GDP), while in theory one would expect a negative relationship. However, variations in GDP were also positively correlated with fluctuations in cumulative fertility rates for birth orders 1 to 3. The positive impact between per capita GDP and cumulative fertility at lags 1 and 2 is much greater than the positive impact between per capita GDP and infant mortality rate. Since Taucher infant mortality rates increase with birth order, a fertility decline shifts the birth structure towards categories of lower mortality risk. Accordingly, she suggests that after controlling for the link between economic fluctuations and fertility, the impact of per capita GDP fluctuations on infant mortality rate could become negative as is theoretically expected.

Bravo (1990) examined the Chilean case as a means of resolving the apparent paradox regarding the relationship between the economic crisis of the second half of the 1970s and the 1980s, and the reduction in infant mortality which occurred Simultaneously. Reviewing prior analyses of the Chilean case, and Taucher's work in particular, Bravo emphasized the importance of distinguishing between trend and short-term fluctuation around the trend. The trend in infant mortality was affected not only by economic performance and per capita income, but also by structural factors such as state policies, especially those on health, public sanitation, water supply, education, etc. If one did not sort out trend from short-term fluctuation, then the paradoxical unpredicted empirical results such as the positive correlation between per capita income growth and the infant mortality rate could lead to implausible causal explanations. In turn, short-term fluctuations are more closely associated with changes in the economic cycle represented by per capita income and the unemployment rate.

Bravo's empirical estimation focused on the short-term fluctuations, inspired by the historical demography methodology advanced by Lee (1981), Galloway (1988), and Reher (1990). After taking the trend out of the series, Bravo estimated correlation coefficients and elasticities relating several mortality and morbidity variables to per capita product, unemployment and wage variables. General results indicated a negative association between short-term fluctuations in product, employment and wages with respect to a number of health indicators (morbidity, mortality, and malnutrition). His results indicate that mortality is less sensitive to fluctuations in economic variables than malnutrition, while malnutrition is less sensitive than morbidity. The economic variable with the strongest impact on health indicators was the unemployment rate.

Bravo (1992) extended his analysis to short- and medium-term changes in other Latin American countries, distinguishing various causes of death. He started by noticing the widespread finding of relatively weak responses of health indicators to economic crisis and recessions. The time series of per capita GDP and infant mortality in Chile, Costa Rica, Guatemala, and Uruguay between 1950 and 1990 show downward trends in infant mortality rates that did not seem to be severely affected by the economic crisis of the 1970s and 1980s. Bravo performed a short-term analysis of deviations around the trend, following the methods previously discussed. The results indicated a clear inverse pattern between the two series in the case of Costa Rica and Guatemala, while the same pattern was found in Chile and Uruguay only after the 1970s. The short-term analysis of mortality by causes of death indicated several patterns of response, but some causes of death (such as malnutrition, influenza, and peptic ulcer) showed consistent negative association with changes in per capita GDP.

Hill and Palloni (1992) also evaluated demographic responses to economic crises in Latin America, with a special emphasis on the most recent crisis of the late 1970s and early 1980s. The analysis was focused on the impact on vital rates (fertility, marriage, and mortality) caused by short-term changes in living conditions.

They also applied the methodology developed by Lee (1981) and Galloway (1988), detrending the series with a 7-year moving average and estimated the regressions using 4 lags (from 0 to 3). Real personal consumption was chosen as the preferred independent variable for capturing welfare variation. The estimations were performed for seven countries from Latin America and the Caribbean. The results found positive responses in the case of marriage and fertility. In the case of mortality, only a few results were statistically significant, but the authors highlight the systematic patterns across the countries, which are consistent with prior expectations.

Short-term Variations: Vital Rates and the Economy in the City of São Paulo

This section presents the results of our empirical analysis of the short-term determinants of vital rates in São Paulo. We have chosen this city for several reasons. First, the city and the state of São Paulo provide the longest reliable time series of vital rates in Brazil. The city is likely to present better vital registration coverage than the state of São Paulo or the other regions of Brazil. Second, São Paulo is at the centre of economic development in Brazil. It was the first city to become a major commercial and financial centre during the Old Republic agrarian export phase, and it is also where import substitution industrialization was concentrated. Even today, the city is the area most affected by the country's macroeconomic adjustment policies, mainly because a large share of Brazilian industry is still located in or near the city. Third, São Paulo has the strongest monetized economy in the country, an important homogeneous factor for the analysis of such a long time series, especially if we intend to evaluate the impact of economic fluctuation on the populations's welfare and on their vital rates. Likewise, it is the city that has experienced the largest number of social policy experiments throughout this century. Finally, São Paulo has received several massive in-migrations over the century. During the agrarian export phase, it received a wave of migrants from Europe, most importantly, immigrants from Italy. After 1930, when the external border was closed, a massive internal migration process took place, with most migrants coming from the Northeast. We have not taken migration into explicit consideration in our analysis, but given the fact that internal migration is cyclical, most of our empirical results will be affected by the impact and interaction of migration with the other demographic variables explicitly considered in our analysis.

The period of the present analysis covers almost the entire twentieth century, from 1916 to 1988, although in some cases we only perform analyses of the second half of the period considered (1940–88). Compared to the estimations available in other Latin American and developing countries, this is a long time series. It is important to note, as we did in the previous section, that the Brazilian economy in this century went through four long economic phases: the agrarian export phase (1900–30), import substitution industrialization (1930–64), 'associated development'—including the so-called 'economic miracle' of 1964–79—and the 'lost decade' of structural adjustment, from 1980 to 1988.

A. Data and method

The vital registration data from the city of São Paulo is published by the SEADE Foundation, a public institution in the State of São Paulo. The Gross Domestic Product series of the Brazilian economy was obtained from an adjusted time series published as *Brasil Em Dados* (1991), which contains time series estimates calculated by Claudio Haddad for the 1900–46 period. These data were then spliced to the GDP time series calculated by the Fundação Getúlio Vargas up until 1970. The figures for the remaining years—up to 1988—were calculated by the Brazilian Census Bureau (IBGE). The cost of living price index is a consumer price index series that was initiated in 1912 for the city of São Paulo. Finally, the minimum wage series was calculated by DIEESE, the Brazilian Union Studies Department. The real minimum wage series began in 1940, when DIEESE was created, and used the consumer price index for the city of São Paulo.

In our analyses we will use the following vital registration measures: number of marriages, number of births, number of non-infant deaths as a proxy for adult mortality, and the infant mortality rate.

The usual procedure for removing the long term uses an 11-year moving average (Lee 1981; Galloway 1988). Bravo (1990) suggested the use of a polynomial curve model for the fitting of the trend when the time series is too short and a reduction in the number of observations is to be avoided. Because we have a large number of observations, sample size is not a major concern in itself; however, we did not want to lose observations during the 1980s, an important period of structural adjustment. Had we applied the moving average procedure, we would have lost these observations.

We decided to try two detrending procedures. The first fitted an exponential trend curve, which required in some cases the calibration of linear trend models in order to adjust for shifts in the slope or intercept through the use of ad-hoc dummy variables. The short-term fluctuations were obtained, as usual, by dividing each observation by the fitted trend value. We call the estimations using variables detrended by this process model A.

In a highly inflationary country such as Brazil, it is a mistake to use a moving average procedure to evaluate price fluctuation. This is so because the price series would present declining deviations from the trend every time the inflationary process was accelerating towards extremely high inflationary levels. Exponential detrending of prices for 1916–80 also proved inadequate, so we decided against using the price series altogether. This confirmed the notion that prices are not a good measure of contemporary fluctuations in the standard of living in Latin American populations, which is very sensitively affected by indexation mechanisms, unemployment, and social policies.

In model B, we remove the trend by the conventional moving average technique. Differences in the estimated parameters (elasticities) could be attributable to the model's sensitivity to different detrending procedures or to the shorter time spanned by the estimates of model B.

Models A and B include only GDP as the independent variable in the longer period. The same models were estimated, adding real minimum wage as an independent variable in the shorter period (after 1940). We did not find usable unemployment series for the period.

The estimation of the magnitude and lag structure of the response of the dependent variables (that is, number of marriages, number of births, number of adult or non-infant deaths, number of infant deaths, and infant mortality rate) to annual

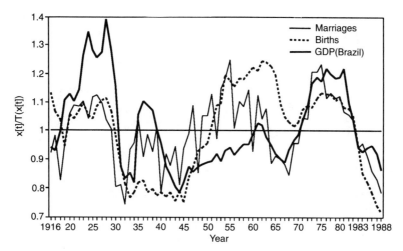

Fig. 8.1 Economic and vital rates fluctuations, Sao Paulo, 1916–88

Note: x[t] is the value of variable x at time t.

T(x[t]) is the estimated trend of variable x at time t.

Source: Fundaçao SEADE, Sao Paulo, Brasil em Dados, 1991.

changes in the independent variables (price level, real minimum wage, and real gross domestic product) in both models is obtained through a distributed lag model in order to allow for the lagged impact of the fluctuations in the independent variables. Following the historical demographic literature, we estimate a model setting five-year annual lags (lags 0, 1, 2, 3, and 4). As is customary in time series models, we incorporated corrections for autoregressive disturbances. After some experimentation, we opted for standardizing our presentation by displaying the correction for second-order autoregressive disturbances.

B. Empirical results: 1916–88

Figure 8.1 shows the annual variations, in detrended marriages, births, and GDP between 1916 and 1988. The series indicate some short-term fluctuations and a positive association between real GDP and marriages and births. They also suggest medium-term cycles in the stationary vital rates and GDP series. These cycles seem to be associated with the economic periodization of the development process in Brazil, as discussed above. Figure 8.2 plots annual variations in the number of adult or non-infant deaths, infant mortality rates and real GDP. The expected negative association between the mortality indicators and economic performance does not seem to hold. We will examine this point further ahead.

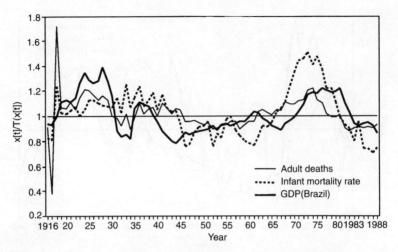

Fig. 8.2   Economic and mortality fluctuations, Sao Paulo, 1916–88

Note: x[t] is the value of variable x at time t.

T(x[t]) is the estimated trend of variable x at time t.

Source: Fundaçao SEADE, Sao Paulo, Brasil em Dados, 1991.

Marriages

The first column of table 8.1 provides the estimated coefficients of real GDP in models A and B. Unlike the pre-industrial experience, the rate of growth in real GDP is a proxy for welfare improvements because it can be positively correlated with nominal wage and the growth in employment opportunities. The preventive check hypothesis of the Malthusian framework predicts a positive elasticity between real income and the number of marriages. This positive elasticity of 0.3 was significant only at lag 0 in model A. When all lags are added, the cumulative elasticity was around 0.28. In model B the positive elasticity occurs at lag 1, with the cumulative elasticity around 0.27. In other words, a continued 10 per cent increase in real GDP would increase the number of marriages by around 2.7 per cent. The GDP elasticities at all lags derived from model B are presented in Figure 8.3.

Births

The preventive check hypothesis of the Malthusian framework would predict a positive link between variations in real GDP and births. Our empirical results for models A and B are presented in the second column of Table 8.1. The estimated elasticities between GDP and births were strong both at lag 0 (0.23) and lag 2 (0.14) in model A, and the cumulative elasticity was both strong and positive (0.59). In model B the estimated elasticity was significant only at lag 1 (0.30), while the cumulative elasticity was also strong and positive (0.47). We conclude

Table 8.1 Regression results, City of São Paulo, estimated coefficients

Variables	Marriages		Births		Adult deaths		Infant mortality rate	
	A	B	A	B	A	B	A	B
Constant	0.712***	0.728 (c)	0.375**	0.537*** c	0.763***	0.246	1.078***	1.501 c
GDP lag								
0	0.301***	−0.025	0.232***	−0.045	0.627**	0.558***	0.004	−0.194
1	0.199	0.401 (b)	0.073	0.298*** c	−0.279	0.306	0.116	0.142
2	−0.232	0.134	0.137*	0.026	0.173	−0.048	−0.184	−0.298
3	0.070	−0.258	0.085	0.087	−0.110	0.148	0.228	0.231
4	−0.058	0.015	0.066	0.100	−0.159	−0.212	−0.258	−0.395** b
V_{t-1}	0.330*	−0.020	1.090***	0.530*** c	−0.090	−0.500***	0.680***	0.320*** c
V_{t-2}	0.350*	0.210 (a)	−0.138	−0.080	0.230**	−0.200*	0.210*	−0.020
R^2	0.519	0.289	0.938	0.617	0.245	0.517	0.741	0.172
R^2 adjusted	0.483	0.233	0.933	0.587	0.189	0.479	0.721	0.106
Durbin–Watson	1.867	1.819	1.955	2.024	2.123	1.998	1.926	1.955
GDP lag sum	0.280	0.267	0.594	0.466	0.253	0.752	−0.094	−0.514

* Significant at 10% level.
** Significant at 5% level.
*** Significant at 1% level.

Model: $Y_t = c + (GDP)_{t-i} + V_{t-1} + V_{t-2} + E_t$
Model A = 1916–88 exponencial detrending.
Model B = 1915–83 moving average.
V_{t-1} = first-order auto regressive estimator.
V_{t-2} = second-order auto regressive estimator.

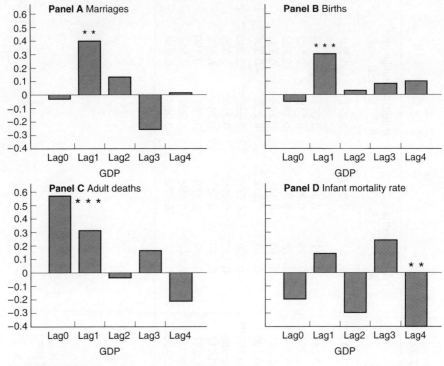

Fig. 8.3   Elasticity values (model B, Table 8.1)
* Significant at 10% level
** Significant at 5% level
*** Significant at 1% level

that the birth variations in Brazil are consistent with the preventive check hypothesis in terms of real GDP variation and are highly procyclical (GDP elasticities from model B are also depicted in Figure 8.3).

Deaths
The positive check hypothesis from the Malthusian framework predicts a negative elasticity between GDP and mortality, although the literature review indicated that the relationship between economic change and mortality is much more complex than the one associated with marriages and births.

We can see the empirical results of the model for the study of non-infant or adult deaths in the third column of Table 8.1. The elasticity between GDP and adult deaths in model A is positive and significant at lag 0 (0.63), a pro-cyclical result that is contrary to that expected by the positive check hypothesis. Overall, most GDP elasticities for the other lags have a negative compensating effect, but the cumulative elasticity for GDP is still positive (0.25). The results of model B are similar and stronger, the estimated elasticity is positive and significant at lag 0 (0.56), while the compensating effect for the other lags is lower. Thus, the cumulative elasticity is much higher (0.75). This pro-cyclical result may be explained by a positive relation between GDP and (internal) in-migration to São Paulo, which would tend to augment the number of deaths registered in the city even without any change in the underlying mortality risks.

The regression using the infant mortality rate as the dependent variable is presented in the last column of Table 8.1. The estimated coefficients for the relationship between GDP and IMR did not present any significant result in model A, the cumulative elasticity was anticyclical as we would predict, but low (−0.09). In model B the estimated elasticity was negative and significant at lag 4 (−0.40), while the cumulative elasticity was high and negative (−0.51). We conclude that IMR is either anticyclical as the positive check hypothesis would predict or insensitive to GDP variations.

C. Empirical results: 1944–88

We have seen that the use of price in these models was suggested by authors who have studied pre-industrial Europe, when the generally accepted assumption was that nominal wage tended to be rigid so that real wage varied inversely with nominal prices. Price variations may not be a good welfare indicator in developing countries, where nominal wages might vary in response to changes in economic activity as well. The Brazilian Government started to regulate the urban labour market in 1940, after the creation of a minimum wage law by President Vargas. Ever since, the nominal minimum wage established by the federal government has been indexed to inflation and has played an important role in determining the real wage rate. We use the real minimum wage time series as an alternative economic measure, one that is most appropriate for examining the Malthusian preventive and positive checks in contemporary Brazil. We kept the GDP in the model in order to allow us to evaluate the net type of cyclical nature of short-term variations in vital rates.

Figure 8.4 shows annual variations in detrended marriages, births, real minimum wage, and real GDP. Figure 8.5 shows annual variations in non-infant deaths, infant mortality rate, real minimum wage, and real GDP. The most interesting point suggested by this figure is the inverse correlation between real minimum wage and the infant mortality rate, a pattern clearly observed in the 1970s and the 1980s.

Marriages
The regression results for marriages are presented in the first column of Table 8.2. The estimated coefficients of the real minimum wage in model A were insignificant, with the exception of lag 4 when the elasticity was −0.27, the opposite direction of that predicted by the Malthusian preventive check framework. The minimum wage lag sum elasticity was −0.18. These findings are partially confirmed by the moving average model (model B). The elasticity at lag 0 was −0.16

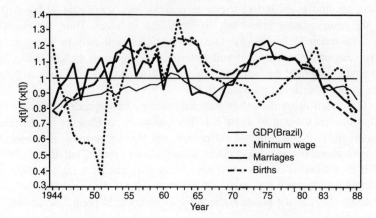

Fig. 8.4 Economic and vital fluctuations (marriages and births), Sao Paulo, 1943–88

Note: x[t] is the value of variable x at time t.

T(x[t]) is the estimated trend of variable x at time t.

Source: Fundaçao SEADE, Sao Paulo, Brasil em Dados, 1991.

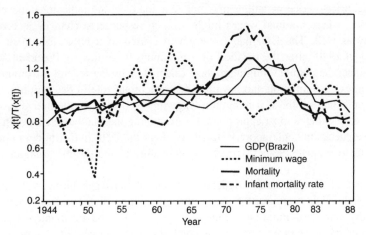

Fig. 8.5 Economic and vital fluctuations (mortality and infant mortality), Sao Paulo, 1943–88

Note: x[t] is the value of variable x at time t.

T(x[t]) is the estimated trend of variable x at time t.

Source: Fundaçao SEADE, Sao Paulo, Brasil em Dados, 1991.

Table 8.2 Regression results, City of São Paulo, estimated coefficients

Variables	Marriages A	B	Births A	B	Adult deaths A	B	Infant mortality rate A	B
Constant	0.626**	0.655***	−0.482	0.170**	0.723***	1.051***	0.823	2.048***
MW lag								
0	−0.091	−0.161***	0.069**	0.073***	−0.023	−0.084**	−0.257***	−0.223***
1	0.139	0.106	−0.012	0.025	0.039	0.034	0.012	0.038
2	0.086	0.151**	0.042	0.050***	−0.005	0.024	−0.155	−0.635
3	−0.047	0.018	−0.016	−0.025	0.045	0.016	0.077	0.125*
4	−0.269***	−0.202***	−0.039	−0.034*	0.073*	−0.004	−0.063	0.011
GDP lag								
0	0.486	0.094	0.221*	0.085	0.425***	0.423**	−0.382	−0.316
1	0.545	0.994**	0.257**	0.217**	−0.192	−0.196	−0.490*	−0.079
2	−0.230	−0.159	0.404***	0.456***	0.124	0.093	1.222***	0.706**
3	−0.562	0.111	0.230*	0.272**	−0.052	−0.224	−0.670**	−0.884***
4	0.341	−0.600**	−0.219*	−0.276***	−0.159	−0.139	0.874***	−0.380
V_{t-1}	0.220*	−0.420**	1.250***	0.150	0.960***	0.560***	1.470***	0.900***
V_{t-2}	0.520***	0.150	−0.250***	−0.150	−0.150	−0.280*	−0.550***	−0.360***
R^2	0.708	0.673	0.969	0.912	0.835	0.520	0.920	0.703
R^2 adjusted	0.622	0.537	0.960	0.875	0.787	0.319	0.897	0.580
Durbin–Watson	1.867	1.952	1.778	1.917	1.920	1.919	2.099	2.089
MW lag sum	−0.182	−0.089	0.044	0.089	0.129	−0.015	−0.386	−0.684
GDP lag sum	0.579	0.439	0.893	0.754	0.146	−0.042	0.555	−0.953

* Significant at 10% level
** Significant at 5% level
*** Significant at 1% level

Model: $Y_t = c + (MWage)_{t-i} + V_{t-1} + V_{t-2} + E_t$
Model A = 1944–88 exponencial detrending
Model B = 1949–83 moving average

and at lag 4 was −0.20, but there was a positive and significant elasticity at lag 2 (0.15). The cumulated elasticity was only −0.09.

In the case of real GDP, the elasticity in model A was positive or pro-cyclical in lags 0 and 1, but there was a rebound in lags 2 and 3. The lag sum elasticity of real GDP was 0.58, but none of the individual coefficients were significant. In the case of model B (see Figure 8.6), the elasticity was near unity and significant (0.99) at lag 1, with a negative rebound at lag 4 (−0.6). The lag sum elasticity of real GDP was 0.44.

Births

The second column of Table 8.2 presents regression results of the births model. The estimated coefficients of real minimum wages in model A were not significant except in lag 0, reaching a low value of 0.07. The minimum wage cumulative elasticity of all lags was positive as predicted, but also small at 0.04. The results did not change much in model B: the estimated elasticities were significant at lags 0, 2, and 4, but the cumulative elasticity of all lags was only 0.09.

The estimated elasticities of real GDP in model A were lower than the ones found in the marriages model, but they were all positive and significant. The lack of rebounds in lags 2 and 3, as previously observed in the marriages estimation, favoured a positive and high lag sum elasticity (0.84). This result revealed a strong procyclical behaviour of births. These results are confirmed in the case of model B, as is depicted in Figure 8.6. The combination of a cyclical pattern in these detrended birth series with the fertility decline trend initiated in the mid-1970s suggests that the structural adjustment of the 1980s was an important factor in explaining the sharp recent fertility decline in Brazil. More importantly, to the extent that the limited availability of contraceptives in Brazil led to an increase in female permanent sterilization, then what would have been a cyclical fluctuation in births might causes a permanent decline in the birth rate.

Deaths

The estimated coefficients for the impact of real minimum wage variations on non-infant or adult deaths obtained from model A reveal again unexpected results. Only in lag 4 was the estimated coefficient significant and positive. The minimum wage lag sum elasticity was 0.13. The results obtained from model B were not very different, showing a wage lag sum elasticity near zero (−0.02).

Adult mortality also presented a weak procyclical pattern in model A. The GDP elasticity was positive and significant in lag 0 (0.43), but some rebound effects, present in lags 1, 3, and 4, reduced the GDP lag sum elasticity to 0.15. The results were a little different in the case of model B. The rebound effects in lags 1, 3, and 4 were larger so that the GDP lag sum elasticity was −0.04.

The last model presented in Table 8.2 concerns the infant mortality rate. In model A, the only significant real wage coefficient was the one of lag 0, and it was negative as expected. Thus, the minimum wage cumulative elasticity of all lags was negative (−0.39), thereby suggesting the operation of the Malthusian positive check.

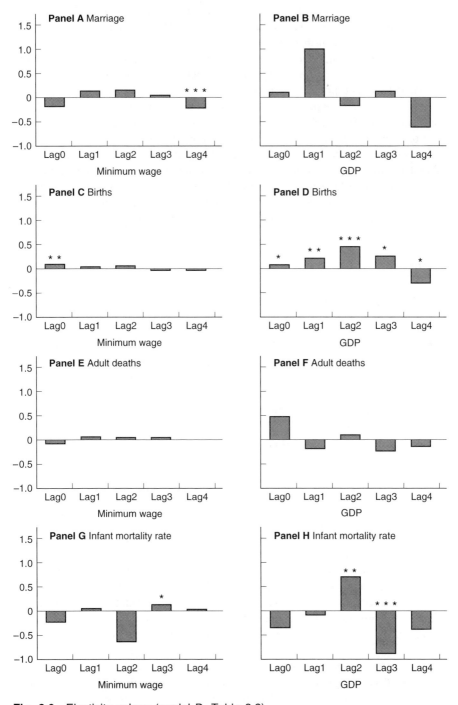

Fig. 8.6 Elasticity values (model B, Table 8.2)

* Significant at 10% level
** Significant at 5% level
*** Significant at 1% level

The results obtained in model B were similar and stronger, due to a high negative elasticity at lag 2 (−0.64). The wage cumulative elasticity of all lags was negative (−0.68) and higher than in model A.

There is one last important finding shown in Table 8.2 (also displayed in Figure 8.6). In model A, the estimated coefficients capturing the impact of variations in real GDP on infant mortality were all significant with the exception of lag 0, and there is wide variability in the elasticities across the other lags. Negative elasticities are found in lags 0, 1, and 3, but the positive elasticities found in lags 2, and 4 were so strong that the lag sum effect of GDP was positive (0.55). This surprising result is not corroborated in model B. Although the elasticities present the same sign as in model A in all but lag 4, the differences in magnitude were such that a negative and almost unitary lag sum elasticity of GDP is obtained. As we said earlier, this difference could be due to the different time spans, or more likely to problems inherent in the exponential detrending implemented in model A.

Conclusion

We applied the empirical methodology derived from the Malthusian framework in the analysis of short-term variations in economic variables and vital rates in the city of São Paulo.

The empirical results obtained from the long-term time series (1916–88) indicated that the impact of GDP on marriages and births was positive in both cases, a fact that is consistent with the preventive check. An unexpected pro-cyclical relation between GDP and adult deaths was obtained in the specifications of models A and B. In the case of infant mortality rate the elasticity between GDP and IMR was negative (close to zero in the case of model A), revealing an anticyclical response consistent with the Malthusian positive check framework.

The empirical results obtained from the post-Second World War period were similar to the previous findings. In this period, we used annual variations in real minimum wages as an alternative to price variations, which proved to be a correct strategy since the results are more clearly in line with both preventive and positive check mechanisms. Marriages and births were highly procyclical with respect to variations in GDP, a result consistent with the preventive check prediction.

The most intriguing result was that of the elasticities between GDP and IMR. The pro-cyclical elasticity found in model A is not consistent with the Malthusian positive check framework. The literature review about the Brazilian 'lost decade' discussed in section III gives us a clue to possible explanations of this result: infrastructure investments in sanitation, health, and nutrition programmes can have compensating effects that are stronger than underlying negative relationships.

A word of caution about techniques is in order. Our empirical estimations may be highly sensitive to the detrending process of both dependent and independent variables. This is suggested by the (expected) countercyclical elasticity between IMR and GDP found in model B of both tables, while the estimates of model A are in the opposite direction. In the future, we should evaluate the robustness of empirical estimations with respect to the different number of observations and to alternative detrending procedures.

REFERENCES

Bravo, J. (1990), 'Fluctuaciones en los indicadores de salud y en la economía chilena, 1960–1986', *Estudios de Economía*, 17/1, Universidad de Chile, Facultad de Ciências Económicas y Administrativas, Departamento de Economía.

Chahad, J. P. Z. and Macedo, R. (1988), 'Ajuste econômico e impacto social no Brasil: 1980–1987. Os efeitos sobre a população infantil', in Chahad, J. P. Z. and Cervini, R. (eds.), *Crise e Infância no Brasil*, São Paulo: IPE–USP, 47–84.

Galloway, P. R. (1984), *Variations in Births, Marriages, Deaths and Prices in Northern Italy: urban and rural differences 1640 to 1830*, unpublished paper, University of California, Berkeley.

——— (1985), 'Annual variations in deaths by age, prices, and weather in London 1670 to 1830', *Population Studies*, 39, 487–505.

——— (1988), 'Basic patterns in annual variations in fertility, nuptiality, mortality, and prices in pre-industrial Europe', *Population Studies*, 42, 275–302.

Goldani, A. M., McCracken, S. D., and Pullum, T. W. (1989), *Demographic Change and Stability in Brazil During a Period of Economic Crisis*, unpublished paper, Austin, Texas.

Hill, K. and Palloni, A. (1992), 'Demographic Responses to Economic Shocks: The Case of Latin America', Proceedings of the Conference on the the Peopling of the Americas, 3, Veracruz: International Union for the Scientific Study of Population, 411–38.

Lee, R. D. (1981), 'Short Term Variation: vital rates, prices and weather', in Wrigley, E. A. and Schofield, R. S., *The Population History of England 1541–1871: A Reconstruction*, Cambridge MA: Harvard University Press.

Monteiro, C. A., Benício, M. H. D., Nunes, R., Gouveia, N. da C., Taddei, J. A. A. G., and Cardoso, M. A. A. (1989), 'O Estado Nutricional das Crianças Brasileiras: a Trajetória de 1975 a 1989', in Monteiro, M. F. G. and Cervini, R. (compilers), *Perfil Estatístico de Crianças e Mães no Brasil: aspectos de saúde e nutrição de crianças no Brasil, 1989*, Rio de Janeiro: FIBGE, 61–78.

Reher, D. S. (1990), 'Coyunturas Económicas y Flutuaciones Demográficas en México Durante el Siglo XVIII', in Nadalin, S. O., Marcílio, M. L. and Balhana, A. P., *História e População: estudos sobre a América Latina*, São Paulo: Fundação Sistema Estadual de Análise de Dados, 276–88.

Richards, T. (1983), 'Weather, Nutrition, and the Economy: short-run fluctuations in births, deaths and marriages, France 1740–1909', in *Demography*, 20, 197–212.

Sawyer, D. R. T. O. (1980), *Mortality–Fertility Relationships Through Historical Socio-Economic Change: the case of São Paulo, Brazil*, Phd dissertation, Faculty of the Harvard School of Public Health, Boston, Massachusetts.

Simões, C. C. S. (1992), 'O Estudo dos Diferenciais na Mortalidade Infantil Segundo Algumas Características Sócio-Econômicas', in Monteiro, M. F. G. and Cervini, R. (orgs), *Perfil Estatístico de Crianças e Mães no Brasil: aspectos de saúde e nutrição de crianças no Brasil, 1989*, Rio de Janeiro: FIBGE, 61–78.

Simões, C. C. S. and Ortiz, L. P. (1988), 'A mortalidade infantil no Brasil das años 80', in Chahad, J. P. Z. and Cervini, R. (eds.), *Crise e Infância no Brasil*, São Paulo: IPE–USP, 243–68.

Taucher, E. (1989), *Behavioural Factors in Demographic Responses to Economic Crisis*, unpublished paper, New Delhi.

Wood, C. H. and Carvalho, J. A. M. de (1988), *The Demography of Inequality in Brazil*, Cambridge: Cambridge University Press.

Part IV

Family Labour Force Responses

9 Structural Adjustment and Family Labour Supply in Latin America

DAVID LAM AND DEBORAH LEVISON

Introduction

Labour markets play a critical role in connecting macroeconomic fluctuations to the living conditions and demographic behaviour of households. Understanding how family labour market activity was affected by short-term economic fluctuations provides evidence about both the impact of the economic crisis and the economic responses made within the family. In analysing family labour supply during Latin America's economic crisis of the 1980s it is important to look beyond the usual measures of labour force participation and unemployment, such as those for prime-age males, and consider the effects of macroeconomic fluctuations on the labour supply of different types of family members. Labour supply responses of married women, children and adolescents, and older people may provide indirect evidence about the flexibility of labour markets and the role that labour market adjustments play in periods of large macroeconomic changes, especially those caused by deliberate policy interventions.

In particular, we are interested in the extent to which negative welfare effects of macroeconomic 'shocks' on individuals are lessened by a change in households' strategies regarding labour force activity of household members. That is, are families able to buffer the impact of macro shocks via a reallocation of the time of family members, presumably from other activities into market work? If so, then evidence on the magnitude of changes in the labour supply of household members is one indirect indicator of the magnitude of the shocks felt by individual households. To the extent that adjustments are made by moving children or young adults out of school or training and into the paid labour force, the long-term effects of macroeconomic shocks may be seriously understated by measured short-term declines in family income. Labour supply behaviour may also provide indirect evidence on the extent to which households experience changes in their overall standard of living during macroeconomic fluctuations: those households with greatest flexibility in family time-use strategies may be most able to maintain their standard of living in the face of falling wages, rising unemployment, and high inflation. In addition, the responsiveness of labour supply of various family members, especially those traditionally considered to be 'secondary' workers, to large changes in

Excellent research assistance was provided by Mary Arends, Suzanne Duryea, and Deborah Reed.

macroeconomic conditions may reveal important information about income and substitution effects in labour supply elasticities that are of general interest.

In this chapter we look at evidence on changes in the labour force participation rates of different family members during the 1980s in a variety of Latin American countries. We attempt, within the limitations of the data, to compare observed changes in labour market activity to economic fluctuations in these economies. As will be seen below, readily available data on economic indicators and labour force participation rates provide very limited information on the relationship between macroeconomic fluctuations and family labour supply. We therefore turn to detailed annual household survey data for Brazil to see whether the highly aggregated published data conceal more systematic labour market changes when we can control more carefully for an individual's position in the household and the household's socioeconomic position. Focusing attention on married women at the lowest education levels, we find some evidence of a counter-cyclical labour supply response, with increases in participation in the worst years of Brazil's recession and decreases in participation in better years. The evidence is not overwhelming, however, with short-term responses often dominated by long-term trends. In the case of children we find no clear, convincing pattern, although there is some limited evidence of procyclial labour supply of 10–15 year-olds in the poorest households. We find little evidence that the labour market activity of children increased significantly in the worst years of the recession.

Theoretical Background

There is a long tradition of research on the effects of business cycle fluctuations on the labour supply of married women in the United States[1]. This research has provided conflicting empirical evidence on the magnitude of an 'added worker effect', defined as a temporary increase in the labour supply of married women in response to an unemployment spell for their husbands. In considering the effects of structural adjustment programmes on labour market activity of family members we need to think not only about the labour supply response of an individual to an unanticipated event such as the unemployment of another family member, but about the way that different types of macroeconomic shocks associated with structural adjustment get transmitted to the household level. To give some structure to our analysis, suppose that there is an exogenous and unanticipated change in the value of some macroeconomic variable M, such as the terms of trade, inflation rate, international price of key exports or imports, or government debt position. We will think of M as capturing the kind of dramatic macroeconomic shocks experienced by many Latin American countries during the 1980s. In general we can think of the effect of M on the labour supply of a particular family member as a combination of responses to changes in wages, prices, and income experienced within the family. The magnitude

[1] See, for example, Mincer (1962) and Lundberg (1985).

of the effect of M on these household-level wages and prices will vary widely across different macroeconomic shocks and may be mitigated or exaggerated by government policy.

If H_1 indicates the number of hours worked in the labour market by some particular member of the household, then we will think of the external variable M as affecting all of the wages, prices, and unearned income relevant to the determination of H_1. The effects of M on different wages are of particular interest since they form the basis for a variety of cross-wage effects on labour supply of various family members. The effects of wages and prices can in turn be decomposed into income and substitution effects. If there are n potential workers in the household, then we will think of the change in M on the labour supply of person 1 as:

$$\frac{\partial H_1}{\partial M} = \frac{\partial H_1}{\partial w_1}\frac{\partial w_1}{\partial M} + \frac{\partial H_1}{\partial w_2}\frac{\partial w_2}{\partial M} + \ldots + \frac{\partial H_1}{\partial w_n}\frac{\partial w_n}{\partial M} + \frac{\partial H_1}{\partial I}\frac{\partial I}{\partial M} \tag{1}$$

where w_i is the wage of the ith member, and I is total household income.

Converting into elasticity form and decomposing the price effects into income and substitution effects, we can rewrite this as:

$$\varepsilon_{H_1,M} = \varepsilon^c_{H_1,w_1}\varepsilon_{w_1,M} + \varepsilon^c_{H_1,w_2}\varepsilon_{w_2,M} + \ldots + \varepsilon^c_{H_1,wn}\varepsilon_{wn,M} + \varepsilon^c_{H_1,I}\varepsilon^*_{I,M} \tag{2}$$

where $\varepsilon^c_{H_1,wi}$ denotes the compensated elasticity of labour supply with respect to the ith wage, and $\varepsilon^*_{I,M}$ represents the complete set of effects of M on the family's budget set, including the income effects of all wage changes caused by M.

We cannot in general observe the complicated set of changes in wages and prices at the household level. Equation (2) provides a useful structure for interpreting observed outcomes, however, since it demonstrates that a variety of own-wage, cross-wage, and income effects may be driving the observed changes. Furthermore, all effects are filtered by the poorly understood links between large macroeconomic fluctuations and the labour market. These links are likely to differ substantially across households. If we observe that the effects of macroeconomic shocks are small, then there are two potential explanations implied by equation (2). First, the elasticity of wages and prices with respect to the macroeconomic shocks may be relatively low. This might be true because the shocks do not affect the sectors of the labour market relevant to particular households, or because social institutions provide a buffer between short-term macroeconomic fluctuations and the wages and prices experienced by households. The extent to which this is true will presumably vary across regions, income classes, and sectors of the economy.

The second reason the demographic effects of shocks may be small is because the elasticities of labour force participation with respect to short-term variations in wages and prices are low. It is important to note that elasticities estimated form cross-section data may not be good predictors of short-term responses. Elasticities based on cross-section variation in wages and prices will reflect some unknown combination of permanent and transitory effects. To the extent that these elasticities reflect life cycle decisions about labour supply based on expected lifetime wages, they may be poor predictors about the response to short-term unanticipated shocks in wages of the kind observed in Latin America in the 1980s.

Another reason that observed responses to short-term fluctuations may be small is simply that large effects are concealed by offsetting longer-term trends. We suspect that this may be an important factor in Latin America in the 1980s, where there continued to be returns to past investments in schooling and social infrastructure in spite of severe short-term economic downturns. Time series analyses using aggregate data to assess the demographic effects of structural adjustment programmes, such as Bravo (Chapter 7 above) and Hill and Palloni (1992) have shown that detrended movements in vital rates do show negative effects of the 1980s recession. These short-term movements are not large enough, however to offset the continued long-term declines in variables such as infant mortality. The distinction between short-term fluctuations and long-term trends may be especially difficult in the case of female labour supply. Labor force participation rates of women have been increasing throughout most of Latin America for several decades.[2] Increases in participation during the recession-plagued 1980s, then, may be attributed to counter-cyclical 'added worker' responses to falling wages and employment of husbands, when in fact they are simply a continuation of historic trends. Although short-term fluctuations should in principle make it possible to separate long-term trends from short-term responses, we will see below that in practice this distinction is not always easy to make given the available data.

Issues and Hypotheses

A set of questions about families' labour supply decisions in the face of structural adjustment or other macroeconomic shocks lead to hypotheses which could be tested, given the appropriate data. Does the institution of the family buffer individuals from bearing the full impact of structural adjustment? Is there a countercyclical added worker effect, such that each individual's welfare falls a little but total or per capita family welfare does not fall as dramatically as might be expected from the magnitude of the external shock? Is there a countercyclical 'discouraged worker' effect, such that some unemployed family members give up searching for jobs, which offsets the added worker effect? These effects might both be relevant in a particular household. For example, an unemployed head may withdraw from the labour force, while 'secondary' household members move into the labour force.

Do family labour force adjustments primarily take place via the time use of children, adolescents, women who would not otherwise be employed, and/or old people? How strong are cross-wage effects? Does the secular trend of rising female labour force participation increase in response to negative macroeconomic conditions, or is it moderated or reversed?

---

[2] See, for example, Psacharopoulos and Tzannatos (1992).

Is there a long-term effect of short-term family labour force adjustments such that, for example, completed education levels of teenagers and young adults are lower than they otherwise would have been?

Are some households more affected by structural adjustment than are others? We expect poorer households to have fewer adjustment mechanisms left to draw upon, since they are using those strategies already, and thus fewer labour force adjustments will be seen in those households. Their welfare levels will fall, correspondingly, by greater amounts.

While it is frequently argued that family adjustments in labour supply were an important part of family 'survival strategies' in the 1980s in Latin America, it is difficult to find clear evidence of the direction or magnitude of the effects. This chapter attempts to survey the evidence that exists and to look for clear patterns in standard data on labour force participation and economic indicators.

Changes in the demand for labour may also result in changes in measured labour force participation. For every possible labour supply explanation for an empirical observation, we can also think of a labour demand explanation for the same phenomenon. For example, a decline in labour force activity of young women which is concurrent with an increase in activity of younger children could mean that young women's labour supply is responding to lower real wages in the market. Since their home productivity may be higher than that of younger siblings, who may command similar market wages, the household could be reallocating the labour force and home production time of its members. That is, children are substituted for young women in the labour market, and young women are substituted for children in tasks related to home maintenance and the provision of child care for even younger children. Alternatively, a demand-side explanation for the same scenario would imply that employers under economic pressure are willing to use cheaper, less experienced labour in order to cut costs.

We are in general unable to differentiate between labour supply and labour demand explanations for changes in observed labour force participation behavior, and we do not attempt to do so. The purpose of this chapter is to observe whether or not measured participation rates for different types of family members change systematically with macroeconomic shocks. Where they do, we can posit underlying supply-side and demand-side explanations, but we cannot choose among them. As we will show, it is the *absence* of sizeable changes in labour force participation rates of various groups which is of greatest interest in our results.

A central issue in any analysis of female labour force participation in Latin America (as in most parts of the world) is that a long-term trend of increasing participation rates may dominate short-term responses to economic fluctuations. Many factors play a role in this trend, with increases in schooling being one of the most important. In the case of Brazil, for example, Lam, Sedlacek, and Duryea (1993) document substantial increases in women's schooling in recent decades. Mean years of schooling rose from 2.7 years for the 1925–7 female birth cohort to 6.3 for the 1961–3 female birth cohort. Also noteworthy is that the mean schooling of females surpassed the mean schooling of males, beginning with cohorts born

during the 1950s. Lam, Sedlacek, and Duryea show that these increases in schooling can explain well over half of the decline in fertility across these cohorts, a
decline directly related to the increase in women's labour force participation. It is
important to keep in mind that while many Latin American countries were experiencing short-term downturns in macroeconomic conditions during the 1980s, it
continued to be the case that women entering the labour force were better educated
that previous cohorts. This exerts a strong upward influence on women's labour
force participation rates that may dominate any short-term effects, especially at
ages above 25 or so.

Another important implication of the increase in women's schooling is that it
may cause younger women's participation rates to decline, creating a divergence in
the trends for younger and older women. At younger ages, especially in the 15–19
age group, increased schooling may exert a downward trend on women's labour
force participation rates, as increasing proportions of women remain in school
during these ages. We are not able to disentangle the role of schooling in most of
the countries we analyse in this chapter. In the case of Brazil, however, we will be
able to analyse participation rates within schooling groups, making it possible to
remove at least that component of the long-term trend in women's labour force
participation.

Empirical Evidence from Latin America

A number of researchers have argued that economic recession in the 1980s played
a direct causal role in explaining increases in labour force participation rates
of women. Garcia and Oliveira (Chapter 10 below) conclude from comparison of
Mexican household survey data from 1981 and 1987 that Mexico's economic crisis
forced more women with little schooling in the manual sector to work. They also
find that both schooling and the presence of young children have smaller effects on
labour force participation rates in 1987, a result they attribute to the increased
economic pressure faced by households in the later period.

Minujin (1992) comes to similar conclusions for the case of Argentina. Using
household survey data from Greater Buenos Aires, he documents increases in
female labour force participation rates from 1974 to 1990 for three socioeconomic
groups he characterizes as 'structurally poor', 'pauperized', and 'non-poor'. Although he emphasizes economic pressure as the major cause of this increase, he
notes that the participation rates for the 'non-poor' increase at a substantially faster
rate than for the 'structurally poor'. The evidence of a direct link between economic
recession on labour force participation of women in Minujin's Argentine data is
indirect at best. The major trend appears to be a steady secular increase in participation rates over time, dominated by rapid increases among the higher income
group. Participation rates for his 'non-poor' group increase from 38.9 per cent in
1980 to 49.5 per cent in 1990. Participation rates increase only slightly for his
lower income groups, rising from 34.3 in 1980 to 38.2 in 1990 for his 'structurally

poor' class, and from 18.3 in 1980 to 21.7 in 1990 for his somewhat better-off 'pauperized' class.

Horton (1994) analyses participation and unemployment rates in Bolivia during a period of severe economic shocks. She finds mixed evidence regarding the extent of 'discouraged worker' and 'added worker' effects. She argues that the recession years of 1982–3 were characterized by falling participation rates for women, implying a 'discouraged worker' effect. Her results are based on participation rates for all women, without controls for age or household position. A secular increase in female participation is the dominant pattern. There is no clear evidence of cyclical responses in female labour market activity, though Horton suggests that increasing female participation during the 1980s may in part be a response to economic crisis.

Gindling (1993) decomposes the determinants of male–female earnings and wage differentials in Costa Rica during the 1980s. The author examines the period of the 1980–3 economic crisis and stabilization, when the differentials increase, as well as the 1983–6 recovery, when the differentials decrease. During the period of crisis and stabilization, the percentage of the labour force consisting of non-heads of households increased from 48.6 per cent in 1979 to 53.3 per cent in 1982, and then fell to 51.5 per cent in 1986. A disproportionate share of these non-head workers were women and, moreover, the new female entrants had lower levels of education than did women already in the labour force. Other secondary workers also increased their participation during the recession of 1980–2: participation rates were significantly higher in 1982 for males and females ages 12–14 and 15–19 than either before or after that year. Gindling concludes that 'the increase in the male–female wage differential during the recession was due primarily to the influx of less educated women into the labour force in response to falling real wages for the primary family worker (1993: 291)', and argues that the increase in female labour force participation during the crisis is differentiated from the long-term trend of increasing female participation by the rapidity of the increase during the economic crisis (1993: 295, note 22).

Edwards and Roberts (1993) survey several case studies of female labour force participation in Latin America during the 1980s, and note that the dominant feature of the evidence is the secular increase in women's labour market activity over time, a trend that appears in most countries during periods of both economic expansion and economic decline. Edwards and Roberts pool data for twenty Latin American countries from 1966 to 1987 to estimate regressions of female participation rates on measures of fertility, school enrolments, urbanization, and the economic cycle. The measure of economic cycle is interacted with overall per capita income in such a way that separate cyclical effects are estimated for three groups of countries ranked by per capita income. The results suggest that women's labour force participation is countercyclical in the lowest income countries, consistent with an 'added worker effect.' The countercyclical effect exists but is smaller in magnitude for middle income countries and is statistically insignificant in the highest income countries.

The analysis of the Argentine experience by Pessino (1991) is one of the few studies which has seriously attempted to deal with issues of causality. Identification of macroeconomic shocks is an important difficulty in studies of the effects of macroeconomic phenomena, and one which is rarely overcome. Pessino uses the brief Argentine hyperinflation of July 1989 as a natural experiment, attributing changes between 'before' and 'after' cross-section data from Greater Buenos Aires to the economic shock of hyperinflation. She examines the structure and distribution of wages of prime-age males in October 1987 and October 1989 and reports three main empirical findings. First, she finds that macroeconomic shocks—inflation, in this case—affected wage profiles of males aged 25–54 in a non-neutral way across experience/age, education, tenure, and sector of the economy. In particular, post-shock returns to education were higher, especially for less-educated groups. Returns to seniority also increased. Second, workers with higher stocks of general and specific human capital were less affected by the negative impact of inflation on real wages. Third, employers, self-employed workers, and those with informal contracts suffered less from inflation than did the wage-employed under formal contracts. Although Pessino's results come from a population of prime-age males, they have interesting—and testable—implications for 'secondary' workers. They suggest that there may have been incentives for such workers to enter the informal sector or to become self-employed workers.

It is possible to construct at least partial series of age-specific labour force participation rates and macroeconomic indicators from published sources for a number of Latin American countries. Figures 9.1–9.5 show data for Argentina, Bolivia, Chile, Costa Rica, and Peru, countries with large economic fluctuations in the 1980s. The data are based on the United Nations Statistical Yearbooks, the International Labour Office's Yearbook of Labour Statistics, and a variety of other sources. We have chosen to focus, in these series, on the labour force participation of young women. This choice was driven partly by a general lack of comparable data for younger teenagers and children or the elderly, but it was also made because women in their twenties are in their peak child-bearing years and thus have been given the most attention in the literature as potential 'added' or 'discouraged' workers.

The economic turbulence of the 1980s in Argentina is reflected by the economic series in the top panel of Figure 9.1. A precipitous fall in GDP in the early 1980s was accompanied by sharply falling industrial production. Real wages (not shown here) also fell sharply. After a mild recovery in 1984, GDP (and real wages) again fell steeply. The bottom panel of Figure 9.1 shows labour force participation rates for young Argentine women during the 1980s. Although few data points are available, it appears that the economic crisis of the early 1980s may have disrupted the secular rise in participation rates. Between 1980 and 1983, female labour force participation rates of the 20–4 and 25–9 age groups actually fell, while participation of 15–19 year-olds increased. After 1983, these patterns were reversed: participation of women in their twenties began to rise again, while participation of teenage women fell.

In Bolivia, the fall in real wages in the early 1980s was even more precipitous than in Argentina. The top panel of Figure 9.2 shows that by 1984 real wages were

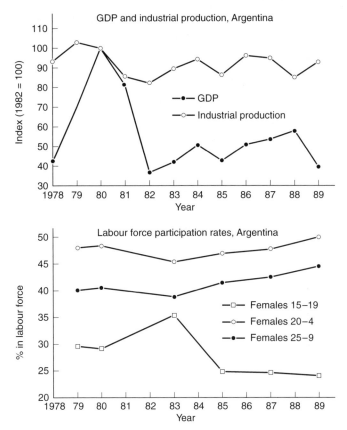

Fig. 9.1 Economic indicators and female labour force participation rates, Argentina, 1978–89

less than 40 per cent of their 1980 level. GDP also fell, gradually until 1984, when it began a sharp decline. Again, our examination of the labour force participation of young women is hindered by a scarcity of data points in the early and mid-1980s. However, like Argentina, it appears that participation of women in their twenties may have been diminished by the crisis of the early 1980s and encouraged by a rise in real wages in 1985, whereas the opposite seems to have held for women aged 15–19.

In contrast, Figure 9.3 shows that after a stabilization-induced recession in 1980, Chile's GDP climbed slowly but steadily throughout the decade of the 1980s. Other evidence shows that Chile experienced a huge level of open unemployment during the early 1980s, and that inequality rose greatly during the decade (Bravo, Chapter 7 below). The lower panel of Figure 9.3 plots labour force participation rates for women aged 20–4 and 25–9. It is interesting that these participation rates show no sign of a secular increase, instead flattening out in the late 1980s.

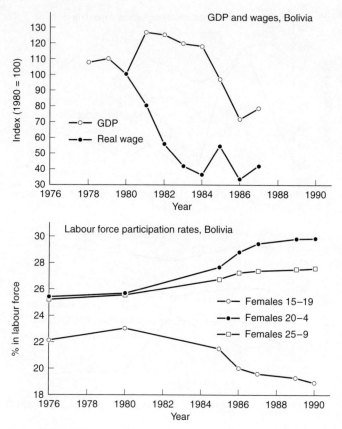

Fig. 9.2 Economic indicators and female labour force participation rates, Bolivia, 1978–90

Figure 9.4 documents the experience of Costa Rica from 1980 to 1986, based on data presented by Gindling (1993). As pointed out by Gindling, the most interesting feature of Figure 9.4 is the substantial increase in the participation rates of women aged 15–19 in 1982, the bottom of Costa Rica's recession. There is also some evidence that participation rates of women aged 20–9 and 30–9 increased during the recession and then fell in the recovery of 1983. Participation rates fell for women aged 15–19 during the economic improvements of 1983–6, but increased for older women.

Figure 9.5 presents data on GDP and female labour force participation rates during the 1980s in Peru. In the Peruvian case the most dramatic economic downturn occurred after 1987. This coincides with what appears to be a decline in the rate of increase in female labour force participation rates. The participation rates of 15–19 and 25–9 year-old women show only slight increases after 1987, while the participation rates of 20–4 year-olds show a decline.

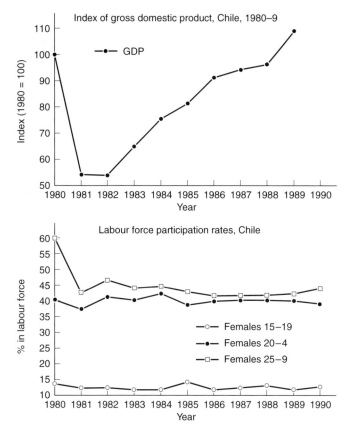

Fig. 9.3 Gross domestic product and female labour force participation rates, Chile, 1980–90

The evidence provided by these five countries is mixed. None of the five sets of figures provides strong evidence that labour force participation rates of young women fluctuate greatly with economic events, even given the dramatic fluctuations observed in each country's macroeconomic indicators. Unfortunately, the data on participation rates have many missing years and are often from inconsistent series.[3] However, some patterns do appear. The secular increase in female labour force participation rates was interrupted in all of these countries at some point in the 1980s. Moreover, participation of women aged 20–4 and 25–9 seems, overall, to be pro-cyclical when we take the secular trends in participation into account. Some of the evidence suggests that, at least in Argentina, Bolivia, and Costa Rica, participation of younger women aged 15–19 is countercyclical. The differing trends

---

[3] The 1980 data for Chile, in particular, are quite problematic. Inspection of the data indicates implausibly large differences in the number of women aged 20–4 and 25–29, the main source of the very high estimated participation rate for 25–9 year-old women in 1980.

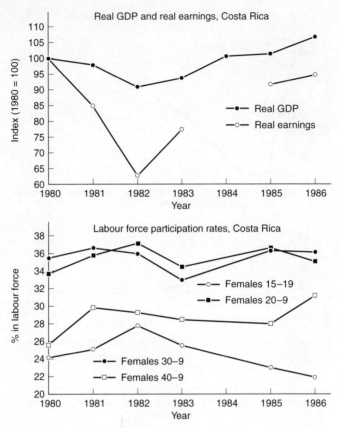

Fig. 9.4 Gross domestic product, earnings, and female labour force participation rates, Costa Rica, 1980–6

for the 15–19 year-olds, however, might be explained by the fact that increasing proportions of women in this age group are remaining in school. The apparent countercyclical tendency for women in this age group may represent a decline in school enrolment (and corresponding increase in labour force) during economic downturns, and an increase in school enrolment (and corresponding decline in labour force) during the economic expansions. Schooling choices become less of an issue for the older women, removing this countercyclical component from the observed response in labour supply.

Analysis of Household Data from Brazil, 1977–90

The previous section showed that published data on labour force participation rates from Latin American countries in the 1980s do not provide a clear picture of any

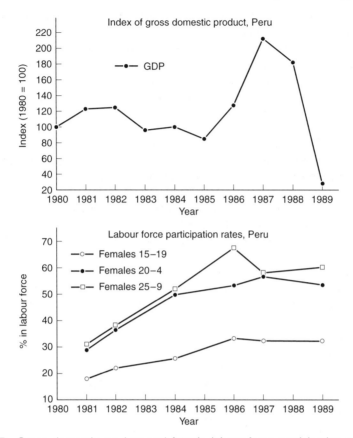

Fig. 9.5 Gross domestic product and female labour force participation rates, Peru, 1980–9

strong systematic relationship between the labour force participation rates for young women and macroeconomic fluctuations, even in cases of extreme macroeconomic shocks. We are reluctant to attach much weight to these data, however, since the empirical record is patchy and imprecise. If true, and not simply the result of poor data, the lack of a strong link between macroeconomic fluctuations and labour force participation rates of young women is important, insofar as it implies that households do not or cannot respond to macroeconomic shocks via adjustments in the employment rates of their members. Further, as will be true throughout our analysis, it is impossible for us to separate effects of labour demand and labour supply. If households are constrained in their employment opportunities then they may not have the ability to adjust labour supply in response to economic conditions. Referring back to our theoretical structure above, we also do not know the extent to which macroeconomic fluctuations show up as significant changes in wages at the household level.

Published data such as these can only be suggestive, then, since they are often only reported for occasional years and are highly aggregated in terms of critical characteristics. More careful analysis of the effects of macroeconomic fluctuations on family labour supply requires detailed household-level data that make it possible to look at separate economic groups and positions in the household. Our strategy will be to take a much more detailed look at one particular country, Brazil, which has detailed and consistent annual survey data that make it possible more finely to test hypotheses about labour market adjustments of particular family members, controlling for household characteristics. The macroeconomic fluctuations of the 1980s in Brazil are similar to those of other Latin American countries, allowing a test of the effects of these shocks on family labour supply.

The data used for this analysis are the core surveys from the Pesquisa Nacional de Amostra de Domicilios (PNAD), an extensive annual economic and demographic survey conducted by the Fundação Instituto Brasileiro de Geografia e Estatística (IBGE). These data have also been used by Jatobá (1993) and Sedlacek (1992) to analyse the relationship between economic recession and family labour supply in Brazil during the 1980s. Jatobá (1993) analyses the labour force participation of the Brazilian family as a unit. He uses PNAD data for 1978–88 to compare family labour force aggregates in the metropolitan areas of Northeast and Southeast Brazil. He creates, for example, a family labour force participation rate defined as the proportion of family members aged 10 and over who are either employed or searching for employment. He also considers the labour force participation of wives and of children over 10 separately. Jatobá concludes from his descriptive evidence for 1978–88 and from his multivariate analysis for 1988 that (1) poor families tend to increase their labour force participation as the income of the head falls; (2) that family labour force participation increases with the level of unemployment among family members, except in the poorest families; and (3) that family participation is more responsive to unemployment in the Northeast than in the Southeast. He argues that although there might have been structural factors pushing up the participation rates of women and children, at least part of the increase in female and child participation is due to the adverse economic conditions —high unemployment rates and falling incomes—in the 1980s. In summary, Jatobá appears to find evidence of an added worker effect. However, since the multivariate analysis is for one year only, his analysis does not overcome our problem of being unable to distinguish added worker effects from time trends.

Sedlacek (1992) also argues that increases in wives' labour force participation rates are an important survival strategy for Brazilian families during periods of recession. Although his evidence of a countercyclical labour supply response by married women is mostly indirect, based on the cross-sectional relationship between husband's income and wife's labour supply, his results confirm the importance of looking separately at women in different household positions in analysing trends in female labour supply. He shows, for example, that part of the observed increase in overall female participation rates from 1979 to 1989 was due to the increase in the proportion of women who were single heads of households. The proportion classified as wives remained relatively constant over this period, while there was a decrease in the proportion of women who were classified as 'daughters of the household head' in the PNAD surveys. Since labour force participation rates of female heads were roughly double the rates for wives, and substantially above the rates for daughters, the increase in the relative proportion of female heads played some role in the observed increase in overall female participation rates. His results also show, however, that the most important trend explaining the overall increase in female labour force participation rates was the large increase in participation rates of wives. Sedlacek's results indicate that the participation rates of wives may behave differently in both long-term trends and short-term fluctuations from the participation rates of women in other household positions.

We will make this same distinction in our analysis, focusing on the participation rates of wives. We have constructed identical household level data from the PNAD surveys from 1977–90. The survey's large size (over 100,000 households until 1985, then about 60,000 households in later years) allows us to make fine controls for age, education, and household status in order to look more carefully at the labour market behavior of households during this period of large economic swings. Future work will also control for urban or rural residence and will attempt to distinguish between formal and informal work; however, those important analyses are beyond the scope of this chapter.[4]

Figure 9.6 shows trends in per capita GDP, industrial production, and female labour force participation in Brazil from 1976 to 1990. The 1970s were a period of sustained economic growth in Brazil, with annual growth in GDP of over 10 per cent in the early 1970s followed by growth rates of around 5 per cent per year in the later part of the decade. As seen clearly in Figure 9.6, the early 1980s showed the dramatic recessionary impact of international shocks and adjustment policies adopted to deal with the debt crisis.[5] At the end of 1980, the Brazilian government adopted a policy of voluntary adjustment to satisfy the demands of the IMF and its other debtors. This policy of restraining internal demand, combined with the Mexican debt payment moratorium of 1982, resulted, in 1983, in the most severe recession of modern-day Brazil. Real wages fell substantially and open urban unemployment rose, as did urban violence. In spite of the large contraction, inflation continued to rise, doubling between 1982 and 1983. A large devaluation of the cruzeiro in February of 1983 contributed to rising rates of import substitution and

---

[4] Jatobá (1990) provides some evidence on the importance of regional differences in his analysis of labour force participation of women and men in the urban regions of Southeast and Northeast Brazil from 1979–86. For both women and men in each year, participation rates in the Southeast are above the urban average for Brazil while those in the Northeast are below the urban average. The gap between Southeast and Northeast participation rates ranges from 3 to 7 percentage points for both females and males over this time period. The trends, however, follow the same patterns of peaks and troughs, with few exceptions. This is also generally true for 10–14 year-old girls and boys and for 20–4 year-old women in the Northeast and Southeast.

[5] See Munhoz (1988), Silva (1991), Chahad and Macedo (1988), Bonelli and Sedlacek (1989), and Amadeo and Camargo (1989) for a discussion of economic trends in Brazil in the 1980s.

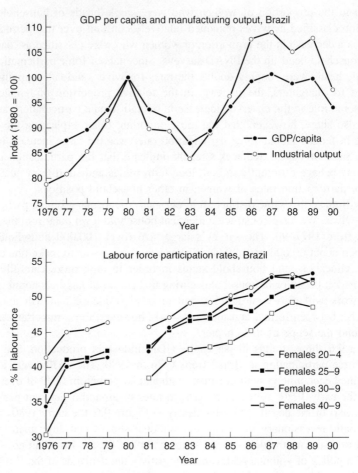

Fig. 9.6 Economic indicators and female labour force participation rates, Brazil, 1976–90

higher sales of exports abroad, eventually leading to a mild recovery in 1984 and 1985. However, inflation rates continued to increase.

The *Plano Cruzado* instituted a general freeze on prices and wages, beginning in February of 1986. It succeeded in reducing the inflation rate to less than 2 per cent per month during its initial months in place, and it also reduced open unemployment rates from 4.4 per cent in February 1986 to 2.2 per cent in December of that year. However, inflation accelerated in 1987, and the *Plano Cruzado* was replaced by the *Plano Bresser* in June of 1987. The Bresser Plan froze prices and wages for about three months, until the end of August, at which time a programme of readjusting wages and prices each month began. Wages were adjusted at less than the inflation rate, leading to declines in real wages.

The *Plano Verão* (Summer Plan) of January 1989 instituted measures to increase government revenues and decrease public sector spending. The Summer Plan has been credited with preventing hyperinflation during the period of political campaigning leading up to Brazil's presidential elections in late 1989 and early 1990 (Silva 1991). Hyperinflation was threatening, however, when the *Plano Collor* came into effect on 15 March 1990, with President Collor's inauguration. The Collor Plan immediately froze access to private sector financial assets, among other measures, drastically decreasing the money supply. This anti-inflationary policy shock presumably played a large role in the economic downturn of 1990.

The bottom panel of Figure 9.6 shows trends in female labour force participation from 1976 to 1989 based on published data from the PNAD household survey. The graph for females demonstrates the important point that increasing female participation rates in the 1980s were a continuation of the strong trend upward during the economic expansions of previous decades. Thus, while economic pressure during the recessionary 1980s may have played a role in the rising female labour force participation rates, it seems unlikely to be the primary explanation.

The patterns for female participation rates in Figure 9.6 do not appear to show a close link between economic fluctuations and female labour market activity and thus appear to offer little support for a countercyclical 'added worker' effect in female labour force participation rates, or at least not for one which dominates a potential 'discouraged worker' effect. The data may be too aggregated, however, to provide a test of the hypothesis that labour force participation of wives moves countercyclically as a buffer to maintain household income. First, the data combine the experience of female household heads with the experience of wives. Female heads without husbands have much higher labour force participation rates than married women do and may behave differently in response to changing wages. Second, the cyclical response of married women may vary substantially across economic levels. It is often argued that the effect will be strongest for poorer households, who are more liquidity constrained and are under greater pressure to maintain household income. Third, if both 'added worker' and 'discouraged worker' effects exist, they may offset each other, resulting in little apparent movement in the aggregate patterns.

The individual data in the PNAD allow us to explore the first two hypotheses more carefully. First of all, we can look at the economic fluctuations during the 1980s for households in different economic situations. Since we are focusing on the labour force participation of wives, we will look at the economic indicators relevant to wives in a particular age group and education level. Figure 9.7 shows real wages and unemployment rates for the *husbands* of wives aged 30–4 by years of schooling of the wives.[6] As the top panel shows, fluctuations in real wages were experienced by households at all education levels, with fairly similar proportional fluctuations in wages experienced at the top and bottom of the schooling distribution. The years

---

[6] Lam and Schoeni (1993) show that the correlation between years of schooling completed by husbands and wives is 0.77.

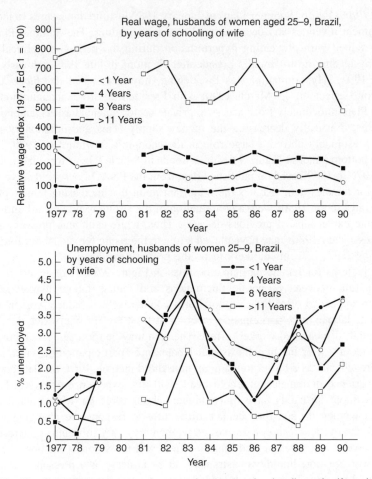

Fig. 9.7 Real wages and unemployment by years of schooling of wife, wives aged 25–9, Brazil, 1977–90

1983 and 1984 appear as recessionary years, while the brief boom of the Cruzado Plan of 1986 shows up for all schooling levels. Looking at the unemployment figures for husbands in the bottom panel of Figure 9.7, 1983 stands out as a year of sharp increases in unemployment at all levels of schooling, with improvements in 1986 and 1987 followed by increases in unemployment at the end of the decade. For example, the group with the least educated wives shows unemployment rising from under 2 per cent in the late 1970s to 4 per cent in the recession of 1983, declining to slightly over 1 per cent in the recovery of 1986, then rising back to 4 per cent in 1990.

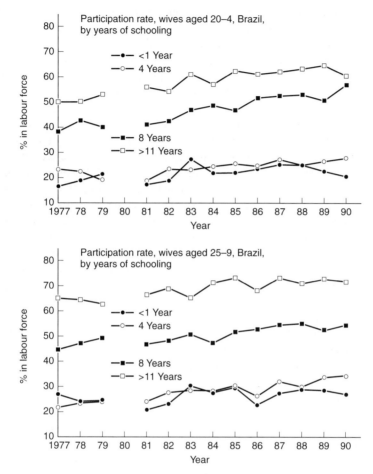

Fig. 9.8 Participation rates for wives aged 20–4 and 25–9, by years of schooling, Brazil, 1977–90

Figures 9.8 and 9.9 look at the labour force participation of wives only[7], controlling for years of education, for separate five-year age groups. The top panel of Figure 9.8 shows the changes in labour force participation rates from 1977 to 1990 for women aged 20–4 for four large schooling categories.[8] One of the most obvious features of Figure 9.8 is the much higher participation rates for highly educated women. The participation rates for the best educated women also increase faster

---

[7] This refers to women whose husbands are present in the household, and is based on the IBGE's broad definition of spouse, which includes both formal marriages and consensual unions.

[8] No estimate is presented for 1980 in all of the following figures. The PNAD was not collected in 1980 because it was replaced by the decennial census.

during the decade than do those for less educated women. Women with the least education show a small upward trend in their participation rates during the decade, and also appear to show larger short-term fluctuations in their labour force participation rates than better educated women. Although the figures do not give a clear picture of cyclical responses in labour supply, the patterns for both 20–4 year-olds and 25–9 year-olds give some evidence of an increase in participation in 1983 and a decrease in participation in 1986 for women in the lowest education categories. The least educated 20–4 year-olds, for example, show an increase in labour force participation of over five percentage points between 1982 and 1983. As noted above, 1983 stands out by most indicators as the worst year of the recession of the early part of the decade, and 1986 stands out as a period of substantial improvement. While these patterns must be interpreted with caution, they appear to offer some support for a countercyclical labour market response of the least educated wives. As emphasized earlier, there may be both labour demand and labour supply interpretations of these effects. Movements in women's participation rates may represent shifts in labour supply, as women enter and leave the labour force in response to shifts in the wages and employment of other household members.[9] Movements in women's participation rates might also represent demand effects to the extent that increases in participation result from increased demand for women workers. In the case of countercyclical movements in participation it is difficult to attribute the changes to labour demand, since we would require that employers increase demand for women workers in the same years that male wages and employment decline. This kind of demand difference could, however, result from labour markets which are segmented along gender lines or from any human capital or institutional reason resulting in lower wages for women than men on average. In other words, if demand shocks affect different sectors of the economy with varying degrees of severity, and/or if female and male workers tend to be substitutes in the labour force, a demand-driven increase in women's participation rates is not incompatible with a demand-driven decrease in men's employment levels.[10]

Figure 9.9 shows the participation rates for women aged 30–4 and 35–9. Once again we see some evidence of countercyclical responses in the participation of the least educated women in 1983 and 1986. Participation rates for better educated women show, if anything, movement in the opposite direction, with participation rates falling slightly in 1983 and increasing in 1986. Among women of 30–4 and 35–9 the increases in participation rates during the 1980s are faster for women with low levels of education. The best educated older women begin the decade with participation rates around 75 per cent and show little change during the decade.

We now look at the labour force activity of children and teenagers, another group traditionally considered 'secondary workers'. We focus attention on the participation

---

[9] Although these can be thought of as labour supply responses, it is important to note that the fundamental shock to the labour market is a labour demand shock affecting the wages and employment of the husband or other household members.

[10] For example, the informal sector generally has a higher proportion of female workers than does the formal sector, and the informal sector also might be less severely affected by macro shocks.

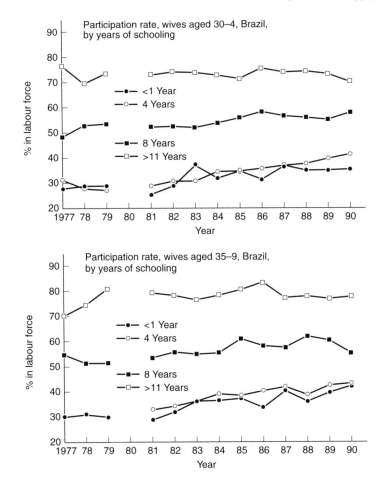

Fig. 9.9 Participation rates for wives aged 30–4 and 35–9, by years of schooling, Brazil, 1977–90

rates of children in households in which the household head has less than one year of schooling.[11] Education of the household head is used as a proxy for socio-economic status both because of its high correlation with household income in Brazil and because it can be measured consistently over time. Analysis of house-holds in which the head has higher levels of education (not shown here) indicates substantial declines in children's participation rates as the schooling of the head increases. About 20 per cent of 10-year-old sons of heads with less than one year of schooling report they are economically active, compared to only 2 or 3 per cent

[11] We use the IBGE definition of 'household head': if the husband is present in the household, he is considered its head.

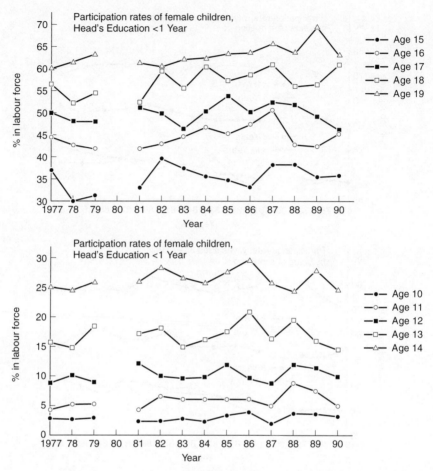

Fig. 9.10 Participation rates for female children, aged 10–19, of household heads with less than one year of schooling, Brazil, 1977–90

of sons of heads with 8–10 years of schooling. Figure 9.10 shows the participation rates of 10–19 year-old daughters of household heads who have less than one year of schooling. Figure 9.11 shows the corresponding participation rates of 10–19 year-old sons.

Overall, Figures 9.10 and 9.11 provide mixed evidence about responses in children's labour force participation to economic fluctuations. The recession trough year of 1983 does show up once again as in these figures, however, although in a somewhat unexpected direction. Boys and girls in several age groups appear to show substantial declines in their participation rates in 1983, suggesting a pro-cyclical response in child labour. For older children, who have much higher labour force participation rates, there does not appear to be a decline in participation in 1983,

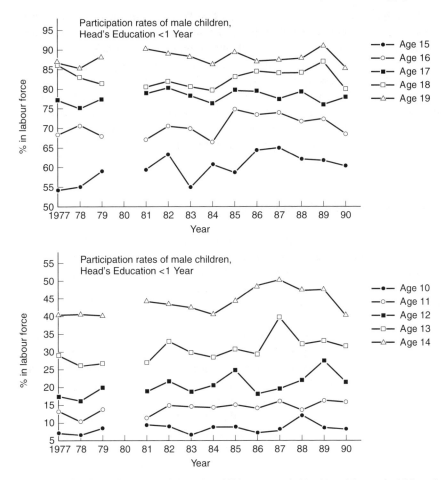

Fig. 9.11 Participation rates for male children, aged 10–19, of household heads with less than one year of schooling, Brazil, 1977–90

although there is evidence of a decline in 1984, a year of lower unemployment but continued recession.

Measured labour force participation rates of 'secondary' workers such as children and young women are always subject to a certain degree of doubt due to problems of measurement, which are likely to affect such workers to a greater extent than they affect 'primary' workers. Unpaid family workers are included in this Brazilian sample;[12] however, other family members who are informal sector workers may be overlooked. Levison (1991) found that an alternative measure of

---

[12] In 1985, for example, 7.6 per cent of urban 10–14 year-olds worked, and 14 per cent of urban 10–14 year-old workers were unpaid (Levison 1991).

work, available for 7–14 year-olds in the 1985 PNAD Supplement, led to a substantially different sample of children being defined as workers. She attributes part of the difference to the child's primary identification being as a student, not a worker. In other words, those household members with a lower degree of labour force attachment may be less readily identified as labour force participants. It is possible that, because of this sort of measurement error, we are unable reliably to identify short-term increases in labour supply for those household members. This would be the case if, for example, children's increased labour force activity were in addition to, not instead of, time spent in school, and if most children worked in the informal sector.

Interpretations and Speculations

The data presented here can only be considered suggestive of the relationship between structural adjustment and labour supply of family members. Although analysis of the detailed annual household survey data for Brazil should provide better evidence of systematic adjustments in family labour supply strategies than can be gleaned from aggregate published data, even the Brazilian data do not provide a consistent picture of clear procyclical or countercyclical behavior in the labour supply of married women or children. Simple comparisons of real wages of husbands and labour force participation rates of wives during the period 1977–90 in Brazil can suggest a strong countercyclical tendency in wives' participation rates. The top panel of Figure 9.12 shows how strong this relationship can appear to be in a simple scatter-plot of wives' participation rates plotted against husbands' real wages.[13] The data are for wives aged 25–9 with less than one year of schooling. Although there is a clear negative relationship in the top panel, it appears to be driven more by long-term trends in labour force participation than by short-term economic fluctuations. The year generating each data point is indicated on the graph. As inspection of the graph makes clear, the major feature is that the 1970s were a period of relatively high real wages of husbands and relatively low labour force participation of wives, while the middle to late 1980s was a period of higher wives' labour force participation and low real wages for husbands. While this is consistent with a strong 'added worker effect' and with the interpretation of the 1980s given by a number of the authors discussed above, it may also be explained as the continuation of past upward trends in female labour supply, with the decline in real wages playing no direct causal role. The bottom panel indicates that the relationship between wives' participation rates and husbands' unemployment rates over this period is much less clear. A positive relationship consistent with a countercyclical 'added worker effect' is partially evident, but is again driven mainly by the increase in participation between the 1970s and the late 1980s. The points generated by the sharp fluctuations of the early and middle 1980s actually map out a

---

[13] These scatterplots are derived from information previously presented in Figures 9.7 and 9.8.

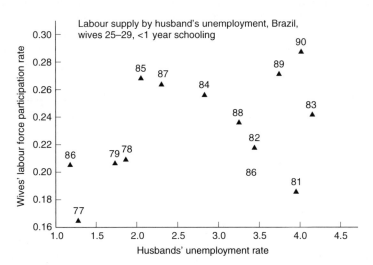

Fig. 9.12 Scatter-plots of wives' participation rates by husbands' real wages and unemployment rates, wives aged 25–9 with less than one year of schooling, Brazil, 1977–90

mostly negative relationship between husbands' unemployment and wives' participation. The evidence overall is quite mixed, then, and is clearly sensitive to the interpretation given to overall increases in female labour supply during the 1980s.

Two of the patterns that we find in the Brazilian data seem especially important. First, married women with little education show a large decline in participation rates in 1986, a year with substantially higher real wages. This is especially true for those at the bottom of the distribution. In terms of labour supply this could indicate a response to the higher wages of husbands: that is, the predicted negative cross-wage effect implied by the conventional 'added worker' hypothesis. Similarly, it could represent an income effect, with wives reducing labour supply in response to the improved economic condition of the household. There may also be quite different explanations relating to labour demand. High real wages may have reduced demand for less educated formal sector 'secondary' workers, who have the least firm-specific human capital. Although we do not observe an increase in reported unemployment for these women, conventional unemployment measures may be poor indicators for them. We also observe an increase in participation for the least educated wives in many age groups in 1983, the trough of the recession. This is also consistent with a countercyclical 'added worker' effect, which dominates any 'discouraged worker' effect.

Second, we find a fall in most of the labour force participation rates for girls and boys aged 10–15 in 1983 in the households with low education for the head. This apparent pro-cyclical response is inconsistent with the common argument that poor households may have their children work more during bad economic times. Labour demand effects may help explain this, to the extent that there are fewer economic opportunities for these children during the trough of the recession. These declines do not appear for older children, however, which poses a challenge for explanations based purely on labour demand. It is tempting to speculate that the decline in labour force participation for children in 1983 is directly related to the observed increase in participation for wives in 1983, especially those with least education. We see increased participation rates in 1983 for women ages 30–4, an increase that could be related to the decrease in participation for 10–12 year-olds. This is consistent with the kind of intrahousehold substitution of labour that has often been suggested by a variety of researchers, but has been difficult to observe in time-series evidence. The poorest households may have responded to the bad economic conditions of 1983 by increasing labour market activity of wives and using older children as substitutes for the mother in household work and care of younger children.

A creative reading of the patterns documented here may provide some support for the arguments found in previous literature linking economic recession in the 1980s in Latin America to increased labour force participation of wives and children. In the final analysis, however, the evidence for such effects appears to be quite weak. The data suggest that the overall increase in participation rates observed in Brazil in the 1980s is much better explained by the increase in schooling of women entering the labour market and by the increases in participation rates for the best educated women than it is by a countercyclical response to bad economic conditions. In the case of children we find virtually no evidence of an increase in labour market activity during the worst years of the recession. Children aged 10–15 show either no adjustment or decreases in their labour force participation rates in the worst year of the recession. Our results do suggest that short-term labour supply responses of both wives and children may be larger for those at the bottom of the scale of education and income distribution. If future research is ever going to identify systematic effects on family labour supply of macroeconomic shocks associated with structural adjustment programmes, it will be essential to control as finely as possible for the socioeconomic characteristics and the position of individuals in the household.

REFERENCES

Amadeo, E. and Camargo, J. M. (1989), 'Brazilian Labour Market in an Era of Adjustment', October, mimeo, Pontificia Universidade Católica, Rio de Janeiro.

Bonelli, R. and Sedlacek, G. (1989), 'Distribuição da Renda: Evolução no ultimo quarto do século,' in Sedlacek, G. and de Barros, R. Paes (eds.), *Mercado do Trabalho e Distribuição de Renda*, Rio de Janeiro: IPEA.

Bravo, J., 'Demographic Consequences of Structural Adjustment in Chile', Chapter 7 below.

Chahad, J. P. Z. and Macedo, R. (1988), 'Ajuste Econômico e Impacto Social no Brasil: 1980–1987. Os Efeitos Sobre a População Infantil', in Chahad and Cervini (eds.), *Crise e Infância no Brasil: O Impacto das Politicas de Ajustamento Econômico*, São Paulo: Instituto de Pesquisas Econômicas da Faculdade de Economia e Administração.

Edwards, Alejandra Cox and Roberts, Judith, 'Macroeconomic Influences on Female Labor Force Participation: The Latin American Evidence', Estudios-de-Economia, 20(0), Special Issue, June 1993, 87–106.

Fundação Instituto Brasileiro de Geografia e Estatística (various years), *Anuário Estatístico do Brasil*, Rio de Janeiro.

Garcia, B. and Oliveira, O. de, 'Economic Recession and Changing Determinants of Women's Work', Chapter 10 below.

Gindling, T. H. (1993), 'Women's Wages and Economic Crisis in Costa Rica', *Economic Development and Cultural Change*, 41/2, 277–97.

Hill, K. and Palloni, A. (1992), 'Demographic Responses to Economic Shocks: The Case of Latin America', Proceedings of the Conference on the Peopling of the Americas, Veracruz: International Union for the Scientific Study of Population, 411–38.

Horton, S. (1994), 'Labor Markets in an Era of Adjustment: Bolivia', in Horton, S. Kanbur, R., and Mazumdar, D. (eds.), *Labor Markets in an Era of Adjustment*, Economic Development Institute, Washington, DC: World Bank.

Horton, S., Kanbur, R., and Mazumbar, D. (1991), 'Labor Markets in an Era of Adjustment: Evidence from 12 Developing Countries', forthcoming, *International Labour Review*, 130/5–6, 531–58.

International Labour Office (various years), *Year Book of Labour Statistics*, Geneva: International Labour Organisation.

Jatobá, J. (1992), 'The Brazilian Family in the Labor Force, 1978–1988: A Study of Labor Supply', Yale Economic Growth Center Working Paper.

Jatobá, J. (1990), 'Ciclo Econômico e Força de Trabalho no Brasil Urbano: 1978/1987', Cadernos de Economia, 01, Programa Nacional de Pesquisa Econômia-PNPE, Rio de Janeiro: IPEA.

Lam, D. and Schoeni, R. (1993), 'Effects of Family Background on Earnings and Returns to Schooling: Evidence from Brazil', *Journal of Political Economy*, 101/4, 710–40.

Lam, D., Sedlacek, G. and Duryea, S. (1993), 'Increases in education and fertility decline in Brazil', paper presented at the Annual Meeting of the Population Association of America.

Levison, D. (1991), *Children's Labor Force Activity and Schooling in Brazil*, unpublished PhD dissertation, University of Michigan, Ann Arbor.

Lundberg, S. (1985), 'The Added Worker Effect', *Journal of Labor Economics*, 3/1, 11–35.

Mincer, J. (1962), 'Labor Force Participation of Married Women', in Lewis, H. G. (ed.), *Aspects of Labor Economics*, Princeton University Press.

Minujin, A. (1992), 'From "Secondary Workers" to Breadwinners: Poor and Non-Poor Women Facing the Crisis', paper presented at the IUSSP Seminar on Demographic Consequences of Structural Adjustment in Latin America, Ouro Preto, Brazil.

Munhoz, D. G. (1988), 'Reflexos Desestabilizadores dos Programas de Ajustamento Externo', in Chahad and Cervini (eds.), *Crise e Infância no Brasil: O Impacto das Políticas de Ajustamento Econômico*.

Pessino, C. (1991), 'From Aggregate Shocks to Labor Market Adjustments: Shifting of Wage Profiles under Hyperinflation in Argentina', July, mimeo, Economic Growth Center, Yale University.

Psacharopoulos, G. and Tzannatos, Z. (1992), *Women's Employment and Pay in Latin America*, The World Bank: Washington, DC.

Sedlacek, G. (1992), 'Estratégia de Sobrevivência da Família Brasileira: Um Estudo da Participação das Esposas', *Perspectivas da Economia Brasileira 1992*, Brasília: Instituto de Pesquisa Econômica Aplicada.

Silva, J. C. Ferreira da (1991), 'Origens, Evolução e Estágio Atual da Crise Econômica', in *Perspectivas da Economia Brasileira—1992*, Rio de Janeiro: IPEA.

United Nations (various years), *Statistical Yearbook*, New York.

10 Economic Recession and Changing Determinants of Women's Work

BRÍGIDA GARCÍA AND ORLANDINA DE OLIVEIRA

Introduction

In 1982, Mexico, like other Latin American countries, began to experience a severe economic recession. Since the mid-1970s the country's economic development, which was based on import substitution, had begun to face difficulties. Public and private investment were at a minimum; fiscal imbalance, inflation and capital flight began to be pronounced. The currency was devalued for the first time in two decades.

In spite of the above, Mexico experienced economic growth towards the end of the 1970s, but this was mainly due to a transitory oil boom. The government began to rely heavily on spending and borrowing in world capital markets; the foreign debt consequently reached unprecedented levels.

At the beginning of the 1980s, oil prices fell, world interest rates rose, and commercial banks stopped lending to the third world. Mexico faced this severe crisis by adopting a set of strict adjustment and reform policies directed towards restoring fiscal balance, promoting exports, liberalizing external trade, and deregulating markets. The negative effects of the debt crisis and the adjustment policies were a series of devaluations of the Mexican currency, high inflation, a severe depression in real wages, and a serious reduction in economic growth. In 1989, the gross domestic product per capita was 9 per cent below the 1980 level; during the same period the real minimum wage declined by 47 per cent. Inflation peaked in 1987 when some estimates placed it above at 150 per cent annually, at which point it began a sustained decline which has continued until the present (Sheahan 1991; CEPAL 1990; Lustig 1992).

The decline in real wages, combined with the deficient social security system and the reduction in subsidies to basic products, have given rise to a clear deterioration in the standards of living of the population. 'The crisis and its aftermath have probably left Mexico with a relatively impoverished middle class, an increasing number of poor households and the poor worse off than before' (Lustig 1992: 95). More visible now is the unequal and exclusionary character of the country's development, which, even in its years of expansion, was characterized by a concentration

Virginia Levin was in charge of the computer programming for this chapter. We appreciate her support and professional dedication.

of wealth and by the persistence of acute social inequalities (see Lustig 1986; Casar and Ros 1987; Tello 1979 and 1987).

Different studies have explored the strategies implemented by Mexican households to cope with the drastic decline in real wages during the 1980s. It has been advanced that the fall in total income and per capita consumption were probably less severe because households sent more members into the labour force, worked additional hours, put into practice different income-generating schemes, and also spent more carefully (Cortés and Rubalcava 1991; Lustig 1992). In this chapter we are interested in one of these possible strategies—the increased presence of Mexican women in the labour market—which went from 25 per cent in 1981 to 32 per cent in 1988 (Pacheco 1988; González de la Rocha 1989; Oliveira 1989; Pedrero 1990).[1]

As we were able to highlight in a previous study, the women who most increased their economic presence during the 1980s were those with family responsibilities (aged over 25, in marital unions, with children) and with less schooling. The data on schooling suggests a greater ease of entrance into the labour market for women from less-privileged social groups; indeed, among all female workers, the proportion of women who were low-income own-account workers increased most (García and Oliveira 1993).

This information sheds light on some of the general characteristics associated with the increase in women's economic participation in the 1980s. Nevertheless, it is of interest to consider the specificities of this increase in different social sectors of the population (agricultural, middle-class, urban working class). Although we argue that women with greater family responsibilities broaden their participation to meet the basic needs of their households, it is essential to determine whether this pattern occurs both among groups with lower income and welfare levels and among more privileged groups. On the other hand, the emphasis on the economic participation of social groups with a lower level of schooling may obscure our knowledge of what happens with women from middle-class sectors. Educational requirements and credentials in traditionally female technical and professional occupations may have become more stringent at a time of reduced demand for salaried labour.

In the light of the above considerations, the purpose of this chapter is to study the determinants of women's work in different social groups in Mexico before and during the economic recession of the 1980s.[2] The aim is to explore through a multivariate analysis how economic constraint may have changed the influence of

---

[1] The tendency in Mexican women's labour force participation in the last decades has been as follows: 13 per cent were economically active in 1950; this figure rose to 16 per cent in 1970; 21 per cent in 1979; 25 per cent in 1981; and 32 per cent in 1988, remaining at the same level in 1991 (data taken from the Population Censuses for 1950 and 1970; the Encuesta Contínua de Ocupación (ECSO) for 1979; the Encuesta Nacional Demográfica (END) for 1982; and the Encuesta Nacional de Empleo (ENE) for 1988 and 1991).

[2] The years examined are 1981 and 1987. The GDP growth in Mexico in the period 1978–81 still recorded annual rates of over 8 per cent. 1987 was the year with the highest inflation, as we have already mentioned. The GDP growth rate over the 1982–8 period, considered as a whole, was negative (−0.2 per cent). (Acosta Díaz 1991; Garza 1992; CEPAL 1990).

age, education, place of residence, and family responsibilities on women's economic performance. Because Mexico is an unequal and polarized society, the changing effect of the different variables during the recession is analysed separately for more and less privileged groups of the population. The Encuesta Nacional Demográfica (END) of 1982, and the Encuesta Nacional de Fecundidad y Salud (ENFES) of 1987 constitute our sources of basic information.[3]

In the next section we will consider first the theoretical and methodological treatment of social groups in our study. Subsequently, we will present the analysed information based on logistic regression models for the different groups in 1981 and 1987. Logistic regression is the appropriate statistical tool when the dependent variable is conceptualized dichotomically (work/non-work), especially when its average probability differs from 0.5 (see Hanushek and Jackson 1977; Christenson, García and de Oliveira 1989; and this chapter's statistical appendix).

Some considerations about social sectors in Mexico

We are particularly interested in analysing how the factors influencing women's economic activity differ among social sectors over time. That is to say, we assume that individual and family characteristics associated with women's work may play different roles in different socioeconomic contexts.

Following this perspective, we form comparable groups of women according to the economic status of the head of household, and consider them as subpopulations within which the effects of age, education, place of residence, and family responsibilities are expected to differ from one year to another. A similar strategy is used in a study conducted by the United Nations (1987), where subpopulations of countries are defined according to their level of development in order to explore the relationship between women's work and fertility. It is also possible to use hierarchical models in order to examine the effect of the socioeconomic status of the head of household on intermediate variables, and then on demographic behaviour (see Rodríguez and Cleland 1980).

The head of household is either the husband or father of the interviewees (1981) or the person upon whom they depend economically (1987).[4] Initially, we shall distinguish between agricultural and nonagricultural socioeconomic groups. In Mexico this is one of the basic social divisions in terms of living standards, measured according to indicators such as education, income, and access to health and communication services. For example, in 1987, 80.8 per cent of heads of household

---

[3] The probabilistic sample of the ENFES, conducted by the Ministry of Health, is representative at the national level and contains 9,310 individual cases. The probabilistic sample of the END, carried out by the National Population Council, CONAPO, consists of 10,206 individual cases and is also representative at the national level (END 1982; ENFES 1988). Although the END sample was taken in 1982, information on women's economic activity refers to the previous year, 1981.

[4] These options were decided beforehand in both surveys.

in the agricultural sector did not complete their elementary schooling, compared
with about 35 per cent of those working in nonagricultural sectors.

The nonagricultural sectors consist of white-collar workers, who generally be-
long to the middle classes, and blue-collar manual labourers who comprise the
urban working classes. The latter are divided into salaried and unsalaried manual
workers. As is well known, middle class workers are generally more privileged in
that they have a better education and a higher income. This group includes profes-
sionals, technicians, teachers, administrators, and clerical workers, 60 per cent of
whom have at least completed their secondary (junior high school) education in
both years considered (data from ENFES 1987; END 1982).

The heads of household who have salaried manual jobs are factory workers,
mechanics, drivers, or workers with diverse manual occupations in the service
sector. We expect this group to have been most affected by the economic crisis of
the 1980s because the buying power of their salaries, upon which, as a rule, they
depend, decreased enormously. As the two surveys show, 44 per cent of heads of
household in 1987 and 50 per cent in 1981 did not finish elementary school; only
a fifth finished or went beyond secondary (junior high school) education (ENFES
1987; END 1982). Those heads of households who are unsalaried manual workers
have the same jobs as their salaried counterparts but they do not have formal work
contracts or receive social security benefits. This is, however, a much more hetero-
geneous group. On the one hand, it includes the most disadvantaged members of
society, forced to create their own employment. On the other, also included are
more privileged groups who can manoevre more effectively in the crisis by raising
the price of their products and the cost of their services within the limits imposed
by the market. The two surveys show that about half the members of this group
finished elementary school, and only a fifth managed to complete their secondary
education (ENFES 1987; END 1982).

The study of the socio-demographic behaviour of different social groups is an
avenue of research which has always interested Latin American scholars. With
regard to labour force participation, some previous analyses of the Mexican case
are a study of Mexico City in 1970 which we carried out, and another study of rural
areas carried out by Zúñiga *et al.* in 1981 (García, Muñoz, and Oliveira 1982;
Zuñiga *et al.* 1986). These two studies focus more on the different work patterns
of women and youth and differential fertility rates by social groups and household
types. In our study of Mexico City we found that the head of household's status
as a white-collar, salaried, or unsalaried manual worker made a great difference in
the participation of women in the labour market. The economic activity rate among
women in households headed by white-collar or self-employed manual workers
was considerably higher than that of women in households headed by salaried
manual workers, especially in young nuclear families. Similarly, in rural areas, the
activity rate was higher among women in households headed by peasants or self-
employed workers. These findings support the well-known fact that the presence of
a family economic unit (agricultural, commercial or other) favours the participation
of women in the labour market. However, they also point to the relevance of

education for the economic participation of women in the middle sectors. In any case—and as we do in this chapter—it is of the utmost importance to analyse the changes in these trends which occur during moments of profound economic change.

Women's work in different social sectors in 1981 and 1987

Tables 10.1 and 10.2 display the percentage of working women by selected socio-demographic characteristics and social groups in the two years considered. We include contextual aspects such as place of residence; individual characteristics such as age and education; and indirect indicators of family responsibility such as marital status and the number and age of children.

These data constitute the variables included in the logistic models (see the statistical note at the end of this chapter in which we specify the algebraic form of these models and the statistical criteria used for evaluating the goodness of fit). We tested two models for each social sector and year. The goodness of fit for each are compared in Table 10.3. Model I considers contextual and individual factors (place of residence, age, level of schooling); Model II evaluates the pertinence of indicators of family responsibility (marital status and number and age of children). In all cases the goodness of fit in Model II is better, for which reason Tables 10.4 and 10.5 display only the Model II coefficients for each social sector and year.[5]

In order to read Tables 10.4 and 10.5 correctly it is important to keep in mind that logistic regression models predict log odds rather than probabilities. To facilitate the interpretation of the results, we establish one of the categories of each independent variable as a reference and compare the value of each other category with it. For example, for the age variable, the 35–9 age group is the referent (omitted) category; coefficients shown in Tables 10.4 and 10.5 indicate the difference, statistically significant or not, between the economic activity of women in this group and that of each of the other age groups. It is important to remember that each time we single out the role of one variable, the effect of the others is controlled.[6]

The greater propensity of older women to work

It is a well-documented fact that a woman's age is closely associated with her family responsibilities and therefore with her ability to carry out extradomestic activities. It is often argued that young women who live with their parents can more

---

[5] Studies similar to our own that fit logistic regression models for women's work in Mexico at different historical moments systematically reaffirm the pertinence of marital status. The number and age, or the presence, of children, may present results in different directions, which shows that it is impossible to attribute a unique sense to the relationship of fertility to women's work at all moments (Myung-Hye 1987; Rubin-Kurtzman 1991).

[6] In the analysis that follows we consider the findings referred to age, education, marital status, and the number and age of children, which are the variables that present more relevant variations. Tables 10.A1 and 10.A2 in the appendix show the distribution of these sociodemographic characteristics for women belonging to different social groups.

Table 10.1 Percentage of women workers by social sector and individual and family characteristics (1981)

	Agricultural		Non-manual		Manual			
					Unsalaried		Salaried	
Total	19.0	(1035)*	35.2	(2755)*	27.7	(958)*	26.7	(4670)*
Age								
15–19	21.2	(267)	16.4	(577)	15.9	(231)	22.7	(1022)
20–4	22.3	(165)	46.4	(631)	41.0	(164)	33.7	(912)
25–9	23.0	(159)	48.5	(452)	37.6	(124)	24.5	(779)
30–4	11.3	(114)	39.5	(365)	29.1	(126)	25.9	(698)
35–9	14.2	(125)	30.5	(287)	25.3	(142)	29.0	(500)
40–4	18.1	(92)	28.0	(267)	23.0	(99)	24.9	(455)
45–9	17.3	(113)	31.8	(177)	26.4	(72)	25.1	(304)
Education								
Without schooling and incomplete elementary	14.6	(753)	17.5	(621)	18.7	(421)	20.0	(2153)
At least complete elementary	20.2	(159)	28.0	(686)	25.1	(228)	26.6	(1231)
At least complete junior high school	40.5	(92)	43.7	(1035)	32.8	(245)	38.2	(1080)
High school and upwards	44.0	(20)	51.6	(344)	76.9	(53)	42.9	(122)

Marital status							
Single	28.0	(337)	36.2	(850)	38.1	(325)	36.4	(1157)
In union	11.1	(619)	31.0	(1745)	17.5	(572)	19.2	(3160)
Widowed/separated/divorced	43.1	(79)	76.9	(156)	69.7	(59)	63.4	(342)
Number and age of children							
Without children	26.6	(376)	39.4	(1056)	34.9	(360)	36.1	(1407)
One or two, youngest 0–3	17.0	(104)	38.7	(507)	19.1	(108)	20.9	(735)
One or two, youngest 4 or above	23.3	(94)	45.1	(302)	44.5	(65)	36.7	(507)
Three or more, youngest 0–3	10.9	(251)	22.2	(390)	19.4	(195)	15.1	(952)
Three or more, youngest 4 or above	12.3	(205)	27.1	(498)	22.5	(229)	23.9	(1066)
Place of residence							
Rural	17.6	(944)	28.5	(1049)	18.4	(407)	21.5	(1854)
Urban	33.8	(91)	39.3	(1706)	34.5	(551)	30.0	(2817)

* Numbers in brackets are absolute numbers. In some cases the individual figures do not add up to this total due to missing information about specific characteristics in the surveys.

Source: Encuesta Nacional Demográfica (END) 1982. Weighted sample.

Table 10.2 Percentage of women workers by social sector and individual and family characteristics (1987)

	Agricultural		Non-manual		Manual			
					Unsalaried		Salaried	
Total	27.7	(2104)*	40.1	(2605)*	35.2	(1131)*	29.2	(2968)*
Age								
15–19	26.3	(517)	15.9	(514)	25.8	(318)	20.0	(726)
20–4	31.4	(327)	41.3	(470)	34.4	(185)	28.4	(602)
25–9	24.0	(343)	47.5	(482)	41.7	(164)	30.7	(530)
30–4	27.9	(276)	49.2	(448)	34.3	(154)	42.7	(380)
35–9	30.4	(240)	51.3	(350)	45.3	(103)	35.5	(289)
40–4	32.3	(211)	41.6	(214)	47.8	(121)	30.8	(240)
45–9	22.9	(190)	40.5	(127)	30.6	(86)	24.9	(201)
Education								
Without schooling and incomplete elementary	30.3	(1423)	39.1	(305)	41.2	(433)	25.9	(1004)
At least complete elementary	19.7	(423)	30.3	(738)	26.0	(356)	26.8	(1041)
At least complete junior high school	23.4	(223)	38.3	(1025)	35.0	(249)	33.2	(763)
High school and upwards	47.4	(35)	57.7	(537)	42.6	(93)	47.4	(160)

Marital status								
Single	32.0	(593)	36.9	(814)	34.3	(446)	39.0	(846)
In union	23.5	(1398)	36.9	(1596)	32.4	(621)	20.4	(1894)
Widowed/separated/divorced	57.5	(112)	80.1	(195)	68.4	(63)	67.1	(226)
Number and age of children								
Without children	30.7	(684)	39.0	(973)	35.8	(479)	35.4	(1025)
One or two, youngest 0–3	29.9	(273)	32.4	(463)	26.1	(118)	16.2	(557)
One or two, youngest 4 or above	36.3	(150)	51.1	(459)	46.0	(121)	42.9	(375)
Three or more, youngest 0–3	23.6	(544)	38.2	(273)	32.5	(176)	19.7	(463)
Three or more, youngest 4 or above	23.9	(452)	40.7	(437)	34.7	(238)	29.7	(547)
Place of residence								
Rural	26.3	(1880)	36.4	(442)	30.6	(367)	21.4	(860)
Urban	39.6	(224)	40.9	(2163)	37.3	(764)	32.5	(2108)

* Absolute numbers

Source: Encuesta Nacional de Fecundidad y Salud (ENFES) 1987. Weighted sample.

Table 10.3 Comparison of different logistic regression models for women's economic participation by social sector

	Agricultural	Non-manual	Manual	
			Unsalaried	Salaried
1981				
L^2 Model I*	907.98	3106.74	976.36	5143.62
L^2 Model II**	854.94	2964.16	863.06	4689.06
L^2I – L^2II	53.04***	142.58***	113.30***	454.56***
Difference in degrees of freedom	6	6	6	6
1987				
L^2 Model I*	2414.70	3209.88	1410.06	3403.36
L^2 Model II**	2331.58	3018.90	1350.00	3022.34
L^2I – L^2II	83.12***	190.98***	60.06***	381.02***
Difference in degrees of freedom	6	6	6	6

* L^2 Model I = –2 (log likelihood) in Model I. This model includes the variables: place of residence, age, and education.
** L^2 Model II = –2 (log likelihood) in Model II. Besides the variables in Model I, Model II includes: marital status and the number and age of children.
*** Significant at a 99% confidence level.

Source: Encuesta Nacional Demográfica (END) 1982, and Encuesta Nacional de Fecundidad y Salud (ENFES) 1987. Weighted samples.

easily accept jobs outside their homes, specially when they are offered by established manufacturing and service industries with fixed schedules. In Mexico and elsewhere in Latin America during the the 1960s and 1970s, women's economic participation conformed to this pattern and the highest participation rate was in the 20–4 age group (García 1975; Negrete 1988; Christenson, García, and Oliveira 1989; Infante and Klein 1991). However, our data suggest that this panorama began to change during the last decade, when we observe a rise in the participation rate of older women.

In 1981 there was already an important economic presence of older women because there was no difference in the propensity to work over the age of 20, regardless of social sector. By 1987 this tendency had become even more pronounced in the nonagricultural subpopulations, with women aged 25–44 being much more likely to work than women in the 20–4 or 15–19 age groups.

Data from occupational surveys for the major metropolitan areas of Mexico confirm the increase in the labour force participation of older women, although this increase is not as pronounced as that observed in the fertility surveys (see Pedrero

Table 10.4 Logistic regression coefficients of women's economic participation in different social sectors (Model II), 1981

	Agricultural	Non-manual	Manual	
			Unsalaried	Salaried
Age				
15–19	−0.587	−2.265**	−2.781**	−1.575**
20–4	−0.105	−0.199	−1.037**	−0.302
25–9	0.459	0.279	−0.037	−0.301
30–4	−0.528	0.191	−0.267	−0.132
35–9*	—	—	—	—
40–4	−0.291	−0.025	−0.194	−0.330
45–9	−0.102	0.077	−0.437	−0.391
Education				
Without schooling and incomplete elementary	−0.871**	−1.169**	−0.364	−0.745**
At least complete elementary	−0.689	−0.639**	−0.131	−0.476**
At least complete junior high school*	—	—	—	—
High school and upwards	0.249	0.020	1.679**	−0.178
Marital Status				
Single	0.996	0.415	1.923**	0.558**
In union*	—	—	—	—
Widowed/separated/divorced	1.788**	−0.936**	2.649**	1.994**
Number and age of children				
Without children*	—	—	—	—
One or two, youngest 0–3	−0.428	−0.072	−0.436	−0.911**
One or two, youngest 4 or above	−0.147	−0.155	−0.475	−0.469**
Three or more, youngest 0–3	−0.346	−0.902**	−0.303	−1.271**
Three or more, youngest 4 or above	0.326	−0.642**	−0.446	−0.896**
Place of residence				
Rural	—	—	—	—
Urban	0.513	−0.029	0.636**	0.248**
Constant	−1.088	0.992	−1.098	0.093
Log likelihood	−427.469	−1482.080	−431.535	−2344.534

* Reference category omitted in the models
** Significance at $P < 0.01$

Source: Encuesta Nacional Demográfica (END) 1982. Weighted sample.

Table 10.5 Logistic regression coefficients of women's economic participation in different social sectors (Model II), 1987

	Agricultural	Non-Manual	Manual	
			Unsalaried	Salaried
Age				
15–19	−0.641**	−2.525**	−1.737**	−2.011**
20–4	−0.246	−1.023**	−1.053**	−0.774**
25–9	−0.366	−0.422**	−0.166	−0.250
30–4	−0.079	−0.071	−0.325	0.469
35–9	—	—	—	—
40–4	−0.008	−0.306	−0.109	−0.380
45–9	−0.545	−0.341	−1.152**	−0.949**
Education				
Without schooling and incomplete elementary	847**	−0.255	0.357	−0.141
At least complete elementary	−0.001	−0.548**	−0.422	−0.181
At least complete junior high school*	—	—	—	—
High school and upwards	0.831	0.585**	−0.100	0.020
Marital status				
Single	0.933**	0.512**	0.206	1.681**
In union*	—	—	—	—
Widowed/separated /divorced	1.333**	1.938**	1.407**	1.990**
Number and age of children				
Without children*	—	—	—	—
One or two, youngest 0–3	0.267	−0.673**	−0.923**	−0.517
One or two, youngest 4 or above	0.204	−0.514**	−0.690	0.147
Three or more, youngest 0–3	−0.213	−0.703**	−1.300**	−0.629**
Three or more, youngest 4 or above	−0.316	−0.701**	−1.189**	−0.068
Place of residence				
Rural*	—	—	—	—
Urban	0.489**	−0.076	0.375	0.414**
Constant	−1.606	0.572	0.374	−0.952
Likelihood logarithm	−1165.787	−1509.449	−675.000	−1511.169

* Reference category omitted in the models.
** Significance at $P < 001$.

Source: Encuesta Nacional de Fecundidad y Salud (ENFES) 1987. Weighted sample.

1991).[7] An increase in extradomestic work among older women has also been observed in other Latin American countries; in Argentina this increase began after 1970 (Pantelides 1976; Wainerman and Recchini de Lattes 1981).

Our data suggest that the change in the pattern of female employment by age during the 1980s occurred across different types of families headed by agricultural and nonagricultural workers. There are at least three possible explanations:

(1) in contrast with earlier periods, young women who tend to live with their parents do not leave their jobs when they age and are faced with different family responsibilities;

(2) the contraction of salaries forced older women to implement income earning activities in order to supplement the family income; and

(3) the number of young working women may have fallen owing to a drop in salaried employment with economic recession.

Variations in the importance of education

Studies that examine the female population as a whole generally conclude that the more schooling a woman has the more likely she is to work. The impact of education on female employment should be assessed in two ways: in terms of the incentives and expectations of working women to become economically independent and obtain a sense of personal satisfaction, and in terms of the operation of the labour market. It is argued that in Latin America highly qualified women are more likely to be economically active because urbanization and diversification of the economic structure offers them better job opportunities and higher salaries. Despite this, it is worth remembering that not all social sectors have equal educational opportunities.

In 1981, the association between education and work presents no surprises: in all sectors studied, a higher educational level corresponded to a greater propensity to work. Women from the agricultural sector who had at least completed their elementary schooling were more likely to work; the same was true for those women from the middle class sectors and salaried manual sectors who had at least finished their secondary (junior high school) education. Finally, women from the manual unsalaried sectors were more likely to work if they had at least finished their high school education.

By 1987, the situation had changed. It was only in the middle class sectors that women with high school or higher education were more economically active than their less-educated counterparts who had at least finished their junior high school studies.

---

[7] In the occupational surveys, economic activity refers to the week before the information is collected; in the fertility surveys the time reference varies, but it tends to be longer (with END it is the year before the survey, and with ENFES the economic activity recorded is the one 'currently' carried out). These differences could account for the possible overestimation of older women's economic activity in the fertility surveys as compared to other sources. Of course, one must also bear in mind possible differences in sampling procedures and in the attention paid to the collection of economic activity data in both sources.

In agricultural families, more workers were found among women who had not finished their elementary education than among those who had completed junior high school. Probably, these women did not have the financial means to study and either worked as agricultural labourers, were self-employed, or performed manual jobs that did not require any formal schooling, such as, for example, remunerated domestic work.

The educational level of women from the salaried and unsalaried manual sectors made little difference with respect to labour market participation. That is to say, the likelihood that they worked in 1987 did not depend upon their schooling. These results show that Mexico's current economic crisis has rendered the relationship between education and work more complex.

On the one hand, in the most disadvantaged nonagricultural sectors, education loses its value as a factor explaining women's economic activity. That is to say, independently of education, the motivation of women from these sectors to work is connected with their need to earn some money in order to compensate for the low salaries of the other members of the family. On the other hand, in the middle-class sectors, education significantly increases the propensity to work, enabling women to compete effectively for the few jobs available in the urban labour market. These results support the argument that the relationship between level of education and the participation of women in the work force may vary in particular situations, depending on the size and nature of the labour market, or the expansion and contraction of qualified and unqualified occupational opportunities (Wainerman and Recchini 1981; García and Oliveira 1993).

The role of female marital status

In various countries of Latin America it has already been well documented that, for the female population as a whole, legally or consensually married women are less likely to work outside the home than single women or women who are separated, widowed, or divorced. The arguments offered to explain this tendency are widely known: the important role of domestic duties and the unwillingness of employers to hire women with family responsibilities. As recent studies document, what has changed in this regard is that the number of women in conjugal union entering the labour market has increased, both in Mexico and elsewhere in Latin America. The same occurred in developed countries in previous decades (Wainerman and Recchini 1981; Pedrero and Rendón 1982; Recchini 1983; Blau and Ferber 1985; Pedrero 1990; García and Oliveira 1993).

The results of the logistic models indicate that, despite this increase in the participation of married women in the labour market, as a group they are still less inclined to work outside the home than their single counterparts. Finally, widows, divorcees, and women who are separated generally have a greater economic presence than women in all other marital categories. Let us now take a look at the situations which do not follow this general pattern.

One such case refers to women in conjugal union from the *middle class sectors*.

In 1981 these women were just as likely to work as single women, and more likely to do so than separated women, widows, and divorcees. In 1987, however, they followed the usual pattern; that is, they were less likely to work than unmarried women. This change in the effect of marital status on female employment among middle class women may be attributed in part to the changing dynamics of the labour market during the 1980s. At the beginning of the decade—a time of economic expansion—the great demand for skilled white-collar workers meant that larger numbers of qualified single and married women began to enter the work force. During the years of economic recession, the situation changed, opportunities for entering white-collar occupations diminished, and, despite their education, it became difficult for middle class women in conjugal unions to maintain the rate of labour force participation that had been registered during the period of economic growth.

The situation is different for women in conjugal union from the *unsalaried manual sectors*. During the years of economic growth, they followed the general pattern: women in conjugal unions were less likely to work. By the late-1980s (1987), however, the proportion of women in marital unions who worked was the same as that of single women and less than that of widows and separated women. There are two ways in which the economic crisis may account for this. On the one hand, we can speculate that when there is a cut-back in demand for salaried workers, this group of women has more possibilities of finding work in small family 'businesses' than women from other social sectors.[8] On the other hand, the participation of married women as family workers is particularly important for small family businesses during a period of crisis when other members of the family take on other jobs to supplement family income.

The presence and ages of children in the household

The association between fertility and work has received growing attention in the field of social demography. One of the central concerns is to establish the causal direction and significance of this association—whether fertility affects work or vice versa—using appropriate sources of information and statistical analyses. Naturally, shared influences are taken into account as well (United Nations 1987; García and Oliveira 1989).

We are interested in exploring the influence of the number of children ever had (cumulative fertility) on women's present economic activity. Other studies underscore the complexity of this relationship. The conclusion most often reached is that the results do not always point in the same direction. In some cases, the expected negative outcome is confirmed, but in others there appears to be no relationship or a positive relation for some social sectors (Standing 1978; Wainerman and Recchini 1981). Using multivariate techniques, our work in Mexico demonstrated that, in 1981, the association between the number of children and work outside the home

---

[8] According to ENFES data (not shown), 53 per cent of these women worked in unsalaried activities.

was negative for all women between the ages of 15 and 49 (Christenson, García, and Oliveira 1989).[9]

A comparison of the surveys carried out in 1981 and 1987 brings to light important differences among the social sectors. In the *agricultural sector* where female labour force participation generally is low, women with children of any age are as likely to work as women who do not have children, regardless of whether the economy is in a period of growth or recession. It is well known that in rural areas there is frequently no division of labour between the home and the workplace so women can work and look after their children at the same time. The 1987 data (not shown) indicate that in 74 per cent of the cases, women with children from the agricultural sectors were involved in agricultural and unsalaried occupations.

In the nonagricultural sectors, the situation changed significantly during the period under study. In the *middle class and the unsalaried manual sectors*, the effect of the number and ages of children on female work outside the home became more restrictive as the economic crisis worsened while it became less so in the *salaried manual sector*. It is worth examing the changes detected in greater detail.

In 1981, controlling for all other factors, *middle class women* with one or two children were as likely to work as women with no children. Only mothers of three children or more were less likely to work. During the same period, most mothers from the *unsalaried manual sector* worked, regardless of the number or age of their children.

By 1987, the panorama had changed. *Among women from the middle class and unsalaried manual sectors*, the propensity to work in the case of those with children significantly dropped. One reasonable interpretation for the behaviour of the *middle class sectors* refers to the diminishing demand for skilled workers in professional, technical, and office jobs. This reduction and the greater emphasis on credentials made it more difficult for the most vulnerable women to keep their jobs or to obtain new ones whereas women without children were in a better position to compete for the few openings available. The corresponding decline for the *unsalaried manual sector* is unexpected and does not follow the hypotheses advanced above. This is a very heterogenous group and with a reduced number of cases, facts that may account for the tendencies shown.

The outcome of our analysis for the *salaried manual sector* is striking and differs from the other social groups. During the period of economic growth, the mere presence of children in the home had a marked effect on reducing the propensity to work. This was presumably because the salaries of the working members of the family were sufficient to maintain the standard of living. This resulted in a reaffirmation that the central role of women with children was their participation in daily housework and child care. Similar findings appear in our study of a previous period of economic growth in Mexico City (1970); the rate of economic participation for women with small children whose husbands were employed in the salaried manual

---

[9] Other multivariate analyses that study this aspect in detail for the case of Mexico are those undertaken by Smith (1981); Zazueta (1981); Wong and Levine (1988).

sector was among the lowest of all social groups (García, Muñoz, and Oliveira 1982). By the late-1980s (1987), however, the aggravation of the economic crisis, the steady reduction in salaries, and the growing need for women to supplement family incomes brought about a change: women were less likely to work only if they were mothers of three children or more, with the youngest child below the age of three. All other mothers were just as likely to work as women without children.

Data for 1987 (not shown) indicate that women in the salaried manual sector used different stategies to enter the work force. Some undertook unsalaried work (25 per cent). This activity is mainly carried out on a part-time basis, and, in a large number of cases, allowed women to look after their children while they worked. Like the head of household, others were employed in the salaried manual sector (35 per cent). These women generally worked on a full-time basis and left the care of their children to relatives or took them to child care centres. Finally, others found jobs as white-collar workers (37 per cent). Although these mothers also often relied on relatives or child care centres to look after their children, in some instances the children were old enough to look after themselves.

Concluding remarks

The information provided by the fertility surveys (END and ENFES) indicate transformations in the level of women's economic activity and the factors influencing these transformations in Mexico towards the end of the 1980s.

The changes regarding age are particularly interesting. In the 1980s female labour force participation does not decline steeply after ages 20–4; rather, it stays relatively high in the other age groups and only declines at the end of a woman's reproductive life. As we have suggested in this text, this can be attributed to the fact that young women do not leave work when they have their first or second child and also to the fact that older women feel a growing necessity to work in order to supplement the family income. According to the ENFES data (not shown), they generally do so in unsalaried activities.

As far as education is concerned, we have pointed out a significant change: the economic crisis forced more women with little schooling in the manual sector to work, and education ceased to be a satisfactory means of explaining women's participation in the labour force.

Also worthy of note is the fact that, under certain conditions, more legally or consensually married women entered the labour market than single women, as in the case of women in the middle sectors in 1981. This may be explained by the rapid expansion of white-collar employment up until the beginning of the 1980s.

Another point is the influence of children on their mothers' propensity to enter the work force, which, as we have seen, varies depending on the social sector and the prevailing economic conditions of growth or recession. In certain circumstances, the influence of children, like that of marital status, depends on the dynamics of the labour market. This is the case, for example, among those women from the middle sectors who entered the labour force at a time of expanding white-collar employment when even women with small children had as good a chance of working as single women. During the economic recession, however, women with children were less likely to work than those without children, because of the cut-back in demand for white-collar workers.

In other circumstances, the influence of children on the labour force participation of their mothers is modified by pressing economic needs. This occurred in 1987 among mothers from the salaried manual sector who traditionally were less likely to work when children were present. The economic crisis placed the urban population of salaried manual workers in such financial straits that, in the majority of cases, children could no longer inhibit women from entering the labour force. Or, put in other and better terms, children and family need are the factors which lead women to implement income-generating strategies and, at the same time, look for alternative means of child care and methods of carrying out their housework.

Thus, as we can see, we are facing considerable changes which may be accounted for not only by the economic crisis affecting the country but also by the long-term modifications in the role of education and the behavioural patterns of the female population. The consequences of these changes on various levels of society, particularly with respect to the women's subordination in Mexico, would be well worth studying in detail in the future.

Statistical Note

Logistic regression is a special case of log-linear models where a dependent variable is specified. This type of regression analysis is preferred when the dependent variable is expressed dichotomously (work–nonwork), as is the case in this study. In this case ordinary least squares regression analysis is inappropriate.

The logistic regression model can be expressed as follows: $\log P/(1 - P) = Bx$. $P/(1 - P)$ is the odds ratio, where P goes from 0 to 1 and represents the proportion of women working. B represents a vector of coefficients corresponding to a constant and a group of independent variables. Error terms do not exist because it is assumed that the model is deterministic.

Logistic regression coefficients are estimated using a maximum likelihood method. Given a joint distribution of the sample results, this method searches iteratively among the possible parameter values for the most probable indicators. The iterative process continues until an arbitrary small difference between the present and previous estimate is reached. The models in this study were fitted using the statistical package STATA.

The likelihood estimate (L^2) that can be used to compare various regression models is expressed as: $L^2 = -2 \log L$, where L is the value of the likelihood function, given a set of parameters. While L^2 normally does not conform to a chi-square distribution, when the sample size is large, model differences take the form of this distribution. For greater details about the use of logistic regressions in the study of economic activity in Mexico, see Myung-Hye 1987; Christenson, García, and Oliveira 1989; Rubin-Kurtzman 1991; and Cortés 1992.

Table 10.A1 Sociodemographic characteristics of women belonging to different social sectors, 1981 (%)

	Agricultural	Non-manual	Manual	
			Unsalaried	Salaried
Total	100.0 (1035)*	100.0 (2755)*	100.0 (958)*	100.0 (4670)*
Age				
15–19	25.8	20.9	24.1	21.9
20–4	16.0	22.9	17.1	19.5
25–9	15.4	16.4	12.9	16.7
30–4	11.0	13.2	13.2	14.9
35–9	12.1	10.4	14.8	10.7
40–4	8.9	9.7	10.4	9.7
45–9	10.9	6.4	7.5	6.5
Education	100.0 (1035)	100.0 (2755)	100.0 (958)	100.0 (4670)
Without schooling and incomplete elementary	73.5	23.1	44.5	47.0
At least complete elementary	15.5	25.5	24.1	26.8
At least complete junior high school	9.0	38.5	25.9	23.5
High school and upwards	1.9	12.9	5.6	2.7
Marital status	100.0 (1035)	100.0 (2755)	100.0 (958)	100.0 (4670)
Single	32.5	30.9	34.0	24.8
In union	59.8	63.4	59.8	67.7
Widowed/ separated/divorced	7.6	5.7	6.2	7.3
Number and age of children	100.0 (1035)	100.0 (2755)	100.0 (958)	100.0 (4670)
Without children	36.4	38.4	37.6	30.3
One or two, youngest 0–3	10.0	18.4	11.3	15.7
One or two, youngest 4 or above	9.2	11.0	6.8	10.8
Three or more, youngest 0–3	24.4	14.1	20.4	20.4
Three or more, youngest 4 or above	19.9	18.1	23.9	22.8
Place of residence	100.0 (1035)	100.0 (2755)	100.0 (958)	100.0 (4670)
Rural	91.2	38.1	42.5	39.7
Urban	8.8	61.9	57.5	60.3

* Absolute numbers. Percentage totals are rounded to 100%.

Source: Encuesta Nacional Demográfica (END) 1982. Weighted sample.

Table 10.A2 Sociodemographic characteristics of women belonging to different social sectors, 1987 (%)

	Agricultural	Non-manual	Manual	
			Unsalaried	Salaried
Total	100.0 (2104)*	100.0 (2605)*	100.0 (1131)*	100.0 (2968)*
Age				
15–19	24.4	19.8	28.0	24.4
20–4	15.5	18.0	16.2	20.4
25–9	16.3	18.5	14.7	17.8
30–4	13.0	17.2	13.5	12.8
35–9	11.5	13.5	9.3	9.8
40–4	10.1	8.2	10.8	8.1
45–9	9.3	4.8	7.5	6.8
Education	100.0 (2104)	100.0 (2605)	100.0 (1131)	100.0 (2968)
Without schooling and incomplete elementary	67.8	11.8	38.4	34.0
At least complete elementary	20.1	28.3	31.5	35.0
At least complete junior high school	10.4	39.3	22.0	25.6
High school and upwards	1.6	20.6	8.1	5.4
Marital status	100.0 (2104)	100.0 (2605)	100.0 (1131)	100.0 (2968)
Single	27.9	31.2	39.2	28.4
In union	66.8	61.3	55.2	64.0
Widowed/ separated/ divorced	5.3	7.5	5.5	7.6
Number and age of children	100.0 (2104)	100.0 (2605)	100.0 (1131)	100.0 (2968)
Without children	32.2	37.3	42.1	34.4
One or two, youngest 0–3	13.2	17.8	10.3	18.9
One or two, youngest 4 or above	7.2	17.6	10.6	12.6
Three or more, youngest 0–3	25.8	10.5	15.8	15.6
Three or more, youngest 4 or above	21.7	16.8	21.1	18.5
Place of residence	100.0 (2104)	100.0 (2605)	100.0 (1131)	100.0 (2968)
Rural	89.5	17.0	32.2	28.9
Urban	11.5	83.0	67.8	71.0

* Absolute numbers. Percentage totals are rounded to 100%.

Source: 1982, Encuesta Nacional Demográfica (END). Weighted sample.

REFERENCES

Acosta Díaz, F. (1991), *Estructura familiar, hogares con jefes mujeres y bienestar en México*, PhD thesis, Centro de Estudios Demográficos y de Desarrollo Urbano, El Colegio de México, mimeo.

Blau, F. D. and Ferber, M. A. (1985), 'Women in the labour market: the last twenty years', in Larwood, L. *et al.*, *Women and Work*, Beverly Hills, Ca: Sage Publications, 19–49.

Casar, J. and Ros, J. (1987), 'Empleo, desempleo y distribución del ingreso', in Tello, C. (coord.), *México: informe sobre la crisis 1982–1986*, Mexico City: UNAM.

Christenson, B., García, B., and Oliveira, O. de (1989), 'Los múltiples condicionantes del trabajo femenino en México', in *Estudios Sociológicos*, 7/20 (May–July), 251–80.

Comisión Económica para América Latina (CEPAL) (1990), *Transformación productiva con equidad. La tarea prioritaria del desarrollo de América Latina y el Caribe en los años noventa*, Santiago: CEPAL.

Cortés, F. (1992), 'Algunas determinantes de la inserción laboral en la industria maquiladora de exportación de Matamoros', Centro de Estudios Sociológicos, El Colegio de México, mimeo.

Cortés, F. and Rubalcava, R. M. (1991), *Autoexplotación forzada y equidad por empobrecimiento*, Jornadas 120, El Colegio de México, 1991.

Encuesta Nacional de Fecundidad y Salud (ENFES) (1988), *Memoria de la reunión celebrada el 30 de septiembre de 1988*, Dirección General de Planificación Familiar, Secretaria de Salud, Mexico.

Encuesta Nacional Demográfica (END) (1982), *Informe General*, Consejo Nacional de Población (CONAPO), Mexico.

García, B. (1975), 'La participación de la población en la actividad económica', in *Demografía y Economía*, 9/1, El Colegio de México, 1–31.

—— Muñoz, H. and Oliveira, O. de (1982), *Hogares y trabajadores en la Ciudad de México*, El Colegio de México and Instituto de Investigaciones Sociales–UNAM, Mexico.

—— and Oliveira, O. de (1989), 'The effect of variation and change in female economic roles upon fertility change in developing countries', 21st Conference of the International Union for the Scientific Study of Population, New Delhi.

—— and Oliveira, O. de (1993), *Trabajo femenino y vida familiar en México*, El Colegio de México.

Garza, G. (1992), 'Crisis del sector servicios de la ciudad de México, 1960–1988', paper presented at the Conference on the Sociodemographic Effects of the 1980s Economic Crisis in Mexico, University of Texas at Austin, April, mimeo.

González de la Rocha, M. (1989), 'Crisis, economía doméstica y trabajo femenino en Guadalajara', in Oliveira, O. de (Coord.), *Trabajo, poder y sexualidad*, El Colegio de México, PIEM.

Hanushek, E. A. and Jackson, J. E. (1977), *Statistical Methods for Social Scientists*, New York: Academic Press, Inc.

Infante, R. and Klein, E. (1991), 'Mercado latinoamericano del trabajo en 1950–1990', *Revista de la CEPAL*, 45 (December), 129–44.

Lustig, N. (1986), 'Economic Crisis and Living Standards in Mexico: 1982–1985', document prepared for the project on the Impact of Global Recession on Living Standards in Selected Developing Countries, organized by Unuwider.

—— (1992), *Mexico. The Remaking of an Economy*, Washington, DC: Brookings Institution.

Myung-Hye, K. (1987), *Female Labor Force Participation and Household Reproduction in Urban Mexico*, PhD thesis, University of Texas at Austin.

Negrete Salas, M. E. (1988), 'Cambios en la estructura y distribución de la fuerza de trabajo en México: la dimensión regional, 1950–1980', in *Memorias de la III Reunión Nacional sobre Investigación Demográfica*, México.

Oliveira, O. de (1989), 'Empleo femenino en México en tiempos de recesión económica: tendencias recientes', in Cooper, J., Barbieri, T. de, Rendón, T., Suárez, E., and Tuñón, E. (complers.), *Fuerza de trabajo femenina urbana en México*, Universidad Nacional Autónoma de México (UNAM) and Miguel Angel Porrúa, México.

Pacheco Gómez Muñoz, M. E. (1988), *Población económicamente activa femenina en algunas áreas urbanas de México en 1986*, Master's degree thesis, Centro de Estudios Demográficos y de Desarrollo Urbano, El Colegio de México.

Pantelides, E. A. (1976), *Estudio de la población femenina económicamente activa en América Latina 1950–1970*, C 161, Santiago: CELADE.

Pedrero, M. (1990), 'Evolución de la participación económica femenina en los ochenta', in *Revista Mexicana de Sociología*, 52/1 (January–March), 133–49.

Pedrero, M. and Rendón, T. (1982), 'El trabajo de la mujer en México en los setentas', in *Estudios sobre la mujer 1. Empleo y la mujer. Bases teóricas, metodología y evidencia empírica*, Serie Lecturas III, INEGI–SPP, México.

Przeworski, A. (1982), 'Teoría sociológica y el estudio de la población: reflexiones sobre el trabajo de la Comisión de Población y Desarrollo de CLACSO', *Reflexiones teórico-metodológicoas sobre las investigaciones en población*, El Colegio de México, 58–99.

Recchini de Lattes, Z. (1983), *Dinámica de la fuerza de trabajo femenina en la Argentina*, Paris: UNESCO.

Rodríguez, G. and Cleland, J. (1980), 'Socio-Economic Determinants of Marital Fertility in Twenty Countries: a Multivariate Analysis', in *World Fertility Survey Conference 1980. Record of Proceedings*, 2, London, 337–422.

Rubin-Kurtzman, J. (1991), *From Prosperity to Adversity: the Labor Force Participation of Women in Mexico City: 1970–1976*. PhD thesis, University of California, Los Angeles, mimeo.

Sheahan, J. (1991), *Conflict and Change in Mexican Economic Strategy*, Center for US–Mexican Studies, University of California, San Diego.

Smith, S. K. (1981), 'Determinants of Female Labor Force Participation and Family Size in Mexico City', *Economic Development and Cultural Changes*, 30/1 (October).

Tello, C. (1979), *La política económica en México*, Mexico City: Siglo XXI.

Tello, C. (1987), 'Introducción', in Tello, C. (coord.), *México: informe sobre la crisis 1982–1986*, Mexico City: UNAM.

United Nations (1987), 'Women's Employment and Fertility', *Fertility Behaviour in the Context of Development. Evidence from the World Fertility Survey*, New York.

Wainerman, C. and Recchini de Lattes, Z. (1981), *El trabajo femenino en el banquillo de los acusados. La medición censal en América Latina*, Mexico City: Terranova and Population Council.

Wong, R. and Levine, R. (1988), 'Labor Force Participation and Reproductive Behaviour among Mothers in Urban Areas of Mexico', paper presented at the annual meeting of the Population Association of America, April.

Zazueta, C. (1981), *La mujer y el mercado de trabajo en México*, Serie Estudios 8, Secretaría del Trabajo y Previsión Social, Centro Nacional de Información y Estadísticas del Trabajo, México.

Zúñiga, E., Hernández, D., Menkes, C. and Santos, C. (1986), *Trabajo familiar, conducta reproductiva y estratificación social. Un estudio en las áreas rurales de México*, Instituto Mexicano del Seguro Social, Programa de Investigaciones Sociales sobre Población en América Latina, Academia Mexicana de Investigación en Demografía Médica, A. C., México.

Index